I0605791

BEYONCÉ

THE STORIES BEHIND THE SONGS

ANNIE ZALESKI

WELBECK

To everyone who's nurtured my passion for music and writing, especially my biggest supporters: my husband and parents.

This book has not been authorized, licensed or endorsed by Beyoncé, nor by anyone involved in the creation, production or distribution of her work.

Unless noted, the single and album release dates in the book correspond to US release dates.

First published in 2025 by Welbeck
An imprint of Headline Publishing Group Limited

1

Cataloguing in Publication Data is available from the British Library

ISBN 978-1-03542-658-4

Publisher: Joe Cottington
Design: Russell Knowles and James Pople
Picture research: Paul Langan
Production: Arlene Lestrade

Printed and bound in China

MIX
Paper | Supporting responsible forestry
FSC www.fsc.org
FSC® C104740

Headline's policy is to use papers that are natural, renewable and recyclable products and made from wood grown in well-managed forests and other controlled sources. The logging and manufacturing processes are expected to conform to the environmental regulations of the country of origin.

HEADLINE PUBLISHING GROUP LIMITED
An Hachette UK Company
Carmelite House
50 Victoria Embankment
London EC4Y 0DZ

www.headline.co.uk
www.hachette.co.uk

The authorised representative in the EEA is Hachette Ireland, 8 Castlecourt Centre, Dublin 15, D15 XTP3, Ireland (email: info@hbgi.ie)

INTRODUCTION

BEYONCÉ HAS BEEN A DOMINANT FORCE IN POPULAR MUSIC FOR CLOSE TO 30 YEARS. THE SECRET IS HER DEEP CURIOSITY AND COMMITMENT TO PUSHING HER MUSIC FORWARD: AFTER ACHIEVING SUCCESS WITH R&B, SOUL AND HIP-HOP, SHE CONTINUES TO EXPAND HER SONIC PALETTE TO INCLUDE GENRES SUCH AS HOUSE MUSIC, COUNTRY, ROCK, AFROBEAT AND ELECTRONIC MUSIC. EVERY STEP OF THE WAY, BEYONCÉ ELEVATES BLACK VOICES, CULTURE AND HISTORY — ENSURING THAT HER SUCCESS SHINES A LIGHT ON BOTH HER PROMINENT INFLUENCES AND FIGURES WHO DESERVE MORE OF THE SPOTLIGHT.

Beyoncé's approach to her music is virtuosic; she hears potential songs within mere fragments of sound and frequently incorporates tracks with imaginative samples. "I don't play any instrument," she once said. "I have writers that I write with, or I have writers that will send me a full song, and I'll rearrange it: change the second verse, change the melody, keep a chord that I like, and recreate it. Just depends. I might bring in whoever I think can help the song."[1]

She also doesn't sweat working with just a beat, she added: "It's the most fun for me. I'll get somebody to play whatever I hum for the bassline. So I'm creating a whole track with my voice."[2] No wonder Diana Gordon, one of the songwriters behind the *Lemonade* track "Sorry", once described Beyoncé as "a scientist of songs" before adding, "I've never seen anyone work the way she works."[3]

Long-time collaborator Rodney Jerkins has compared her to Michael Jackson, while Stuart White, her personal engineer and mixer since 2012, called her "a true genius at producing – and she's brilliantly right on it, all the time."[4] Then there's producer Dre, who witnessed Beyoncé flawlessly singing a tune she had never heard before – in *French*, no less – after hearing it just three times. "In three listens, she picked up on a sample in a different language and sang the whole thing," he recalled. "When I saw that, I was like, 'This is a totally different level.'"[5]

Beyoncé: The Stories Behind the Songs chronologically explores her entire music career, beginning with the influential R&B/hip-hop she created with Destiny's Child in the late 1990s and early 2000s, then moving on to cover her solo work, including features, collaborations and rarities. Pairing musical and visual analysis with quotes from Beyoncé and her musical collaborators, this book celebrates the power of her voice and her culture-changing platform, her commitment to activism – and the ambition and brilliance that has made her one of the most successful (and innovative) musicians of all time.

Opposite: Beyoncé dazzles onstage wherever she goes – like the Barcelona, Spain, date of the On The Run II Tour in 2018.

PART I

DESTINY'S CHILD

group was on their way.

Released in February 1998, their debut album *Destiny's Child* featured big names like Jermaine Dupri, Wyclef Jean and Pras of the Fugees, Master P and D'Wayne Wiggins of Tony! Toni! Toné!

eventually bloomed into harmony-driven catharsis. "Illusion", meanwhile, is a cover of the 1982 electro-disco hit "Just an Illusion" by the UK band Imagination. The latter song in particular gave Destiny's Child a chance to flex their hip-hop skills, something

they'd revisit on subsequent albums, while a dance remix of the song called "DubiLLusions" offered glimpses of Beyoncé's powerhouse diva future.

The album ends with the lovely ballad "My Time Has Come" (Dedicated to Andretta Tillman)", a tribute to their former manager, who died of lupus in 1997. Majestic strings and piano call to mind an elegiac church hymn, as Beyoncé sings about trusting yourself and how you feel, and not letting fear stand in the way of moving forward.

The international edition of *Destiny's Child* includes the TLC-esque "Know That", an upbeat R&B song produced by Father Shaheed of Poor Righteous Teachers that interpolates Suzanne Vega's "Tom's Diner". The Japanese edition, meanwhile, features a rendition of "Amazing Grace". And the 2001 European reissue edition includes "You're the Only One", a love song driven by funky grooves.

Destiny's Child was certified platinum on the strength of the single "No, No, No", which became the group's first major hit, peaking at No. 3 on the *Billboard* Hot 100. And while the album itself peaked well outside of the top 40, it was successful enough that when Destiny's Child returned a few years later with *The Writing's on the Wall*, they were poised to come into their own.

Below and opposite: As a kid, Beyoncé was in a group called Girls Tyme with Latavia Robertson and Kelly Rowland. Later, this trio teamed up with LeToya Luckett and reorganized as Destiny's Child.

NO, NO, NO

[SINGLE]

Released: October 27, 1997 (single) / February 17, 1998 (album)
Writers: Mary Brown, Rob Fusari, Calvin Gaines, Vincent Herbert
Producers: Rob Fusari and Vincent Herbert
Select Alternate Versions: Part 1, Part 2 (featuring Wyclef Jean), Camdino Soul extended remix

The protagonist of "No, No, No" has a simple request: she'd like her romantic crush to stop being cagey about his feelings *and* stop denying that he likes her. The song was co-written by Rob Fusari, who was then an aspiring songwriter hunkered down in a studio in his mother's basement trying to make his music career happen. His fortunes changed when writer/producer Vincent Herbert came to visit, heard "No, No, No", and suspected it might work for Destiny's Child. "I gave him a cassette, and he calls me that night and says, 'We're cutting the record'," Fusari later recalled. "'And I've got a guarantee it will be their first single.'"[2] Herbert kept his promise: the tune was released in 1997 as a single under the title "No, No, No". Not long after, the song ended up evolving into two distinct versions, both of which appeared on Destiny's Child's 1998 debut album. Part 1 is a sparkling R&B slow jam, while the brisker Part 2 features Wyclef Jean and boasts an insistent rhythmic sample of Love Unlimited Orchestra's "Strange Games & Things".

WITH ME

[SINGLE]

Released: April 20, 1998 (single) / February 17, 1998 (album)
Writers: Jermaine Dupri, Master P, Manuel Seal (Part 2 also features the Destiny's Child members)
Producers: Jermaine Dupri and Manuel Seal
Select Alternate Versions: Part 1, Part 2

As with "No, No, No", *Destiny's Child* contains two distinct versions of this song. Although both are based around the spiralling piano line of TRU's 1997 song "Freak Hoes", Part 2 is distinguished by vocal contributions from rapper Master P. Lyrically, "With Me" was meant as a response to Usher's "You Make Me Wanna", a song from the perspective of a man who's ready to break up his stable relationship because he's met someone new. In contrast, Destiny's Child's song is from the perspective of that other woman, who is telling the unsuspecting girlfriend about the cheating and subterfuge.

KILLING TIME

[SOUNDTRACK / ALBUM TRACK]

Released: Summer 1997 (*Men in Black: The Album*) / February 17, 1998 (album)
Writers: Taura Stinson and D'Wayne Wiggins
Producer: D'Wayne Wiggins

In June 1997, on ads for the soundtrack to the blockbuster film *Men in Black*, Destiny's Child received billing alongside hip-hop heavyweights such as De La Soul, Nas and A Tribe Called Quest. The occasion was their neo-soul song "Killing Time", co-written and co-produced by D'Wayne Wiggins of Tony! Toni! Toné!. Slow and melancholy, the tune depicts a lonely narrator who's waiting for her absent partner to return. Until then, she's biding her time and assuring him that she's remaining loyal.

Opposite: Destiny's Child started their career off strong with 1997's "Killing Time," a song that appeared on the *Men In Black* soundtrack.

02 THE WRITING'S ON THE WALL

THE WRITING'S ON THE WALL WAS A MAJOR STEP FORWARD FOR DESTINY'S CHILD. CHALK IT UP TO EXPERIENCE: IN THE YEAR AND A HALF SINCE RELEASING THEIR SELF-TITLED DEBUT ALBUM, THE GROUP HAD OPENED FOR BOYZ II MEN AND FIGURED OUT WHAT WORKED FOR THEM MUSICALLY. "THEY GOT MORE INVOLVED IN THE [*THE WRITING'S ON THE WALL*] CREATIVE PROCESS," SAID MATHEW KNOWLES, BEYONCÉ'S DAD AND THE GROUP'S MANAGER. AMONG OTHER THINGS, HE NOTED THAT BEYONCÉ STARTED CO-PRODUCING SONGS AND ALSO BEGAN CO-WRITING TUNES ALONG WITH SOME OF THE OTHER GROUP MEMBERS. "THEY HAD BEEN A PART OF THE WRITING [PROCESS] AND PUTTING THEIR OWN MARK ON THE RECORDS IN TERMS OF HOW THEY FELT THEY SHOULD BE."[3]

But Destiny's Child also worked with new collaborators who favoured a younger sound, such as Kevin "She'kspere" Briggs and Kandi Burruss – who were having a huge 1999 after co-writing TLC's smash "No Scrubs" – and producer Rodney "Darkchild" Jerkins. "The first record was successful but not hugely successful," Beyoncé said. "It was a neo-soul record and we were 15 years old. It was way too mature for us."[4]

Unsurprisingly, *The Writing's on the Wall*'s sound was immediately much more contemporary, drawing on influences from Southern hip-hop and vibrant pop production. Briggs and Burruss especially favoured colourful, popping-bubble beats alongside other instruments: "Bills, Bills, Bills" pairs a wary harpsichord with cascading harmonies; "Hey Ladies" boasts a slipshod backdrop with stuttering rhythms; and acoustic guitar flutters propel "So Good". Elsewhere, "If You Leave" is a collaboration with the R&B troupe Next, while Immature member Marques Houston co-wrote "Where'd You Go". And even songs with retro flair – the Jody Watley co-write "Sweet Sixteen" and the sophisticated soul-jazz number "She Can't Love You" – feel fresh.

Thematically, the album focused on relatable matters of the heart – namely, romantic ups and downs. Lead-off track "Intro (The Writing's on the Wall)" pays tribute to the *Godfather* scene from the 1996 movie *Set It Off*: the spoken-word tune cheekily references "Beyoncé Corleone" and outlines relationship commandments that the group references throughout the album.

The slinky R&B number "Temptation" is about feeling torn between your partner and a handsome stranger; another slow jam, "Now That She's Gone", slams a man for his indecisiveness and lack of commitment, because he was hedging his bets between two women; "Stay" pleads for a boyfriend not to leave; and the Missy Elliott-featuring "Confessions" is from the perspective of a woman divulging that she was unfaithful. Poignantly, the album ends with another heartfelt tribute to their late manager Andretta Tillman, an a-cappella take on "Amazing Grace" that allows the group to show off their gospel influences.

The Writing's on the Wall's international edition features the funky, syncopated "Get on the Bus" – which has a guest appearance by Timbaland and is also on the soundtrack to 1998's *Why Do Fools Fall in Love* – while the '90s R&B girl-group jam "Can't Help Myself" is a lost classic released only in the group's hometown of Houston.

It all added up to a blockbuster album that reached the top 10 in both the US and UK. Years later, Beyoncé noted that Destiny's Child "had no idea that *The Writing's on the Wall* would be as big a record as it was, especially worldwide. You have to remember at that time that we'd talk to people at the record company and they'd say, 'Look, they don't even play R&B in Europe right now.'"[5] But the album and Destiny's Child changed this perception – and helped usher in a golden age of modern hip-hop and R&B.

Opposite: Destiny's Child, pictured in summer 1997 in a recording studio in southwest Houston, very quickly became involved in production and songwriting.

BUG A BOO

[SINGLE]

Released: September 7, 1999 (single) / July 27, 1999 (album)
Writers: Kevin Briggs, Kandi Burruss, Beyoncé Knowles, LeToya Luckett, LaTavia Roberson, Kelly Rowland
Producer: Kevin "She'kspere" Briggs
Select Alternate Versions: Refugee Camp Remix featuring Wyclef Jean, Maurice's Xclusive "Bug a Boo" Club Mix

"Bug a Boo" is all about the importance of setting boundaries. The narrator references charmingly obsolete communication methods (the telephone company MCI, America Online email) while telling someone to back off, stop lovebombing and respect her wishes for no contact. "Bug a Boo" was "written for the fellas," Beyoncé later said, "but there are some female bug a boos out there. We wanted everyone to be able to relate to it."[6] Driven by a syncopated sample of Toto's 1978 song "Child's Anthem" that flashes like a camera shutter, the brisk "Bug a Boo" boasts sassy, exasperated vocals and uptempo hip-hop rhythms. "At the time, people weren't really singing over those types of tracks," said co-writer Kandi Burruss. "You'd look at it as something they'd rap over."[7] The members of Destiny's Child actually weren't into the song at first, she added: "I remember Beyoncé was telling the rest of the girls, 'Y'all, if we really don't like this, maybe we should let [producer She'kspere] know.'" However, Burruss worked with the group and they came around – and "Bug a Boo" became a US top 40 hit and peaked at No. 2 in the UK.

JUMPIN', JUMPIN'

[SINGLE]

Released: July 18, 2000 (single) / July 27, 1999 (album)
Writers: Chad Elliott, Beyoncé Knowles, Rufus Moore
Producers: Jovonn Alexander, Chad Elliott, Beyoncé Knowles
Select Alternate Versions: So So Def remix clean version featuring Jermaine Dupri, Da Brat and Lil Bow Wow, Maurice's Jumpin' Retro mix, Azza's remix

One of the most inventive, circa-Y2K, hip-hop club jams, the buoyant "Jumpin', Jumpin'" combines honey-sweet R&B harmonies and fiery pop hooks. Incredibly enough, this song emerged from a musical mix-up. Co-writer/co-producer Chad Elliott and his collaborators Rufus Moore and Jovonn Alexander sent Mathew Knowles a CD of in-progress tracks for Destiny's Child to check out. Much to Elliott's dismay, the disc accidentally included a tune called "The Ambush Crew" that he was working on for a separate, personal project. However, Beyoncé happened to like the track and came up with new lyrics, christening the song "Jumpin', Jumpin'".

Elliott was "blown away" by the transformation, he says. "Now it was a call for women to leave their significant others at home and go clubbing. It was a female twist that took me by surprise .... [But] there was something democratic about it, too, because it was also telling men to do the same thing, without their women."[8] Elliott gave his blessing to the song – and it became a massive global hit.

BILLS, BILLS, BILLS

[SINGLE]

Released: May 31, 1999 (single) / July 27, 1999 (album)
Writers: Kevin Briggs, Kandi Burruss, Beyoncé Knowles, LeToya Luckett, Kelly Rowland
Producers: Kevin "She'kspere" Briggs
Alternate Versions: Digital Black-N-Groove Club Mix, Remix with Sporty Thievz

The boyfriend depicted in "Bills, Bills, Bills" is a capital-F freeloader. He drives his girlfriend's car and doesn't fill up the gas tank, ruins her credit by maxing out her cards, makes her pay for tons of things and even has the gall to ask to borrow money. Despite this terrible behaviour, Beyoncé stressed that the song wasn't a "male-bashing song about women who just want to get paid", but about an irresponsible guy who's careless with money. "And now we're wondering if he can pay for what he created."[9]

As it turns out, co-writer Kandi Burruss drew on her previous relationships for lyrical ideas. Years later, she revealed that certain things in the song were true – and hit *very* close to home. "One of the girls that was in [Destiny's Child] was dating my ex at the time," Burruss said. "So I didn't tell them that some of the lyrics in there were inspired by him."[10] (She didn't name names, but savvy online sleuths deduced the ex in question appeared to be Jagged Edge member Brandon Casey, who was dating Destiny's Child member LaTavia Roberson.) The exasperation of "Bills, Bills, Bills" certainly resonated, becoming Destiny's Child's first No. 1 on the *Billboard* Hot 100 and earning two Grammy nominations.

SAY MY NAME

[SINGLE]

Released: Early 2000 (single) / July 27, 1999 (album)
Writers: LaShawn Daniels, Fred Jerkins III, Rodney Jerkins, Beyoncé Knowles, LeToya Luckett, LaTavia Roberson, Kelly Rowland
Producer: Rodney "Darkchild" Jerkins
Alternate Versions: Timbaland Remix

In 2006, Beyoncé deemed "Say My Name" one of Destiny's Child's best songs. It's easy to hear why: the tune combines a powerful message – the narrator is suspicious of her man's shifty behaviour and demands he treat her with respect – with vibrant music dominated by crisp, synthesized strings and throwback, funk-flecked guitars. "Say My Name" was the first song that Destiny's Child and Rodney Jerkins worked on together. However, both parties were lukewarm on the results; Beyoncé didn't even think it was going to make the album. "There was just too much stuff going on in it," she said. "It just sounded like this ... jungle. I don't even know to this day how we wrote that song over that track."[11] But Jerkins kept tinkering with the song – and when Destiny's Child was in a photo shoot, Beyoncé's dad brought the group a new version. "[He] said, 'Rodney's done a new mix of that song that you hate but you just have to take a listen to it,'" she recalled. "He played the mix to us and we couldn't even focus on anything. He had turned it into an amazing, timeless R&B record." The tune reached No. 1 on the *Billboard* Hot 100 and earned Destiny's Child their first Grammy win, for Best R&B Performance by a Duo or Group with Vocal.

Opposite: Destiny's Child put the work in to become a success. Here the group is seen performing at a Virgin Megastore in Paris.

03 SURVIVOR

IN THE LINER NOTES OF THEIR THIRD STUDIO ALBUM, *SURVIVOR*, THE MEMBERS OF DESTINY'S CHILD THANKED EVERYONE WHO "MADE IT THROUGH" A LITANY OF CHALLENGES – TO NAME A FEW, SADNESS, LONELINESS, BAD RELATIONSHIPS, HEALTH ISSUES, DISCRIMINATION, THE DEATH OF A LOVED ONE AND LOW SELF-ESTEEM – "AND SURVIVED".[12]

The pep talk might as well have been geared towards the group itself, which weathered several major lineup changes upon *Survivor*'s release. Most notably, original members LeToya Luckett and LaTavia Roberson were no longer in the group; instead, Destiny's Child was now a trio featuring Beyoncé Knowles, Kelly Rowland and new member Michelle Williams.

These changes attracted plenty of high-profile negative attention that detracted from the trio's growing musical skills and confidence. But instead of letting critics bring them down, Destiny's Child doubled down on themselves *and* their vision for their music. Among other things, Beyoncé co-wrote and co-produced *Survivor*. "I've never before seen or heard of anybody have that degree of acuity and memory and, you know, savant type of control over what she was doing in the studio," engineer Dan Workman recalled of watching her bring "Bootylicious" to life.[13]

However, Knowles went out of her way to stress that *Survivor* wasn't a Beyoncé solo effort: "Everybody is singing lead on all of the songs, so it gives it a more Destiny's Child feel."[14] (To that end, the title track even won a Grammy for Best R&B Performance by a Duo or Group with Vocal.) Instead, *Survivor* possesses a distinct empowering edge built around the idea of friendship, unity and independence.

That translates to songs like "Sexy Daddy", a celebration of a debauched night out with your girls where you're looking to let loose with a handsome guy, or "Independent Women Part II", a no-nonsense reinforcement of the ladies-first, self-empowerment

vibe of the song's first part. Other moments are deeply moving: the group wrote "The Story of Beauty" to provide support to a fan who wrote a letter and shared that she was sexually abused.

Musically, *Survivor* continued where *The Writing's on the Wall* left off by encompassing sophisticated soul ("Apple Pie à la Mode"), bustling hip-hop tracks with melodic R&B vocals ("Nasty Girl", "Fancy") and plush ballads ("Brown Eyes"). Elsewhere, however, the album also includes curveballs like the electronica-influenced "Happy Face" and "Outro (DC-3) Thank You". The international edition of *Survivor* also boasted several unique tracks, including the robotic funk percolations of "Perfect Man" and the stutter-stepping "Dance with Me".

Still, the elegant bonus track "My Heart Still Beats" and another gospel medley honouring their late manager Andretta Tillman ("You've Been So Good" / "Now Behold The Lamb" / "Jesus Loves Me") demonstrated the group's vocal ebullience. And, fittingly, *Survivor* was the group's first album to reach No. 1 on the *Billboard* 200 – a reflection of not just Destiny's Child's burgeoning superstardom, but also the album's encouraging vibe. "It's the type of album you'd listen to if you're feeling kind of down or you feel like you need to conquer something or survive something," Beyoncé said. "It gives you that confidence and self-esteem."[15]

Opposite, above and below: Destiny's Child eventually evolved into the trio of Beyoncé, Michelle Williams and Kelly Rowland. Hit after hit soon followed, as the women toured tirelessly and picked up awards like Best R&B/Soul Single for "Say My Name" at the Soul Train Lady of Soul Awards.

INDEPENDENT WOMEN PART 1

[SOUNDTRACK / SINGLE]

Released: August 29, 2000 (single) / May 1, 2001 (album)
Writers: Samuel Barnes, Beyoncé Knowles, Jean-Claude Olivier, Cory Rooney
Producers: Samuel Barnes, Beyoncé Knowles, Jean-Claude Olivier, Cory Rooney
Select Alternate Versions: Maurice's Independent Man remix, Victor Calderone club mix

"Independent Women Part 1" is an anthem for women who rely on nobody but themselves for money, clothes and jewellery – and wouldn't have it any other way. Beyoncé wrote the song when she was just 18 years old, envisioning it as a riposte to haters who misunderstood and criticized Destiny's Child. "They called us male-bashers," she said. "They called us gold diggers. And I had enough. So I wrote my own theme song."[16] She intentionally recorded a demo of the song by herself in the studio, she added: "I wanted to make it very clear that we paid our own bills."[17]

Unbeknownst to Beyoncé, however, her dad took this demo and played it for Sony Pictures, who was planning the 2000 *Charlie's Angels* movie. Weaving film references into the song helped it become a massive No. 1 hit that spent 11 weeks atop the *Billboard* Hot 100. Perhaps even more importantly, "Independent Women Part 1" reflected Beyoncé's growing impact as an icon. During a trip to Japan, she encountered women "saying how proud they were to have their own jobs, their own independent thinking, their own goals," she said. "It made me feel so good, and I realized that one of my responsibilities was to inspire women in a deeper way."[18]

SURVIVOR

[SINGLE]

Released: March 6, 2001 (single) / May 1, 2001 (album)
Writers: Anthony Dent, Beyoncé Knowles, Mathew Knowles
Producers: Anthony Dent and Beyoncé Knowles
Select Alternate Versions: Extended Remix featuring Da Brat, Calderone Drum Dub mix, CB200 Club Anthem mix

Contrary to rumours, Beyoncé didn't write *Survivor*'s title track about anybody specific – "People automatically assume that it's about former members, and it's not," she said[19] – but instead directed it to sceptics who doubted Destiny's Child's staying power. She reportedly penned the lyrics quickly, on an airplane while Destiny's Child was on tour with Christina Aguilera, after being irked by a radio station that compared the group's lineup changes to a reality TV show. "They were saying, 'Oh, Destiny's Child is like *Survivor*, trying to see which member is going to last the longest on the island', and everyone laughed," she said. "I was like, 'Ah, that's cute, but you know what? I'm going to use that negative thing and turn it into a positive thing and try to write a great song out of it.'"[20] When it came time to record the song, co-producer/co-writer Anthony Dent was duly impressed with Beyoncé's focus and vision. "She's really a woman who knows what she wants," Dent said. "She sat down and told me what type of direction she wanted to go. And once I made the music, she was like, 'That's it. Let me do my thing.'"[21]

BOOTYLICIOUS

[SINGLE]

Released: May 22, 2001 (single) / May 1, 2001 (album)
Writers: Rob Fusari, Beyoncé Knowles, Falonte Moore
Producers: Rob Fusari, Beyoncé Knowles, Falonte Moore
Select Alternate Versions: Rockwilder remix featuring Missy Elliott, Richard Vission's V-Quest, Big Boyz remix

In 2000, Beyoncé was on a long flight and came upon a track written by collaborator Rob Fusari that was propelled by the distinctive, corrugated, guitar riff of Stevie Nicks' 1981 song "Edge of Seventeen". The part "reminded me of a voluptuous woman" showing off her shimmying dance moves, Beyoncé said – and inspiration struck. "I said, 'I don't care what anybody says about me. I'm gonna write a song to celebrate a woman's curves,'" she later explained. "And I didn't care what they were saying about me: I was *bootylicious*!"[22]

That confidence carried over into the studio, where Beyoncé spent long hours refining the lyrics and recording vocal parts, layering and doubling harmonies to form a vocal tapestry. "She'd listen to the playback of all those Beyoncé voices and say, 'You know, that one take, in the middle, that second one? I need to do that one over again,'" recalls engineer Dan Workman. "'I made a mistake there. My inflection wasn't quite the same as the others, and my breath was a little different.'"[23] Her attention to detail paid off: "Bootylicious" spent two weeks at No. 1 on the *Billboard* Hot 100 – and the song to this day makes being bootylicious something to *celebrate.*

EMOTION

[SINGLE]

Released: September 4, 2001 (single) / May 1, 2001 (album)
Writers: Barry Gibb and Robin Gibb
Producers: Mark J. Feist, Beyoncé Knowles, Mathew Knowles
Select Alternate Versions: The Neptunes Remix, With Strings

At the 2001 Soul Train Lady of Soul Awards, Destiny's Child opened the show with a tender performance of "Emotion" dedicated to Aaliyah, as the R&B star had died in a plane crash just days before. "She was one of the most beautiful people on the inside as well as out," Beyoncé said at the show. "It's tragic. Every night we pray for her family and everyone else's family."[24] Written by Bee Gees members Barry and Robin Gibb, "Emotion" was originally recorded as a frothy soft-pop ballad in 1978 by the Australian artist Samantha Sang. As their awards show performance demonstrates, Destiny's Child took a different approach to the song, emphasizing the heartbreak and resignation in the lyrics via passionate vocal performances that exude longing. "[We] added our Destiny's Child flavor to it," Beyoncé said. "Vocally, it's the strongest song on our album. It features everybody; you can really hear all our voices."[25] "Emotion" reached No. 3 in the UK and entered the top 10 in the US.

Opposite and above: MTV and Destiny's Child had a great relationship. The group attended the taping of *MTV ICON: Janet Jackson* and headlined MTV's TRL Tour alongside Nelly and the St. Lunatics, Eve, and 3LW.

*NSYNC, 98 DEGREES AND CHRISTINA AGUILERA RELEASED CHRISTMAS ALBUMS — SETTING THE STAGE FOR DESTINY'S CHILD TO RELEASE A HOLIDAY RECORD OF THEIR OWN, *8 DAYS OF CHRISTMAS*, IN OCTOBER 2001.

It was clear the group had been planning this release for a while, as the title track originally appeared on a deluxe edition of *The Writing's on the Wall.* It's a playful remake of the "12 Days of Christmas", where the group members receive gifts like clothes, jewellery, a romantic dinner and even a poem from their beloved.

"8 Days of Christmas" was a solid indicator of the direction in which Destiny's Child went with their album: reverent to classic songs and styles, but with a modern twist. "There hasn't been a Christmas album like this – it's kind of like a 2000 version of *Motown Christmas*," Beyoncé said, referencing the infamous 1973 LP that featured label greats such as Stevie Wonder, Smokey Robinson and The Jackson 5. "There's nothing traditional about the album, even with the traditional songs."[26]

That's clear from the impressive "A 'DC' Christmas Medley", which incorporates lyrics from six seasonal staples, including "Santa Claus is Coming to Town", "Frosty the Snowman" and "Have a Holly Jolly Christmas" over a sizzling track co-produced by Rob Fusari and Falonte Moore. But Beyoncé also noted that Destiny's Child "totally remade" many of the standards that appeared in full on the album (for example, "Do You Hear What I Hear?", "O' Holy Night" and "Silent Night") with "really different harmonies and arrangements."[27]

This was especially evident on "White Christmas", which included both intricate backing vocals and syncopated rhythms; a soulful "Little Drummer Boy" with new melodies and cascading girl-group harmonies throughout; and completely deconstructed versions of "Silver Bells" and "Carol of the Bells" retitled (respectively) "Platinum Bells" and "Opera of the Bells".

Even more radical is the classic soul song "This Christmas", which was popularized in 1970 by Donny Hathaway. On *8 Days of Christmas,* it's an ultra-modern house music tune with skittering beats and chilly electronic textures. "You know Destiny's Child has to have beats, right?" Kelly Rowland said. "Even at Christmas. We put the DC 'stank' on it." Added Michelle Williams: "We wanted to make a Christmas album to wrap gifts to but that could also be listened to after the holidays."[28]

The originals on *8 Days of Christmas* display that same spirit of adventure. "Spread A Little Love on Christmas Day" expresses gratitude for family and faith and reassures that Santa has plans to visit kids no matter where they live, while the chilly synthpop song "Winter Paradise" interpolates the melody of George Michael's 1987 song "Father Figure" while also praising what matters at the holidays. A 2005 reissue of the album tacked on an exuberant cover of "Rudolph the Red-Nosed Reindeer" and another dynamite original song, "Home for the Holidays", with co-writing and production from the Bama Boyz. In the end, Destiny's Child's *8 Days of Christmas* is the rare album that brings something new to the holiday music landscape.

Opposite: Destiny's Child at their festive best during the Rockefeller Center Christmas Tree Lighting in New York City.

05 DESTINY FULFILLED

IN LATE 2000, EACH MEMBER OF DESTINY'S CHILD ANNOUNCED PLANS TO RELEASE A SOLO RECORD. "WE'RE GOING TO ALL DO DIFFERENT TYPES OF MUSIC AND SUPPORT EACH OTHER'S ALBUM," BEYONCÉ SAID, WHILE NOTING THESE RELEASES WEREN'T MEANT AS COMPETITION. "AND WE'LL COME BACK AND DO ANOTHER ALBUM FOR DESTINY'S CHILD, AND HOPEFULLY IT WILL BROADEN OUR AUDIENCE, SO IT WILL HELP US ALL OUT."[29]

This strategy worked like a charm. Michelle Williams released two gospel studio albums, 2002's *Heart to Yours* – which reached No. 1 on *Billboard*'s Top Gospel Albums chart – and 2004's *Do You Know*. Kelly Rowland, meanwhile, spent 10 weeks at No. 1 on the *Billboard* Hot 100 with the Grammy-winning 2002 Nelly duet "Dilemma", from her solo debut *Simply Deep*. And Beyoncé had even more commercial success with her 2003 debut solo LP *Dangerously in Love*, to the tune of two No. 1 hits and five Grammy Awards.

When the group reconvened in summer 2004 to record what would become *Destiny Fulfilled*, they worked quickly. "We probably recorded all the songs in about a month and every day it was a new song coming out," said Sean Garrett, who co-wrote and co-produced multiple songs.[30] The music was cohesive, leaning into harmony-forward R&B with prominent chill grooves and a '70s soul influence ("If", "Love", "Free"), and built upon casual conversations the trio had in the studio.

This approach was deliberate, Beyoncé revealed, as she wanted the individual talents of each member to shine through. "You can really sing on those songs," she said. "It was important for me, the vocal producer of the record, for people to hear Michelle, to hear how soulful and raspy her voice is. To hear how colorful and clear Kelly's voice is and to hear all of us and how different we are. And you can't do that as much with uptempos."[31]

Indeed, although the lead-off track "Lose My Breath" is a quintessential upbeat Destiny's Child smash, the *Destiny Fulfilled* album tracks are more sophisticated and contemplative. Highlights include the seductive "T-Shirt", which chronicles the many ways a man's T-shirt is sexy; "Bad Habit", a tortured tale of trying to shake off an ex for good; and the piano-driven "Through with Love", which details a woman reclaiming her sense of self and power after a bad relationship. Another standout, "Is She the Reason", incorporates Melba Moore's "I Don't Know No One Else to Turn To" while expressing pain and confusion after the ultimate betrayal: being rejected for another woman.

The international edition included the steamy "Game Over", while a Japanese version featured two neo-soul-leaning bonus tracks – "Got's My Own" and "Why You Actin'". And a Walmart edition of the album featured two lost classics, the retro-influenced "My Man" and the sinewy "2 Step".

Destiny Fulfilled closed the book on Destiny's Child's active musical career – and although the group has reunited in various ways in the decades since, the album is an accomplished swan song that positioned Beyoncé, Kelly and Michelle for future solo career success.

Opposite and above: Destiny's Child released their last studio album, *Destiny Fulfilled*, in 2004, and then went on tour, leading to opportunities like performing at the 2006 NBA All-Star Game.

NBA

LOSE MY BREATH

[SINGLE]

Released: October 5, 2004 (single) / November 15, 2004 (album)
Writers: Shawn Carter, LaShawn Daniels, Sean Garrett, Fred Jerkins III, Rodney Jerkins, Beyoncé Knowles, Kelly Rowland, Michelle Williams
Producers: Sean Garrett, Rodney Jerkins, Beyoncé Knowles, Kelly Rowland
Select Alternate Versions: Maurice's Nu Soul Mix, Paul Johnson's Club Mix

When Destiny's Child came back together after a few years apart to release 2004's *Destiny Fulfilled*, the group wanted to make a *statement*. Enter "Lose My Breath", which is tailor-made for a marching band, given its burst of drumline beats, staccato strings that resemble a horn section, and precise coordinated vocals. Beyoncé and Michelle Williams initially heard just the song's rhythm track, but immediately knew it set the perfect tone for the album. "When I saw their excitement, I got excited without even hearing it," Kelly Rowland said. "That track has so much presence, and the fact that we've been on hiatus for two or three years, it's a great comeback song. It sounds like 'We're back!'"[32] The members of Destiny's Child then wrote the verses and bridge – all of which playfully challenge a man to see if he is on the level with his woman – around a chorus written by Jay-Z. "I told him we heard this crazy track and it's going to have everyone losing their breath," Beyoncé said. "He was like, 'I got it, [singing] "Can you keep up?"' He actually came up with the chorus without even hearing the track."[33]

SOLDIER

[SINGLE]

Released: November 9, 2004 (single) / November 15, 2004 (album)
Writers: Dwayne Carter, Sean Garrett, Clifford Harris, Rich Harrison, Beyoncé Knowles, Kelly Rowland, Michelle Williams
Producers: Rich Harrison and Beyoncé Knowles
Select Alternate Versions: Maurice's Nu Soul Mix, Peter Rauhofer's Breathless Club Mix, Grizz Blackmarket Remix

Featuring appearances by rappers T.I. and Lil Wayne, "Soldier" illustrates Destiny's Child's talent for shapeshifting between hip-hop and R&B: the women embrace a laid-back vocal delivery that veers between beestung harmonies and Southern hip-hop twang. Sean Garrett wrote "Soldier" in a taxi, when he was heading to the studio. "I loved how Destiny's Child evolved and became this really incredible pop group," he said. "But I wanted to introduce them to the hood from the perspective of having the world look at them in a different way."[34] That extended to the lyrics of "Soldier", which Rowland said reflected the group's romantic preferences. "What you want is a soldier that is going to stand up for you. ... And we actually really get into detail about the kind of men that we like, whether he's from the East Coast or the West Coast or the South side with gold grills."[35] In Beyoncé's case, her part alludes to Jay-Z – the first time she referenced her future husband in a song.

GIRL

[SINGLE]

Released: March 14, 2005 (single) / November 15, 2004 (album)
Writers: Angela Beyincé, Don Davis, Patrick "9th Wonder" Douthit, Sean Garrett, Beyoncé Knowles, Eddie Robinson, Kelly Rowland, Michelle Williams
Producers: Patrick Douthit, Beyoncé Knowles, Kelly Rowland
Select Alternate Versions: Junior Vasquez Club Dub, Kardinal Beats Remix, The Freshman Remix

Driven by a sample of the Dramatics' lush "Ocean of Thoughts and Dreams", "Girl" is one of the most personal moments in Destiny's Child's catalogue – and the embodiment of the group's sisterhood. The song begins with Beyoncé expressing concern about a friend trapped in a romantic relationship where she's not being treated well. On verse two, Kelly Rowland takes the lead and justifies the boyfriend's actions, though it's clear she's making excuses to cover up his lying and infidelity. However, the rest of the group isn't convinced: on the bridge, Beyoncé and Michelle Williams join forces vocally to comfort their friend, note she's not looking great, and offer help. As it turns out, "Girl" is based on a true story, as Beyoncé and Williams wrote the song for Rowland, who was in an abusive relationship at the time. "Destiny's Child is deeper than what people see on the surface," Rowland said in 2013. "Those are my homies for life. For life! Those girls, we stuck with each other – period."[36]

Opposite and right: Beyoncé, Kelly Rowland and Michelle Williams closed out their career as an active group with the 2005's Destiny Fulfilled... And Lovin' It Tour alongside television appearances.

CATER 2 U

[SINGLE]

Released: June 7, 2005 (single) / November 15, 2004 (album)
Writers: Rodney Jerkins, Beyoncé Knowles, Ricky Lewis, Kelly Rowland, Robert Waller, Michelle Williams
Producers: Rodney Jerkins, Beyoncé Knowles, Ric Rude
Select Alternate Versions: Storch Remix Edit, Grizz to the Club, J. Beck Dance Remix

The narrator of the R&B ballad "Cater 2 U" is so grateful for her man that she's ready to pamper him with all of his favourite things – which means she's (among other things) running a bath, rubbing his feet, getting his slippers and grabbing him dinner. "It basically talks about how a guy inspires you," Beyoncé said of the neo-soul slow jam. "You want to make him happy."[37] This might seem like an odd thematic switch from a group that touted female empowerment and independence, but Beyoncé stressed that wasn't the case. "I know it's going to be surprising to a lot of people that the independent survivors are being submissive to their man," she explained, "but it's important that people know that, you know, it's fine if your man deserves it and gives that back to you."[38] "Cater 2 U" ended up accounting for two of the last Grammy nominations for Destiny's Child; the song was up for Best R&B Performance by a Duo or Group with Vocals and Best R&B Song.

OTHER SONGS

OUTSIDE OF THEIR STUDIO ALBUMS, DESTINY'S CHILD RELEASED A REMIX ALBUM (2002'S *THIS IS THE REMIX*) AND MULTIPLE COMPILATIONS. THESE RELEASES OFTEN INCLUDED SONGS YOU COULDN'T GET ANYWHERE ELSE.

For example, the 2001 Target-exclusive EP *Love: Destiny* included "My Song". Dating from the *Survivor* era and produced by D'Wayne Wiggins, the tune captures the unfettered joy of hearing your favourite song in the wild while out at night. Destiny's Child's 2005 hits collection *#1s* included three new songs, including the piano ballad (and 2005 World Children's Day Anthem) "Stand Up for Love"; a Beyoncé-led "Check on It" with Slim Thug; and the breathy "Feel the Same Way I Do", which is about hoping that your love is reciprocated. And 2013's *Love Songs* included the dreamy '90s dance throwback "Nuclear".

Between 1997 and 2015, Destiny's Child was also the featured artist on multiple songs by pop acts (Jessica Simpson's "Woman in Me"), gospel artists (Mary Mary's "Good to Me") and rappers (Cam'ron's "Do It Again"; 50 Cent's "Thug Love"; Silkk the Shocker's "Just Be Straight with Me"). They also contributed original songs to multiple soundtracks, appearing with Da Brat on "Big Momma's Theme" (from 2000's *Big Momma's House*), collaborating with Solange on 2004's "The Proud Family Theme Song" and creating the 1999 original "No More Rainy Days" for the soundtrack to TV show *The PJs*.

And when Kelly Rowland and Michelle Williams continued their solo careers, they never forgot the rest of Destiny's Child. Rowland enlisted Beyoncé and Williams for "You Changed" on 2013's *Talk a Good Game*, while Rowland and Bey returned the favour for Williams on 2014's "Say Yes".

Below and opposite: Although Destiny's Child did their last world tour in 2005 (below), the group has reunited occasionally for live performances; for example, they performed "Say Yes" (opposite) during the 30th Annual Stellar Awards in 2015.

PART II

BEYONCÉ

06 EARLY SOLO

UNLIKE MANY ARTISTS WHO FIRST CUT THEIR TEETH IN A BAND OR GROUP, BEYONCÉ SOFT-LAUNCHED HER SOLO MUSIC CAREER WHILE STILL THRIVING IN DESTINY'S CHILD. SHE DID SO WHILE SIMULTANEOUSLY BEGINNING AN ACTING CAREER, FIRST WITH THE MTV-PRODUCED MUSICAL *CARMEN: A HIP HOPERA* AND NEXT IN THE HIGH-PROFILE *AUSTIN POWERS IN GOLDMEMBER*. EVEN THEN SHE WAS PUTTING TOGETHER A BLUEPRINT FOR HER EVENTUAL SUPERSTAR CAREER, AS SHE RECORDED SAVVY COLLABORATIONS (MISSY ELLIOTT) AND SOUNDTRACK TUNES ("WORK IT OUT") THAT GAVE HER VOICE A CHANCE TO SHINE.

AFTER ALL IS SAID AND DONE (BEYONCÉ AND MARC NELSON)

[SOUNDTRACK]

Released: October 12, 1999 (album)
Writers: Gordon Chambers and Phil Galdston
Producer: Warryn "Dub" Campbell

Many early Beyoncé solo songs were associated with movies. Case in point: "After All Is Said and Done" – a duet with Marc Nelson, an early member of Boyz II Men who found success as a solo artist and as part of the group Az Yet – appeared on the soundtrack to 1999's *The Best Man*, alongside tracks by R&B stars Maxwell, Faith Evans and Eric Benét. As the film's title implies, the plot of the Taye Diggs-Nia Long movie revolves around a wedding filled with drama, romantic and otherwise. "After All Is Said and Done" – which was co-written by Phil Galdston, the writer who is also credited for co-writing Vanessa Williams' "Save the Best For Last" – comes across like heartfelt wedding vows given by two people who are grateful to have found solace in each other. Accordingly, Beyoncé sings in a tender voice that exudes vulnerability, which enhances the tune's emotional sincerity.

Opposite and right: Beyoncé began recording solo music while still with Destiny's Child and even crossed paths creatively with her future boyfriend, rapper Jay-Z (opposite), on a 2000 single.

CRAZY FEELINGS (MISSY ELLIOTT FEATURING BEYONCÉ)

[ALBUM TRACK]

Released: June 22, 1999 (album)
Writers: Missy Elliott and Timothy "Timbaland" Mosley
Producer: Timbaland

Beyoncé and hip-hop virtuoso Missy Elliott collaborated multiple times in the late 1990s and early 2000s, including on "Crazy Feelings", a subdued highlight on Elliott's second album, *Da Real World*. Led by a trip-hop-inspired groove, dusk-dark electronic production and downtrodden vocals, the song is from the perspective of a woman who realized she stayed in a relationship too long. Her now-ex didn't even try to hide his lies; instead, she ignored her instincts and overlooked his shady behaviour because she was so madly in love. The brute honesty of "Crazy Feelings" reflects Elliott's approach to songwriting. "If you listen to my songs, they tell stories," she said. "I don't write in song form, I write almost as if I'm in conversation with somebody. That's my way of getting something off my chest."[1]

HAVE YOUR WAY (KELLY ROWLAND AND BEYONCÉ)

[SOUNDTRACK]

Released: February 2000 (album)
Writers: LaShawn Daniels, Fred Jerkins III, Beyoncé Knowles
Producers: LaShawn Daniels and Fred Jerkins III

"Have Your Way" is one of Beyoncé's most obscure songs. The sombre R&B tune, which is actually a collaboration with Kelly Rowland, appeared on the soundtrack to a gospel-inspired musical called *His Woman His Wife*, which starred actor Malik Yoba and ran at New York City's Beacon Theatre in February 2000. Lyrically, "Have Your Way" is a song about relying on faith when things become difficult. Having been promised that an engagement is imminent, the song's narrator has made personal sacrifices for their partner. Unfortunately, a ring doesn't appear to be coming anytime soon – so she's now looking for support and guidance from God to help her navigate these rough waters. Beyoncé and Rowland clearly have compassion for the woman within the song, as their vocal performances are sensitive and empathetic.

I GOT THAT (AMIL FEATURING BEYONCÉ)

[SINGLE]

Released: July 5, 2000 (single) / August 29, 2000 (album)
Writers: Samuel Barnes, Shawn Carter, Makeda Davis, LeShan Lewis, Jean-Claude "Poke" Olivier, Tamy Smith, Amil Whitehead
Producers: L.E.S. and Trackmasters
Alternate Versions: Radio Edit, Instrumental

New York City rapper Amil first rose to prominence in the late 1990s as a protégé of Jay-Z, appearing on songs like "Can I Get A…" as a secondary voice. By 2000, she was ready to step out on her own as a solo artist with her debut album, *All Money Is Legal.* Thanks to some record label matchmaking, Beyoncé appeared as a featured artist on Amil's first single, "I Got That". Perhaps unsurprisingly, the tune is very reminiscent of Destiny's Child. Thematically, Amil and Beyoncé sing about being independent women who are fiscally responsible and don't need a man to pay for their rent, credit cards or cars. Amil's tenacious rapping alternates with Beyoncé's soulful singing, a perfect textural match for a funky, stuttering track that samples Gwen Guthrie's 1983 electro classic "Seventh Heaven". Sadly, "I Got That" wasn't a huge hit, although it did reach No. 1 on *Billboard*'s Bubbling Under R&B/Hip-Hop Singles chart and is remembered today for being Beyoncé's first musical collaboration with Jay-Z.

CARMEN: A HIP HOPERA

IN 2001, BEYONCÉ LANDED THE LEAD ROLE IN THE MUSICAL FILM *CARMEN: A HIP HOPERA*, A CONTEMPORARY SPIN ON GEORGES BIZET'S 1875 OPERA *CARMEN*. AS THE TITLE IMPLIES, THE MTV-PRODUCED MOVIE FEATURED ORIGINAL HIP-HOP, SOUL AND R&B SONGS PERFORMED BY BEYONCÉ, HER CO-STAR MEKHI PHIFER AND RAPPERS LIKE DA BRAT, MOS DEF, RAH DIGGA AND WYCLEF JEAN.

Her entrance into the movie business came about almost on a lark. "MTV came to a Destiny's Child show with the script," Beyoncé said, "and at the time, acting wasn't something I was planning to do."[2] However, she thought the script was good – and sensed immediately that branching out into movies was a smart career move. "Music is something that can, and should, be used to get you into different things," she theorized, "because eventually what goes up must come down – we're not going to be the number one group in the world forever – so you have to have something else to fall back on."[3]

Despite being a novice actress, Beyoncé held her own with the rest of the cast, particularly vocally. She added jazzy flair to "Cards Never Lie", which also featured Rah Digga and Wyclef Jean, and embraced the '80s hip-hop throwback vibes of "Girls' Cali Dream" with gusto. Beyoncé's steely rapping on the Mos Def-featuring "If Looks Could Kill (You Would Be Dead)" and her melodic flow on the Mekhi Phifer collaboration "The Last Great Seduction" also foreshadowed the directions she'd explore on subsequent solo records.

Director Robert Townsend, who helmed movies such as 1987's *Eddie Murphy Raw* and 1991's *The Five Heartbeats*, brought a wealth of experience to his role that also guided the film's development. "I'm a fan of *Carmen Jones*," he said, referencing a stage musical based on the opera, "but I was aware of the opera as well. I grew up in the theater in Chicago. I knew all the classics."[4]

Thanks to all of this support, Beyoncé had a "great experience" filming *Carmen* in Los Angeles, she said. Outside of music, being part of the cast was just as formative, as it marked the first time she lived and worked by herself. "All my life, because I was in a group, I've been taught to compromise," Beyoncé said. "Someone says, 'What do you want to eat?' My first instinct is to ask, What y'all want me to eat? Okay, this is what we want."[5] After filming was done, her takeaways from *Carmen* endured. "Besides Kelly and Michelle, I'm not around people our age for more than forty-five minutes," she says. "So I was around people my age for a month and a half, and I made friends. So it was way more than a movie for me."[6]

Above and opposite: In 2001, Beyoncé co-starred with Mos Def (pictured with her at the Grammy Awards) in the film *Carmen: A Hip Hopera*.

WORK IT OUT

[SOUNDTRACK / ALBUM TRACK]

Released: June 11, 2002 (single) / July 16, 2002 (album)
Writers: Chad Hugo, Beyoncé Knowles, Pharrell Williams
Producers: The Neptunes
Select Alternate Mixes: Maurice's Nu Soul Mix, Rockwilder Remix, Victor Calderone's Blow Your Horn Dub

Beyoncé's career as a solo artist officially kicked off with "Work It Out", the first single released from the *Austin Powers in Goldmember* soundtrack. The hip-shaking tune sounds beamed straight from a flashy 1970s nightclub, between its funky grooves, disco-rock underbelly, and Beyoncé's ecstatic, soul-diva vocals.

Co-written and produced by Chad Hugo and Pharrell Williams of The Neptunes, "Work it Out" was, unsurprisingly, "a blast to record in Los Angeles," recalled John Houlihan, the movie's music supervisor. "[It was an] incredibly small vocal session with only Beyoncé, Pharrell and me."[7]

Beyoncé's performance on "Work It Out" also captured the exuberant, worldly vibe of her character in *Austin Powers in Goldmember:* Foxxy Cleopatra, a stealth FBI agent inspired by the legendary actress Pam Grier. "Before the movie, I watched every one of her films I could find," Beyoncé said. "At the reading with Mike [Myers], I wouldn't talk unless I was talking like her. She helped me tremendously. She's who I based everything on. She was my inspiration."[8] To director Jay Roach, this method acting paid off big time. "What Beyoncé contributed to *Goldmember* is so huge," he said. "Its lasting presence is very much due to her involvement, and the fact that she's become this mega-mega-megastar can't hurt."[9]

HEY GOLDMEMBER (BEYONCÉ, DEVIN AND SOLANGE)

[SOUNDTRACK]

Released: July 16, 2002 (album)
Writers: Harry Wayne Casey, Richard Finch, Mike Myers, Paul Myers
Producers: Damon Elliott and Beyoncé Knowles

Disco music plays an outsized role in *Austin Powers in Goldmember* and its soundtrack. Case in point: "Hey Goldmember" is a horn-heavy groovefest that mashes up three KC and the Sunshine Band disco hits ("That's The Way (I Like It)", "Get Down Tonight" and "(Shake Shake Shake) Shake Your Booty") and Earth, Wind & Fire's "Sing a Song". For good measure, the song also features cheeky (and occasionally risqué) new lyrics about the film's villain, Goldmember, written by *Austin Powers'* star Mike Myers and his brother, the journalist and musician Paul Myers.

In the studio, Beyoncé and her younger sister Solange Knowles, who features on the track, "rolled in together, very low-key but enthusiastic," said music supervisor John Houlihan. "As we hoped, Beyoncé took control of her vocal tracking. She was a super-pro and had a great ear for perfecting her lead vocal and the backing tracks."[10] Beyoncé also "guided [Solange] to perfection" on the backing tracks, Houlihan added, a prelude to Mike Myers coming to the session after filming and putting the finishing touches on the tune. "We all laid down a disco clap track. We were all laughing our heads off."[11]

NOTHING OUT THERE FOR ME (MISSY ELLIOTT FEATURING BEYONCÉ)

[ALBUM TRACK]

Released: November 12, 2002 (album)
Writers: Craig Brockman, Missy Elliott, Nisan Stewart
Producers: Craig Brockman, Missy Elliott, Nisan Stewart

On Missy Elliott's fourth album, *Under Construction*, the rapper once again teamed up with Beyoncé for another gem, "Nothing Out There for Me". The song takes the form of a phone conversation between the two women. Missy first tries to coax Beyoncé out of the house to the club, but the latter demurs because she insists that she's happier being at home with her man. (Relatable!) Although Missy is concerned about her friend, she eventually comes around after Beyoncé stresses that her relationship is rock-solid and healthy.

Beyoncé also shows off her vocal versatility on "Nothing Out There for Me", dabbling in both soaring soul runs and brisk rap-singing. "I said: 'Hey, I want you to rap a little bit,'" Elliott later recalled. "And she was like: 'Miss, if I sound crazy, don't put this out!' And I said: "Trust me, B, I'm not gonna allow you to sound crazy.' She went in there and now she's rapping better than me!"[12]

SEXY LIL' THUG

[MIXTAPE]

Released: Early 2003 (song) / 2005 (mixtape)
Writers: Mike Elizondo, Curtis Jackson, Andre Young

"Sexy Lil' Thug" is one of the more unfairly under-the-radar songs in Beyoncé's catalogue. Over the backing track of 50 Cent's massive hit "In Da Club", she gender-flips the lyrics, turning the song into a celebration of a powerful woman who's ruling the night (and wowing any man in her path) with fancy clothes and a confident attitude. Beyoncé's version of "In Da Club" reached No. 67 on *Billboard*'s Hot R&B/Hip-Hop Singles and Tracks chart in April 2003 – coincidentally enough, the same week 50 Cent's version of the song was perched at No. 1 – and had started to pick up radio airplay. However, according to a report at the time, her version was "pulled from the airwaves after 50 Cent's record company issued a 'cease and desist' order."[13] (No wonder manager Mathew Knowles told MTV News the song wasn't going to be on her forthcoming debut album *Dangerously In Love*.[14]) However, Beyoncé's "In Da Club" eventually did surface on the 2005 mixtape *Speak My Mind*.

Below: When Beyoncé portrayed stealth FBI agent Foxxy Cleopatra in 2002's *Austin Powers in Goldmember*, she also recorded several songs for the film's soundtrack.

07 DANGEROUSLY IN LOVE

BEYONCÉ ANNOUNCED HER SOLO DEBUT ALBUM WITH A BRASSY SPLASH: THE 2003 SINGLE "CRAZY IN LOVE", WHICH SAILED TO THE TOP OF THE CHARTS IN THE US AND UK ON THE STRENGTH OF A CRISP CHI-LITES SAMPLE, AN EFFERVESCENT JAY-Z GUEST SPOT, AND BEYONCÉ'S BOLD, CONFIDENT VOCALS. *DANGEROUSLY IN LOVE* ITSELF REACHED NO. 1 AROUND THE WORLD (AND WON A GRAMMY FOR BEST CONTEMPORARY R&B ALBUM) ON THE STRENGTH OF FLIRTY SINGLES "NAUGHTY GIRL" AND "BABY BOY", AS WELL AS A TRACKLIST THAT CRYSTALLIZED HER UNIQUE BLEND OF R&B, POP AND HIP-HOP.

CRAZY IN LOVE

[SINGLE]

Released: May 14, 2003 (single) / June 24, 2003 (album)
Writers: Shawn Carter, Rich Harrison, Beyoncé Knowles, Eugene Record
Producers: Rich Harrison and Beyoncé Knowles
Select Alternate Versions: *Fifty Shades of Grey* re-recorded version, Rockwilder remix, Maurice Joshua's Nu Soul remix

When Beyoncé started working on *Dangerously in Love*, she had a very specific vision. As a result, she oversaw every bit of the songwriting, song selection, production and mixing on the album, and was deliberate about her chosen collaborators. "I had meetings and interviews with every producer from the East Coast and every producer from the West Coast – all day for two days, every 30 minutes someone else," she said.[1] One of the producers she met with was Rich Harrison, who had worked with Mary J. Blige, Alicia Keys and Kelly Rowland.

Harrison ran late for their meeting and, on top of that, wasn't feeling great; by his own admission, he was totally hungover from an epic night of clubbing. But Harrison had an advantage: he had saved a striking musical track to play for Beyoncé, one that sampled the extroverted horn bursts from "Are You My Woman? (Tell Me So)" by '70s soul group the Chi-Lites.

"I knew I was going to have to sell it a little bit," he recalled, "because when it comes on it doesn't sound like anything that was being done at the time."[2] Beyoncé was also initially on the fence about the sample. "It has this go-go feel to it, this old-school feel. I wasn't sure if people were going to get it."[3] Still, she had Harrison try to build a song around the track – and gave him a tight deadline of two hours to do so.

The producer came through, powering through his hangover and putting together the verses and the hook. The results are like a dynamite soul revue: "Crazy in Love" goes from zero to 60, exploding in a burst of brass, drumline rhythms and Beyoncé's hiccupping uh-ohs. It's the sonic equivalent of being deliriously head over heels for someone, when your heart starts pounding with desire and happiness whenever you see them.

Lyrically, "Crazy in Love" also captures this ecstatic feeling, as it "talks about a young lady who is realizing that she's so in love that she's doing things she wouldn't normally do," Beyoncé explained. "She's basically not even conscious of some of the things she's doing. It's almost driving her crazy and she doesn't care because she loves the feeling."[4]

However, the initial lyrical inspiration wasn't being crazy in love. Instead, Beyoncé was in the studio and wanted to go buy Kelly Rowland a birthday present, but was worried about being seen in public looking less than her best. "I was looking crazy with my clothes," she said. "And I kept saying, 'I'm looking crazy right now.'... [I was wearing] things that weren't matching, my hair wasn't combed, just looking crazy! And [Harrison] said, "That's the hook!"[5] Much to Harrison's delight, Jay-Z also loved the music track – and when Beyoncé asked him to appear on the track, he added a perfect verse.

"Crazy in Love" won Grammy Awards for Best R&B Song and Best Rap/Sung Collaboration and reached No. 1 in the US and UK pop singles charts, including an eight-week run atop the *Billboard* Hot 100. To this day it remains one of Beyoncé's signature songs – and it created a blueprint for her vibrant solo career.

Left and opposite: At the 2003 MTV Video Music Awards, Beyoncé performed and won three awards for "Crazy in Love," including Best Female Video.

NAUGHTY GIRL

[SINGLE]

Released: March 14, 2004 (single) / June 24, 2003 (album)
Writers: Pete Bellotte, Angela Beyincé, Beyoncé Knowles, Giorgio Moroder, Scott Storch, Donna Summer, Robert Waller
Producers: Beyoncé Knowles and Scott Storch
Select Alternate Versions: Calderone Quayle club mix, Featuring Lil' Flip, Featuring Lil' Kim

In the mid-1970s, disco queen Donna Summer landed a massive hit with the disco-funk smash "Love to Love You Baby", which paired babymaking grooves with seductive (if at times sexually explicit) vocals. A quarter-century later, Beyoncé paid tribute to the groundbreaking song with her own seduction tune, "Naughty Girl". She interpolates the airy "Love to Love You Baby" chorus hook and Summer's coquettish croon, pairing them with flirty, confident lyrics that exude a sexy vibe. "Many of the songs on the album examine aspects of relationships," Beyoncé says, "and this is one element."[6]

"Naughty Girl" was the first song Beyoncé and Scott Storch worked on together. Although she already liked his production style – in the preceding years, he had worked with the Roots and Dr. Dre – she was more interested in finding people she "vibed with well" from a personality standpoint in the studio, because she knew it would lead to better music. "And that's what happened," Beyoncé said. "His beats were really different, [and] didn't sound like anything else."[7] Driven by slinky grooves propelled by flourishes from dancehall and Arabic music, "Naughty Girl" topped US dance charts and reached No. 3 on the *Billboard* Hot 100 and the UK top 10.

BABY BOY

[SINGLE]

Released: August 3, 2003 (single) / June 24, 2003 (album)
Writers: Shawn Carter, Sean Paul Henriques, Beyoncé Knowles, Scott Storch, Robert Walker
Producers: Beyoncé Knowles and Scott Storch
Select Alternate Versions: Junior Vasquez Club Anthem remix, Maurice's Nu Soul mix

For the second single from *Dangerously in Love* – the dancehall-oriented duet "Baby Boy", which describes sizzling romantic fantasies – Beyoncé once again turned to a red-hot collaborator: Jamaican dancehall artist Sean Paul. The pair first met years before, when he played a show on the same bill as Destiny's Child, and she specifically sought him out for "Baby Boy".

Sean Paul sat in his car in his backyard to write lyrics, leaning into a seduction vibe. "She's telling me about her fantasies and picturing me and her going here and there, all over the world," Paul said. "I'm answering back, like, 'I'm wit' it.'"[8] During the writing process, something unexpected happened: a juicy mango fell out of a tree through his car window and landed directly in his lap. He took the unexpected gift as a good omen for "Baby Boy": "And I'm like, 'That's a hit song right there.'"[9]

Sean Paul was correct. Completed near the end of the recording process for *Dangerously in Love*, "Baby Boy" became Beyoncé's second *Billboard* Hot 100 solo No. 1 hit, spending nine weeks atop the chart, and also topped the Hot R&B/Hip-Hop Singles and Tracks chart. It was also the second No. 1 hit for Sean Paul, although he was even prouder that an artist of Beyoncé's stature chose to record a "dancehall-oriented track" with him. "It really made me feel that dancehall-style was coming into its own and that my music or my genre was being accepted by a lot of people."[10]

Opposite and below: Beyoncé performed "Baby Boy" with Sean Paul at the 2003 MTV Europe Music Awards and (for good measure) took home Best Song for "Crazy in Love."

HIP HOP STAR (FEATURING BIG BOI AND SLEEPY BROWN)

[ALBUM TRACK]

Released: June 24, 2003
Writers: Shawn Carter, Makeda Davis, Beyoncé Knowles, Antwan Patton, Bryce Wilson
Producers: Beyoncé Knowles, Antwan Patton, Bryce Wilson

After Beyoncé finished recording *Dangerously in Love,* she sensed that several songs needed an extra voice or two. In a nod to her confident approach to the album, she boldly called up her chosen guests, sent them music and invited them to collaborate. Among those saying yes to a song called "Hip Hop Star" was Atlanta producer Sleepy Brown and rapper Big Boi from Outkast. "It's a very different hip-hop song," Beyoncé said. "It's a very rock and roll, very street, almost Broadway. It sounds like Marilyn Monroe mixed with rock and hip-hop."[11] On paper, that combination seems like it might clash – but in practice, "Hip Hop Star" works perfectly. Built on a foundation of heavy blues-rock riffs and snaky percussive grooves, the song resembles a mini Shakespearean play. "Hip Hop Star" starts with a man (voiced by Big Boi) who proclaims he's a dynamite lover. The swaggering female narrator, portrayed by Beyoncé, considers this boast a challenge: calling herself a rockstar *and* a hip-hop star, she dares him to turn words into action. In the end, it's Sleepy Brown who chimes in and accepts her offer with soulful glee.

BE WITH YOU

[ALBUM TRACK]

Released: June 24, 2003
Writers: Angela Beyincé, George Clinton Jr., William Collins, Gary Cooper, Rich Harrison, Beyoncé Knowles, Shuggie Otis
Producers: Rich Harrison and Beyoncé Knowles

Beyoncé's early records often had a retro vibe thanks to choice samples culled from funk and soul songs. These moments also made her music quite diverse – as evidenced by *Dangerously in Love*, which she noted with pride was "very eclectic. I have a different variation of different types of music, from reggae to hip-hop to Middle Eastern to jazz."[12] The quiet storm slow jam "Be With You" was especially diverse, as it subtly interpolates Bootsy's Rubber Band's "I'd Rather Be with You" and Shuggie Otis's sparkling "Strawberry Letter 23". To Otis, an American R&B musician active since the late 1960s, having his music used in this way meant the world. "When I made *Freedom Flight* in 1971, I knew I needed a pop song so I wrote 'Strawberry Letter 23'," he said. "It came out as a single but it didn't hit, even though it's still my pride and joy."[13] The usage in "Be With You" is especially poignant, as Beyoncé wrote a vulnerable song about connecting with your partner on a deep level: emotionally, physically and sexually.

Opposite: Beyoncé enjoyed great success with her debut solo album, *Dangerously in Love*, thanks to collaborators like Big Boi (pictured opposite with his Outkast partner André 3000 and Destiny's Child).

ME, MYSELF AND I

[SINGLE]

Released: October 19, 2003 (single) / June 24, 2003 (album)
Writers: Beyoncé Knowles, Scott Storch, Robert Waller
Producers: Beyoncé Knowles and Scott Storch
Select Alternate Versions: Bama Boys Sexy Remix, Eastern Delight Mix, Grizzly Remix featuring Ghostface Killah

The sleek R&B ballad "Me, Myself and I" isn't a De La Soul cover, but it is "basically a celebration of a breakup," Beyoncé said, based on a real-life experience she had with a relationship that went south. (Her lips were sealed on who the ex was; as she told one interviewer who wanted specifics, "Well, that was about a time in my life when I was with a guy that was wrong!"[14]) "In relationships, it's not always good, it's not always great, not always smooth," she says. "Sometimes the guy disappoints you. And then most women look back and they're thinking, 'God, I'm smarter than that. What was I thinking?'"[15] Rather than wallow in regrets or should-have-beens, "Me, Myself and I" encourages women to acknowledge the bad parts of their previous relationship – and recognize their occasionally poor judgement – so they can move on and hopefully find a better situation. "The way I looked at it was, you just take that experience and just think of it as a growing experience," she said. "You always have yourself, and you can always depend on yourself. You will never disappoint yourself."[16] "Me, Myself and I" was another big hit that peaked at No. 4 on the *Billboard* Hot 100.

YES

[ALBUM TRACK]

Released: June 24, 2003
Writers: Shawn Carter, Bernard Edwards Jr., Beyoncé Knowles
Producers: Focus... and Beyoncé Knowles

Beyoncé's approach to songwriting is rooted in deep listening – and deep empathy. "I love to come up with concepts," she says. "I usually get that from just sitting down, talking to people and seeing what people go through, and seeing what people want to hear songs about."[17] On *Dangerously in Love*, this process led to relatable songs like "Yes", which she produced alongside Bernard Edwards Jr., son of the late Chic bassist Bernard Edwards. The narrator of this leisurely slow jam agrees to date someone as long as he respects her boundaries – but she promises to cut him off immediately if he doesn't listen when she says no. Beyoncé based the underlying concept of this song on things she's gone through. "I can sign a million autographs and the first time I have to say, 'Sorry, I'm gonna miss my plane', it's like I never signed the other million," she explains. "That happens all the time with all different situations of life. That's why I thought it was such a good concept."[18]

SIGNS (FEATURING MISSY ELLIOTT)

[ALBUM TRACK]

Released: June 24, 2003
Writers: Craig Brockman, Missy Elliott, Nisan Stewart
Producers: Craig Brockman, Missy Elliott, Beyoncé Knowles, Nisan Stewart

On the sinewy psychedelic R&B song "Signs", the proud Virgo Beyoncé muses about her compatibility with a Sagittarius partner. After noting that her lover has embodied various characteristics of other Zodiac signs along the way (i.e., a flirty Aries, a fun-loving Libra), she decides not to stress too much because every sign has its pros and cons. Upon release, some wondered whether "Signs" referred to her rumoured relationship with Jay-Z. "People can come to whatever conclusion they like," Beyoncé said when a journalist asked her about the connection. "That's the beauty of music."[19] Still, these relationship sleuths were on to something: years later, rapper Missy Elliott – who said she wanted to write "something grown and sexy" for Beyoncé with "Signs" – spilled the beans. "I remember saying, 'What can I write about for her that everyone can feel a part of?' And at the time people didn't really know how deep her and Jay's relationship was."[20] Elliott didn't want to come right out and namecheck Jay-Z, but she had a brilliant idea. "I thought, 'I wonder what his sign is?' and I said, 'Oh he's a Sagittarius.' Then it clicked."[21]

SPEECHLESS

[ALBUM TRACK]

Released: June 24, 2003
Writers: Sherrod Barnes, Angela Beyincé, Andreao Heard, Beyoncé Knowles
Producers: Sherrod Barnes, Andreao Heard, Beyoncé Knowles

On *Dangerously in Love*, Beyoncé deliberately sought out collaborators because she knew working with other people would help her evolve as an artist. "I'm always looking for a way to grow, and I didn't want to do it by myself, because I wanted to go to the next level," she said. "So, for the majority of this record, I wrote in the studio with the other producers."[22] One of the biggest evolutions on *Dangerously in Love* is the luxurious "Speechless", which Beyoncé compared favourably to The Isley Brothers. "As soon as I heard the track it inspired me," she says. "It's very sexy, very sensual," she continued. "The sort of ballad that I've never done before. This song is definitely a population increaser!"[23] That's an understatement: an airy funk song with a Prince-esque guitar solo, "Speechless" is a sophisticated song about being in a passionate (and steamy) romantic relationship.

THAT'S HOW YOU LIKE IT (FEATURING JAY-Z)

[ALBUM TRACK]

Released: June 24, 2003
Writers: Delroy Andrews, Brian Bridgeman, Shawn Carter, Eldra DeBarge, Randy DeBarge, Etterlene Jordan, Beyoncé Knowles
Producers: Mr. B, D-Roy, Beyoncé Knowles

Although Beyoncé and Jay-Z were still keeping their relationship private upon the release of *Dangerously in Love*, they weren't necessarily keeping it a secret. Exhibit A: the playful "That's How You Like It" – which interpolates resung lyrics from DeBarge's 1982 hit "I Like It" – finds Beyoncé outlining everything she loves about a man who bears a striking resemblance to Jay-Z. On the third verse, Jay-Z himself even pops up to reassure Beyoncé that their relationship is sound. "Basically, the song talks about all the things in a relationship you like, all of the characteristics in a man that you like," she says. "It's really happy. It's a feel-good song."[24] Co-producer D-Roy later noted that the "the writing process was actually initiated by Jay-Z. After hearing the track we produced, he wrote the hook and recorded a demo before sending the record over."[25] The couple penned the other verses – and the rest is history.

Opposite and above: Missy Elliott (pictured opposite) and Beyoncé were frequent collaborators and even toured together as co-headliners of 2004's Verizon Ladies First Tour (above, top); Beyoncé and Jay-Z forged a creative partnership as well as a romantic one.

THE CLOSER I GET TO YOU

[SINGLE]

Released: June 13, 2004 (single) / June 24, 2003 (album)
Writers: Reggie Lucas and James Mtume
Producer: Nat Adderley Jr.

Several months before the release of *Dangerously in Love* and his own highly-anticipated solo album *Dance with My Father*, Luther Vandross had a massive stroke. This sadly prevented him from promoting "The Closer I Get to You" – a duet with Beyoncé that appeared on both of their albums – but it didn't diminish the impact of the song. An '80s soft-rock throwback with stylish arrangements and polished production, "The Closer I Get to You" exudes classic (and classy) romantic vibes.

The tune – which was co-written by James Mtume and Reggie Lucas, who previously played with Miles Davis – was originally a major hit for R&B icons Roberta Flack and Donny Hathaway in 1978. Beyoncé grew up listening to these artists and also deeply admired Vandross, so covering the song was "a dream come true," she said. "[It's] one of the most beautiful songs on my record, and it showcases my voice and I had no idea that the collaboration with us to our voices would complement each other so well."[26] Other people agreed; in fact, "The Closer I Get to You" took home a Grammy Award for Best R&B Performance by a Duo or Group with Vocals.

DANGEROUSLY IN LOVE 2 / BEYONCÉ INTERLUDE

[ALBUM TRACK]

Released: June 24, 2003
Writers: Beyoncé Knowles and Errol "Poppi" McCalla Jr.
Producers: Beyoncé Knowles and Errol "Poppi" McCalla Jr.

Your ears weren't deceiving you: the love song "Dangerously in Love 2", the de-facto title track of Beyoncé's debut solo album, previously surfaced on Destiny's Child's 2001 full-length *Survivor* in a slightly different version under the title "Dangerously in Love". The two songs share the same gratitude-filled lyrics, although the Beyoncé solo version starts with elegant piano before giving way to plaintive guitar strums. "I always liked that title, because sometimes when you fall in love, it's a little dangerous," she said. "I'm a young lady basically evolving into a young woman now, I thought that was a great title, because there's so many steps in relationships and love. And that's what the album is about."[27] After the song is a 16-second "Beyoncé Interlude" that feels like a private (if poetic) love letter that ushers in the rest of the record.

"Dangerously in Love 2" earned a Grammy for Best Female R&B Vocal Performance – one of five Grammys Beyoncé won at the 2004 ceremony. In a nod to the album's creative depth, *Dangerously in Love* itself also took home Best Contemporary R&B Album. "There are some songs that talk about making love, but it talks about all different steps of relationships, from the first time you meet a guy and you're attracted to him to the first time you tell him no," Beyoncé said of the full-length. "Everything. First time you say you love someone, first time he disappoints you. It just talks about everything that women go through."[28]

Above: Beyoncé dueted with R&B/soul legend Luther Vandross (pictured) on the song "The Closer I Get to You" on her debut album, *Dangerously In Love*.

GIFT FROM VIRGO

[ALBUM TRACK]

Released: June 24, 2003
Writers: Beyoncé Knowles and Shuggie Otis
Producer: Beyoncé Knowles

"Gift From Virgo" is the second song on *Dangerously in Love* to sample Shuggie Otis. This time around, Beyoncé incorporates the gentle guitar of 1974's "Rainy Day" as the basis for a lovely song extolling the virtues of a relationship's simplest pleasure: simply spending time together. The narrator checks off what she appreciates about her beloved – long conversations, a first kiss, a shared dance –and dreams that one day they will be together and making love.

Sonically, "Gift From Virgo" is distinct from the rest of *Dangerously in Love*. Vocally, Beyoncé sounds meditative and sentimental, singing in a yearning, dainty voice reminiscent of the 1970s soul/R&B great Minnie Riperton. "This record was a chance for me to grow as a writer and a singer," she says. "There are more ballads. The vocals aren't as precisely produced and because it's just me, there aren't as many harmonies."[29]

The topics she covered also made a difference. "This time, because I only had to write for myself, my songs are much more personal," she said, while adding, "The experience was very liberating and therapeutic. I felt free, because I could go into the studio and talk about whatever I wanted."[30] For Otis, having his music recirculated into pop culture was equally inspiring: "Beyoncé sampling two of my songs has kept me living."[31]

DADDY

[PROMO SINGLE]

Released: June 3, 2003 (single) / June 24, 2003 (album)
Writers: Mark Batson and Beyoncé Knowles
Producers: Mark Batson and Beyoncé Knowles

Beyoncé executive-produced *Dangerously in Love* alongside Mathew Knowles, her father and manager. But she kept the album's closing ballad, "Daddy", a secret, mainly because she didn't write the tune for the record; she wrote it for him. "And he was speechless," Beyoncé adds. "He didn't know what to say or how to react really, because it is really a heavy song."[32]

Indeed, "Daddy" is a tearjerker in which Beyoncé shares memories of her childhood and adolescence – including his response to her getting a tattoo, which was to get one himself! – and expresses how grateful she is for his unyielding support. In fact, she says she wants her future husband *and* unborn son to be like him.

"My mother and father have been together for 23, 24 years, and I've seen them go through a lot," Beyoncé explains. "And he has always supported his wife and supported his family and supported me and my sister and [my cousin] Kelly. That loyalty and that strength that he has, those certain qualities I just want in all the people around me."[33]

"Daddy" ended up as a hidden bonus track on the CD version of *Dangerously in Love*. In fact, Beyoncé admitted she felt conflicted about putting the song on the album at all. "So I put it last," she said. "They can find it if they want. I think it's a beautiful song, but it's really personal, and people don't want to hear that all the time."[34]

Opposite: Destiny's Child posed for a photo with Beyoncé's dad, Matthew Knowles – the subject of "Daddy" – in 2000.

I CAN'T TAKE NO MORE

[BONUS TRACK / MIXTAPE]

Released: June 24, 2003
Writers: Mike Jones, Beyoncé Knowles, Mario Winans
Producer: Mario Winans

Several decades ago, record labels went to great lengths to entice fans to buy albums. As a result, those who preordered *Dangerously in Love* from the online Sony Music Store were given a free download of "I Can't Take No More". The midtempo R&B ballad is an uncharacteristically uncertain song in which Beyoncé admits the haters have got under her skin. In fact, she's befuddled as to why they dislike her so much *and* persist in criticizing her. In the end, however, Beyoncé's resilient attitude prevails: she tells the critics to knock it off because she's fed up with their lies and slander. "I Can't Take No More" eventually surfaced in a more widespread way on the 2005 *Speak My Mind* mixtape.

BIENVENUE (IAM FEATURING BEYONCÉ)

[*DANGEROUSLY IN LOVE* FRENCH AND BELGIAN EDITION / *REVOIR UN PRINTEMPS*]

Released: June 2003
Writers: Akhenaton, Deni Hines, Shurik'n
Producers: IAM

Back in the 2000s, record labels would release different versions of mainstream pop albums in different countries. To convince fans to buy them, these releases often had unique bonus tracks, such as original songs or remixes. The French and Belgian version of *Dangerously in Love* included a duet with the French hip-hop band IAM on the song "Bienvenue". (The song, whose title translates to "Welcome", also appeared on IAM's 2003 album, *Revoir un printemps*.) Musically, "Bienvenue" takes inspiration from a variety of genres: jazzy '90s hip-hop, scorching blues rock and funky French electro-disco. Lyrically, it's a rather serious song that takes a cynical view of the world by pointing out the foibles of modern politics, culture and society; the "welcome" is a bit sarcastic. However, Beyoncé serves as the song's optimistic voice: she notes that despite all these challenges, we have to keep going and remember that the world is big enough to include everybody – and, even more importantly, that our core foundation is love.

Opposite and above: In 2004, Beyoncé (opposite) was part of a gladiators-themed Pepsi commercial alongside Britney Spears and Pink; the women covered Queen's "We Will Rock You." She also kept busy collaborating with French hip-hop group IAM (above).

03 BONNIE & CLYDE (JAY-Z FEATURING BEYONCÉ)

[SINGLE / *THE BLUEPRINT²: THE GIFT & THE CURSE*]

Released: October 10, 2002 (single) / November 12, 2002 (album)
Writers: Shawn Carter, Darryl Harper, Prince Nelson, Ricky Rouse, Tupac Shakur, Kanye West, Tyrone Wrice
Producer: Kanye West
Select Alternate Versions: Radio Edit, Instrumental

Beyoncé and Jay-Z's first musical collaboration was an indirect one. Back in 2000, she was a featured artist on rapper Amil's debut single, "I Got That", which Jay-Z co-wrote. However, the pair stepped out in an even bigger way in 2002 with "03 Bonnie & Clyde", the lead single from Jay-Z's *The Blueprint²: The Gift & The Curse*.

Even though the couple's romance was still under wraps, "03 Bonnie & Clyde" heavily insinuates that Beyoncé and Jay-Z are in a relationship and compares them to the thieves Bonnie and Clyde. (Jay-Z frequently references the legendary lawbreakers in other songs; the comparison is meant to be complimentary, less about their shared criminal acts and more about their love and loyalty.) The chorus references a boyfriend and girlfriend who are each other's ride or die. During the first verse, Jay-Z gushes about his girl and compares their relationship to that of musicians Bobby Brown and Whitney Houston; at the start of verse two, he chides men for not treating their romantic partners with respect.

To those in Jay-Z's life, these lyrics were telling. "If y'all know Jay, a lot of times everything comes out in music," Roc-A-Fella Records co-founder Kareem "Biggs" Burke said years later. "When he does interviews, he's a little more reluctant to speak about certain things. But it always comes out in his albums – so at that time when 'Bonnie & Clyde' came out we knew he was in love with Beyoncé."[35]

Produced by rapper Kanye West, "03 Bonnie & Clyde" appropriately feels like the soundtrack to a cinematic heist, what with its evocative Spanish guitars and low-key hip-hop grooves. West ended up hiring his collaborator Eric "E-Bass" Johnson to handle the musical aspect. "I programmed the drums in ten minutes," West said, "and then he played all the different parts. This version is all live bass, live guitars, live chords on it."[36]

The bridge features a nod to Prince's "If I Was Your Girlfriend", while the chorus borrows heavily from 2Pac's "Me and My Girlfriend". Using the latter song was also West's idea – "[Jay-Z] said, 'We got this joint, it has to be the best beat you ever made'"[37] – although obtaining permission was a challenge, as they only had one day to clear the sample. But the stress was worth it: "03 Bonnie and Clyde" became a huge hit that reached the top 5 in the US and UK and topped the UK hip-hop charts – and laid the groundwork for Beyoncé's future solo success.

Right: In 2002, Beyoncé and Jay-Z twinned with double denim on MTV's popular daily show *TRL*.

WHAT'S IT GONNA BE

[DIGITAL SINGLE / *DANGEROUSLY IN LOVE* JAPANESE EDITION]

Released: June 25, 2003 (album)
Writers: Corte Ellis, Beyoncé Knowles, Kandice Love, Karrim Mack, LaShaun Owens, Larry Troutman, Roger Troutman
Producers: Beyoncé Knowles and Soul Diggaz
Select Alternate Versions: Live at Wembley, Instrumental A Cappella

With its shuffling grooves and warm-syrup melodies, "What's It Gonna Be" is the kind of hip-hop/R&B hybrid at which Beyoncé excels. The song continues the throwback vibe of *Dangerously in Love*, thanks to a prominent sample of the soulful rhythmic track of 2Pac's "I Wonder If Heaven Got a Ghetto (Hip-Hop Version)", which itself incorporates elements of Cameo's 1978 song "Two of Us". (Roger Troutman's "Do It Roger" is also in the music mix, owing to a version of the 2Pac song sampling the funky tune.)

Lyrically, "What's It Gonna Be" describes a potential love connection. While at a club, the narrator spots a sexy guy staring at her and senses they have chemistry. She suggests going somewhere less crowded and getting to know each other better. Crucially, the ball's in his court to say yes – hence the song's anxious-if-direct title – but she's hopeful he'll take a chance.

"What's It Gonna Be" was released in many ways circa *Dangerously in Love*, including on the Japanese edition of the album and as a digital single on iTunes. But in 2004, it also appeared on the limited-edition Walmart version of Destiny's Child's *Destiny Fulfilled* and became a promotional single for Beyoncé's L'Oréal Paris advertising campaign.

Opposite and below: As a solo artist, Beyoncé quickly became popular enough to headline big venues like Wembley Arena.

THE FIGHTING TEMPTATIONS

IN 2003, BEYONCÉ RETURNED TO THE SILVER SCREEN WITH A ROLE IN *THE FIGHTING TEMPTATIONS* ALONGSIDE CUBA GOODING JR. IN THE FILM, SHE PORTRAYS SINGLE MOM LILLY, A CHARACTER THAT WAS A DEPARTURE FROM FOXXY CLEOPATRA, HER FLAMBOYANT *AUSTIN POWERS IN GOLDMEMBER* CHARACTER.

"[Foxxy] was so over the top I wanted to do something opposite," she said. "I gained some weight for the film and tried to dread my hair and wore no makeup. I wanted to look as natural and unglamorous as possible, because I wanted to basically be taken serious."[38]

Beyoncé wasn't the only musician in the movie. In fact, the cast read like a who's-who of the R&B and soul world; other stars include Faith Evans, Walter Williams Sr. of The O'Jays, Melba Moore, Eddie LeVert and Angie Stone. In a charming bit of foreshadowing, Chloe Bailey played the younger version of Beyoncé's character; years later, she and her sister Halle opened for Beyoncé and Jay-Z's *On the Run II Tour*.

At the time of *The Fighting Temptations'* release, Beyoncé was also fighting off persistent tabloid gossip that Destiny's Child were splitting up. "We haven't broken up," she assured. "We're going to continue to tour and record and be a group."[39] To underscore their commitment, she noted they recorded the laid-back "I Know" for *The Fighting Temptations'* soundtrack.

Left, below and opposite: In 2003, Beyoncé starred in (and contributed to the soundtrack of) *The Fighting Temptations* alongside actor Cuba Gooding Jr. and musicians such as Angie Stone, Faith Evans and Walter Williams Sr. of The O'Jays.

For the movie, Beyoncé also collaborated with multiple other marquee artists from the film's cast, including Walter Williams Sr. (the uplifting, gospel R&B number "He Still Loves Me"); Bilal (the neo-soul highlight "Everything I Do"); and Angie Stone and Melba Moore ("Time To Come Home"). She also teamed up with P. Diddy for "Summertime" and, more notably, joined forces with long-time friend Missy Elliott, hip-hop legend MC Lyte and rapper (and *106 & Park* host) Free for "Fighting Temptation". Driven by a sample of Uncle Louie's disco-funk tune "I Like Funky Music", the song is an all-star throwback jam with soulful overtones.

In hindsight, *The Fighting Temptations'* soundtrack also hinted at future Beyoncé musical directions. Her slinky version of the Little Willie John 1956 R&B hit "Fever" is both playful and sensual, and her gospel-infused take on the African American spiritual "Swing Low, Sweet Chariot" is stunning.

The Fighting Temptations wasn't a huge hit at the box office, grossing only $34 million worldwide. And, sadly, its soundtrack feels almost obscure today despite the star power involved. However, the music is worth paying attention to – and Beyoncé herself made a strong case for the film upon its release. "It's really a feel-good movie," she said. "The whole message is coming back home and finding out the things that are really important to you."[40]

OTHER SONGS

AS A SOLO ARTIST, BEYONCÉ WASTED NO TIME APPEARING ON MOVIE SOUNDTRACKS. FOR 2003'S *BAD BOYS II*, SHE CONTRIBUTED "KEEP GIVING YOUR LOVE TO ME", A FLIRTY HIP-HOP SONG WITH COME-HITHER LYRICS THAT WAS INDICATIVE OF THE UPBEAT PRODUCTION STYLE SHE FAVOURED CIRCA *DANGEROUSLY IN LOVE*.

In April 2004, Beyoncé released her own movie, the concert film *Live at Wembley*, which had been recorded at Wembley Arena. The setting was fitting, as she's always possessed strong ties to the UK. (Among other things, while with Destiny's Child she provided backup vocals on *Coronation Street* actor Matthew Marsden's cover of Daryl Hall & John Oates' "She's Gone".) *Live at Wembley* proved she could more than hold her own as a solo artist – showcasing her powerful stage presence and awe-inspiring vocals.

"There is hardly an overdub on this project – it's 95 percent live Beyoncé," said Rick Camp, the engineer who was the front of house mixer for the live show. "In my 22 years of mixing, I've never come across anyone who could deliver like she does: vocally and her ability to do a show."[41]

In addition to featuring "My First Time" [*see* page 84] and "What's It Gonna Be" [*see* page 57], the CD from Beyoncé's *Live at Wembley* release included a delicate, soulful cover of Rose Royce's

"Wishing On a Star"; the Japanese edition of the album also includes an HR Crump remix of Solange's solo song "Naïve" with Beyoncé and Da Brat. Both of these songs are on the *True Star: A Private Performance* EP, while the former is on the *Roll Bounce* soundtrack.

"Wishing On a Star" is also on 2005's unofficial *Speak My Mind* mixtape, which gathers Beyoncé b-sides and rarities found on other releases, as well as a few unique original songs: the Destiny's Child-esque "I'm Leaving" and the old-school electro-funk jam "Sexuality". Another rarity comes on *The Katrina* CD from Recording Artists for Hope, where Beyoncé and Kelly Rowland collaborated with Kitten Sera on "All That I'm Lookin' For".

In 2003, Beyoncé and Luther Vandross dueted on "The Closer I Get To You". Two years later, she teamed up with another legend, Stevie Wonder, for a duet on *So Amazing: An All-Star Tribute to Luther Vandross*. The pair lovingly captured the icon's tender soul on "So Amazing", and won a Grammy Award for Best R&B Performance By A Duo Or Group With Vocals in the process.

And, finally, there's "A Woman Like Me", which Beyoncé intended for the soundtrack of the 2006 film *The Pink Panther*. The brassy song "has the strength of a Tina Turner song but the drama of a Bond tune,"[42] she says – a perfect description for the old-fashioned, horn-heavy tune.

Opposite and below: Beyoncé rubbed elbows with music royalty on 2004's Verizon Ladies First Tour (opposite) and the *VH1 Divas Duets* special; at the latter, she sang with Stevie Wonder.

08 B'DAY

BEYONCÉ WENT FROM FILMING THE MOVIE *DREAMGIRLS* DIRECTLY INTO WRITING AND RECORDING *B'DAY*; IN FACT, SHE KEPT THE SESSIONS A SECRET FROM ALMOST EVERYBODY IN HER LIFE. IN ANOTHER POWER MOVE, SHE ALSO TOOK RECORDING INSPIRATION FROM THE APPROACH USED BY JAY-Z AND OTHER HIP-HOP ARTISTS ON THE ROC-A-FELLA LABEL: BOOKING PRODUCERS INTO INDIVIDUAL STUDIO ROOMS WITHIN A GIVEN SPACE. HAVING ENLISTED TRUSTED COLLABORATORS LIKE SWIZZ BEATZ, RICH HARRISON AND RODNEY JERKINS, SHE ENDED UP WITH *B'DAY*, A WILDLY CREATIVE ALBUM THAT TOOK AN EXPANSIVE VIEW OF R&B, POP AND HIP-HOP, ENCOMPASSING SWEEPING BALLADS ("IRREPLACEABLE") AND KICKY DANCE NUMBERS ("GET ME BODIED") ALIKE.

DÉJÀ VU (FEATURING JAY-Z)

[SINGLE]

Released: June 24, 2006 (single) / September 5, 2006 (album)
Writers: Shawn Carter, Rodney Jerkins, Beyoncé Knowles, Keli Nicole Price, Makeba Riddick, Delisha Thomas
Producers: Beyoncé Knowles and Darkchild
Select Alternate Versions: Freemasons Radio Mix, Maurice's Nusoul Mix

Beyoncé was profoundly affected by portraying Deena in the 2006 movie *Dreamgirls.* After filming wrapped, she was supposed to go on vacation but instead secretly headed into the studio and recorded her second solo album, *B'Day*, in just two weeks. "I didn't allow myself to go in the studio [while filming] because I didn't want to get myself confused with this character," she said. "So I had so many things bottled up, so many emotions, so many things I wanted to say."[1]

This solitary work wasn't necessarily a big change for Beyoncé; as she points out, she also produced multiple Destiny's Child songs and always loved songwriting "just for fun" in the studio. But recording under the radar freed her up to focus on art and creativity. "I wanted to go back to that, where it was just me and the songwriters, and we just had little jam sessions and had conversations and made it fun again," she said. "It allowed me to not think about labels or think about radio stations or think about what's commercial."[2]

Among other things, she wanted to use live instruments on her songs. Luckily, co-producer Rodney "Darkchild" Jerkins was on the same wavelength. Right before going to New York City to work on *B'Day*, he and bassist Jon Jon Webb were driving to 7-Eleven to get Slurpees while listening to Michael Jackson's "Don't Stop 'Til You Get Enough". Jerkins was inspired. "I told Jon Jon, 'Man, what if we gave Beyoncé some Michael Jackson-type stuff?' I worked with Michael and I'm a big fan, but Beyoncé was probably the only female artist that was challenging herself in a way that Michael would."[3]

The result was *B'Day*'s adventurous lead single, "Déjà Vu", which hit No. 1 in the UK and reached the top 5 on the US pop charts. Driven by live instruments like brassy horns, sizzling bass and an 808 drum machine, it merges the vintage feel of '70s disco-soul with vibrant, modern hip-hop. At the beginning of the song, Beyoncé brilliantly calls out these instruments individually by name as they're added into the mix, "like some James Brown-type stuff," Jerkins observed.[4] Beyoncé was thrilled with how it turned out. "It's still young, still new and fresh, but it has the old soul groove," she said. "The energy is incredible."[5]

Jay-Z also ended up contributing a few verses, including one in which he says he's straightened out his behaviour now that he's with Beyoncé. "I never planned for him to be on [the song]," she said. "But once he heard it, I saw his lips start moving. So I was like, 'Would you like to go into the studio and record what you just did?'"[6] Still, "Déjà Vu" isn't a straight-up love song – or strictly about the couple's relationship – but a tune about trying to shake off an ex who you think you see everywhere.

As the song progresses, Beyoncé channels powerful vocal idols like Tina Turner and starts to belt out the lyrics, which amplifies the desperation within lines about moving on from a former partner even though you miss them dearly. "['Déjà Vu'] was intricate," Jerkins says. "That song had a lot of harmonies and notes that were somewhat unconventional for regular, mainstream music. She just goes at it with such intensity."[7]

Left and opposite: Rodney Jerkins (pictured), who started working with Beyoncé while in Destiny's Child, co-wrote and co-produced her hit "Déjà Vu", which she performed with Jay-Z at the 2006 BET Awards.

GET ME BODIED

[SINGLE]

Released: July 10, 2007 (single) / September 5, 2006 (album)
Writers: Angela Beyincé, Kasseem Dean, Sean Garrett, Beyoncé Knowles, Solange Knowles, Makeba Riddick
Producers: Swizz Beatz, Sean Garrett, Beyoncé Knowles
Select Alternate Versions: Extended

When Swizz Beatz started working on *B'Day* with Beyoncé, he figured it was going to be just the two of them. How wrong he was. "She was like, 'I got Rodney Jerkins upstairs, I got this guy upstairs ...'" he recalled. "It forced me to go left."[8] Feeling slightly intimidated by the other producers' pedigrees ("These guys started in church. They can play anything. Me, I'm a kid from the Bronx"), Swizz Beatz decided to lean into his strengths. "[I said], 'You know what? I'm in here because of what I do.' And I stripped everything out the beat, and then that's how 'Get Me Bodied' happened."[9]

What Swizz Beatz created are beats that resemble the kind of cheers you might hear during an intense playground game – handclaps, foot stomps, hyped-up chants – to capture the jubilant experience of going to a club with your friends (and, hopefully, finding a hottie to seduce). Beyoncé co-wrote the song with her younger sister, Solange, and deliberately references her tight bond with her Destiny's Child bandmates Kelly Rowland and Michelle Williams. "When I wrote it, I said 'three best friends' because I was thinking about them," she said. "They make me laugh so hard, and we are so silly together."[10] Fittingly, Beyoncé leans into a Texas twang for her vocals – and Solange, Rowland and Williams all appeared in the "Get Me Bodied" video.

SUGA MAMA

[ALBUM TRACK]

Released: September 5, 2006 (album)
Writers: Rich Harrison, Beyoncé Knowles, Chuck Middleton, Makeba Riddick
Producers: Rich Harrison and Beyoncé Knowles

Driven by an easygoing sample of Jake Wade and the Soul Searchers' 1968 garage-funk single "Searching for Soul", the throwback number "Suga Mama" flips the script on the concept of a sugar daddy. Instead of a man showering a woman with gifts and affection, the song centres on a female narrator – with an accountant standing by, she notes – ready to spoil her man with all the finer things in life (and in the bedroom). The title is a clever double entendre that also cheekily refers to the colloquial phrase "give me some sugar", while the narrator expresses her burning desire by comparing herself to a melting ice cream cone or sticky-sweet candy. "I love this song so much," Beyoncé says. "It's funky and sexy and [has] the role reversal. I was able to show a harder side, a cool, tougher side."[11]

"Suga Mama" was co-written by Makeba Riddick, who had been collaborating with Rihanna, girl group Danity Kane and Toni Braxton, and ended up "pulling 14-hour days" co-writing the bulk of *B'Day*. "I see the reason why [Beyoncé] is the biggest artist of our generation: her work ethic is unlike anything I've ever seen," Riddick says. "She would tell us to be there at 11 o'clock in the morning and we would be there until, like, four or five in the morning .... [But] when we got there, she was already there, working."[12] In a nod to women putting in the work, Beyoncé named her all-female band from this era Suga Mama.

Opposite and below: Beyoncé and her younger sister Solange (pictured together in 1990) have a special creative bond (opposite); Beyoncé performs "Suga Mama" in Spain in 2006.

UPGRADE U (FEATURING JAY-Z)

[PROMO SINGLE]

Released: November 27, 2006 (promo single) / September 5, 2006 (album)
Writers: Angela Beyincé, Shawn Carter, Willie Clarke, Sean Garrett, Beyoncé Knowles, Solange Knowles, Clarence Reid, Makeba Riddick
Producers: Swizz Beatz, Sean Garrett, Beyoncé Knowles, Cameron Wallace
Select Alternate Versions: Instrumental, A Cappella

Built around a stuttering sample of Betty Wright's 1968 song "Girls Can't Do What the Guys Do" that sounds like a marching band, "Upgrade U" is a savvy song about power dynamics in relationships, careers and the business world. However, it's also one of *B'Day*'s more playful songs. Beyoncé asserts that being with her is an upgrade, in the sense that she's a successful woman who has her life together *and* can give her man luxury goods. Jay-Z jokes that he'll upgrade his woman, but also references the fact he's been elevating the business world with his moves and perspective.

Beyoncé and Jay-Z ultimately acknowledge that they're good for each other; their partnership represents a mutual upgrade. It's a case of art imitating life. "When we work together, we weren't thinking, 'Okay, let's do this so you can help my career [or] so I can help your career,'" Beyoncé says. "He is one of the best – if not the best – hip-hop MCs, and he feels the same about me with R&B music."[13] In that sense, "Upgrade U" resembles a contemporary update of Sonny and Cher's "I Got You Babe", another song about a power couple conquering the world together.

RING THE ALARM

[SINGLE]

Released: September 10, 2006 (single) / September 5, 2006 (album)
Writers: Swizz Beatz, Sean Garrett, Beyoncé Knowles
Producers: Swizz Beatz, Sean Garrett, Beyoncé Knowles

The title *B'Day* has special significance for Beyoncé: Not only is it a reference to her nickname ("B"), but in many places around the world the album was also released on her actual birthday. But from a musical standpoint, co-producer Swizz Beatz says the tune "is just one of the many presents I gave her for her *B'Day,*" while noting that Beyoncé outdid herself with her performances on his songs. "I've never heard a singer singing on tracks like this. It hasn't been done in R&B yet, and if she can pull this off, it's going down. We're taking stuff to the next level."[14] Indeed, *B'Day* often resembles the forward-thinking music of 1970s trailblazers like Labelle or Rufus featuring Chaka Khan.

Thematically, however, "Ring The Alarm" is about the kind of birthday present you *don't* want to receive: news of a cheating partner. "Ring The Alarm" begins with the sound of a wailing siren, which segues immediately into Beyoncé snarling about the unfaithful man, her voice manipulated by distortion. As the song progresses, her passionate, tough-as-nails vocals seethe with anger and jealousy, while clipped, insistent syncopated beats and the occasional siren combine for uneasy stress and bubbling rage. "I love working with Swizz," Beyoncé said. "He's challenging. His beats are so complex it's hard to find a melody. But this just clicked."[15] Indeed, "Ring The Alarm" earned a Grammy nomination for Best Female R&B Vocal Performance.

Above and opposite: Swizz Beatz (pictured, above) worked with Beyoncé on the song "Ring The Alarm," which she performed at the 2006 MTV Video Music Awards (opposite).

P
M

KITTY KAT

[ALBUM TRACK]

Released: September 5, 2006
Writers: Shawn Carter, Beyoncé Knowles, Makeba Riddick, Pharrell Williams
Producers: Beyoncé Knowles and The Neptunes

Like her good friend Taylor Swift, Beyoncé is a cat person. "My first pet was a Himalayan-Persian cat named Gizmo, like in *Gremlins*," she once said.[16] But the song "Kitty Kat" isn't about an adorable pet; instead, the title is a euphemism for another kind of cat, a colloquial slang term for female genitalia. You see, the woman at the heart of the song is kicking her man to the kerb because she's tired of being disrespected. But it's absolutely his loss: Beyoncé assumes a coy tone and coos that she and her "kitty kat" are leaving him. "The song is very sexy, talking about a man who is out with friends all night and you're left at home," Beyoncé says. "And you're like, 'No more of this. It's time to go.'"[17] Slipshod, electro-tinged R&B production by The Neptunes adds just the right amount of sexual tension – and serves as a reminder of what the lame dude will be missing.

FREAKUM DRESS

[ALBUM TRACK]

Released: September 5, 2006
Writers: Angela Beyincé, Rich Harrison, Beyoncé Knowles, Makeba Riddick
Producers: Rich Harrison and Beyoncé Knowles

Everybody has an outfit that makes them feel cool, confident and sexy. But when you need to grab the attention of your significant other, the right move is slipping on a freakum dress. "You know, [it's] when your man starts taking you for granted and you put on that one dress that makes him go, 'Wow', and not want you to leave the house," Beyoncé says.[18]

Beyoncé stresses that there's no one kind of freakum dress, however. "You can't really explain it," she says. "You have to see it. Everyone has their own version."[19] She demonstrates this in the song's music video, where a diverse crowd of women all sport their own take on the dress: "Because we all have those dresses we pull out when we need to shut it down."[20]

In the studio, "Freakum Dress" was a "Crazy in Love"-style tune with horn blasts. Live, it was also a showstopper, particularly on the *I Am ... World Tour,* between high-stepping choreography and a blazing electric guitar solo by Bibi McGill that made Beyoncé exclaim: "Take me higher!"

GREEN LIGHT

[SINGLE]

Released: July 27, 2007 (single) / September 5, 2006 (album)
Writers: Sean Garrett, Beyoncé Knowles, Pharrell Williams
Producers: Beyoncé Knowles and The Neptunes
Select Alternate Versions: Freemasons Remix, Remix featuring Young Buck

When Beyoncé started to make *B'Day*, she took inspiration from the recording method employed by Jay-Z and other hip-hop artists on the Roc-A-Fella label: booking producers into individual studio rooms. "They get this positive competitive energy going by moving from one room to the next and comparing what everyone is doing," she said. "I said to myself, 'Why don't I do that with R&B?'"[21] She enlisted a trio of her most trusted collaborators, including Rich Harrison, Sean Garrett and Rodney Jerkins, and hunkered down at Sony Studios in New York City. The resulting songs included "Green Light", which ended up being a collaboration with The Neptunes. Beyoncé uses the metaphor of a traffic signal to give a stalled-out romantic partner two options. On the one hand, she reassures him that she's still interested in moving forward with their relationship; on the flip side, she tells him that if he's no longer into her, he needs to move along because he's (figuratively) blocking traffic for her future romantic pursuits. The jazzy music is classic Neptunes, with taut horns, simmering drums and bass, and bustling percussion.

Opposite: Beyoncé performed in Times Square on the TV show *Good Morning America* in 2006.

IRREPLACEABLE

[SINGLE]

Released: October 23, 2006 (single) / September 5, 2006 (album)
Writers: Amund Bjørklund, Mikkel Eriksen, Tor Erik Hermansen, Beyoncé Knowles, Espen Lind, Ne-Yo
Producers: Beyoncé Knowles, Ne-Yo, Stargate
Select Alternate Versions: Featuring Ghostface Killah, Maurice Joshua Radio Mix, Ralphi Rosario & Craig J Club Mix

"Irreplaceable" is one of Beyoncé's biggest hits ever: it spent ten weeks at No. 1 on the *Billboard* Hot 100 and was nominated for Record of the Year at the Grammys. The song features a protagonist who wants her now-ex *gone* from her life. After all, he underestimated his partner and made the grave mistake of assuming he was irreplaceable in the relationship. Now his stuff is in boxes, she's calling him a taxi, and then she's cutting ties. Beyoncé delivers this news in a steely, no-nonsense voice that makes it quite clear that his behaviour is unforgivable.

The "Irreplaceable" origin story has many twists and turns; in fact, the song wasn't written for Beyoncé at all. Instead, the Norwegian production team Stargate, a.k.a. the duo of Tor Erik Hermansen and Mikkel Eriksen, wrote a song at the suggestion of their early manager Jay Brown, the co-founder of Roc Nation. "He said, 'I think you guys should make a song that has acoustic guitar and hip-hop beats,'" Hermansen recalled. "That's all he said. We had no idea what to do with the song because it was so different."[22]

When the R&B star Ne-Yo heard a version with just guitars, his mind immediately went to country stars Shania Twain and Faith Hill, not Beyoncé. But once the drums kicked in, he settled on "making an R & B country western music song"[23] instead and came up with lyrics from a male point of view. "When we wrote it with Ne-Yo it was done first with a male vocal, and we thought, 'This is more of a female vocal part,'" Hermansen said. "We liked it and so did Ne-Yo, but he said, 'Who will cut this?'"[24]

Enter a label A&R rep who thought a woman could sing "Irreplaceable" better – and then Beyoncé, who heard and liked the song, and recorded it after requesting some modifications to the arrangement and drums "to make it more current-sounding," Hermansen said.[25] Still, "Irreplaceable" sounded like nothing else on *B'Day*; in fact, Beyoncé was only persuaded to put the song on the album at the urging of producer Swizz Beatz.[26]

Ne-Yo also considered recording "Irreplaceable" himself before Beyoncé took on the song. Years later, he expounded on this decision. "I realized in the lyrics of the record that, well, first and foremost, a good 90 percent of my fan base was female," he said, while noting that certain sentiments wouldn't go over well with them. "It's not so much the message as it is the messenger. The messenger's also very important. See, a man saying that comes across mean, misogynistic. A woman saying that comes across [as] empowering."[27]

Indeed, "Irreplaceable" became an empowerment anthem – and turned out to be influential within Beyoncé's career. Foreshadowing her live collaboration with the Chicks and 2024's *Cowboy Carter*, Beyoncé performed "Irreplaceable" with the country act Sugarland at the 2007 American Music Awards.

Above and opposite: To promote *B'Day*, Beyoncé performed on NBC's *The Today Show* (above) and also sang "Irreplaceable" (opposite) at the 2006 American Music Awards.

RESENTMENT

[ALBUM TRACK]

Released: September 5, 2006
Writers: Beyoncé Knowles, Curtis Mayfield, Walter Millsap III, Candice Nelson
Producers: Beyoncé Knowles, Candice Nelson, Lil Walt

On "Resentment", Beyoncé portrays a proud woman navigating the ups and downs of romantic betrayal. Propelled by a sample of Curtis Mayfield's evocative, stripped-down guitar instrumental "Think", the torchy R&B ballad understandably oozes sadness. The narrator is heartbroken over her partner's infidelity and (understandably) views the deception as unforgivable. At the same time, she's struggling to move forward and overcome her resentment and anguish. Addressing these complicated emotions requires vocal nuance, and Beyoncé rises to the occasion. She channels the narrator's pain with equal parts anger and despair via a vulnerable, gospel-tinged performance. Her voice breaks with weary exasperation as she sings about attempting forgiveness, even as she feels inferior to her partner's mistress. Near the end of the song, she likewise sounds delicate and wounded as she wonders why her ex wasn't honest with her. "Resentment" is by far Beyoncé's most emotional vocal performance on *B'Day* – and the song of which she's understandably deeply proud. "I feel like vocally I've grown," she said. "I feel like all the chord changes and the beautiful harmonies and the lyrics is something that I really am proud of."[28]

CHECK ON IT (FEATURING BUN B AND SLIM THUG)

[BONUS TRACK / SINGLE]

Released: December 13, 2005 (single) / October 21, 2005 (*#1's* album)
Writers: Angela Beyincé, Bun B, Sean Garrett, Beyoncé Knowles, Swizz Beatz, Slim Thug
Producer: Swizz Beatz
Select Alternate Versions: Bama Boyz Remix, Junior Vasquez Club Mix, King Klub Mix

The laid-back "Check on It" is "all about checking on yourself and making sure you're moving right and your man admiring how you move," Beyoncé said. "It's simple."[29] Despite being so straightforward, "Check on It" had a convoluted history. Through a quirk of the time, the R&B/hip-hop hybrid appeared as a bonus track on several editions of *B'Day* and on Destiny's Child's 2005 compilation *The #1's*. And while the final version of the song ended up as a Houston homecoming that featured Beyoncé in collaboration with rappers Slim Thug and Bun B, the latter wasn't initially on the track.

Additionally, the song was also used in the 2006 movie *The Pink Panther*, in which Beyoncé co-starred as the popstar Xania, a character she described as a "modern-day Josephine Baker".[30] The music video nodded to the movie by including an abundance of pink clothing and set pieces, among other things. "['Check on It'] is so fun, it makes you feel like a child again," Beyoncé said, "and we wanted to put some of that in the choreography and the feel of the video."[31] Despite the lighthearted vibe, "Check on It" didn't make the cut for *The Pink Panther* soundtrack and only appeared in the movie. However, the song was a massive success, reaching No. 1 on the *Billboard* Hot 100.

Opposite and above: Beyoncé won Best R&B Video for "Check On It" at the 2006 MTV Video Music Awards (opposite) and turned heads at the premiere for the film *The Pink Panther* (above).

CREOLE

[*B'DAY* JAPANESE EDITION]

Released: September 4, 2006
Writers: Rich Harrison, Beyoncé Knowles, Makeba Riddick
Producers: Rich Harrison

Although Beyoncé is closely associated with Texas, she also has deep Louisiana roots via her mother, Tina Knowles, who is of Louisiana Creole heritage. This fact turns up on "Creole", a lesser-known *B'Day* bonus track on which Beyoncé celebrates how the different parts of her heritage (including and especially her Creole roots) come together to make her who she is. The metaphorical second verse is particularly meaningful, as she compares various coloured bones (representing her diverse background) to ingredients; when mixed, these create a unique, rare dish.

Producer Rodney Jerkins observed that on *B'Day*, Beyoncé was interested in honouring her heritage through music. "The mood that she was in, and she was feeling, she wanted New Orleans-inspired music to be incorporated to the stuff she was doing," he says. "Creole-type stuff. Zydeco."[32] Jerkins didn't work on "Creole" – co-producer/co-writer Rich Harrison did instead – but this song certainly aligns with this vibe, given the flashy horns, rhythmic nods to New Orleans bounce and Beyoncé's forceful vocals. Consider "Creole" of a sonic piece alongside *B'Day* tracks "Suga Mama" and "Freakum Dress".

Below and opposite: Beyoncé is extremely close to her mom, Tina Knowles (below, pictured together in 2012). In 2007, Beyoncé and Justin Timberlake joined forces for the duet "Until The End Of Time."

UNTIL THE END OF TIME (JUSTIN TIMBERLAKE AND BEYONCÉ)

[*FUTURESEX/LOVE SOUNDS* DELUXE EDITION]

Released: November 13, 2007 (single) / November 27, 2007 (album)
Writers: Nate "Danja" Hills, Timbaland, Justin Timberlake
Producers: Nate "Danja" Hills, Timbaland, Justin Timberlake
Select Alternate Versions: Jason Nevins Extended Mix, Mike Rizzo Global Club Mix, Ralphi Rosario BIG Radio Mix

Back in the late 1990s and early 2000s, Justin Timberlake and Beyoncé ran in similar circles owing to the success of (respectively) their groups *NSYNC and Destiny's Child. After these acts took a breather, both musicians also became massive solo stars. Teaming up for a duet was the next logical step – and the love song "Until the End of Time", which initially appeared as a Timberlake-only cut on his 2006 solo effort *FutureSex/LoveSounds,* was a winner.

Musically, it's reminiscent of a Prince-esque slow jam from the 1980s, between the moody, chilly production and hints of Minneapolis funk. Lyrically, the song's protagonist notes that the only thing he needs in his life is the love of his woman; her presence provides solace, as well as shelter from the storms of the outside world.

On the "Until the End of Time" remix, Beyoncé adds extra depth with a simple gesture: flipping the gender references. Instead of the song being a male-centred soliloquy, the song now gives the woman a voice – and she makes it clear that the feelings of love and protection are mutual. Given the star power, the new version of "Until the End of Time" landed in the top 20 of the *Billboard* Hot 100.

BEAUTIFUL LIAR [BEYONCÉ AND SHAKIRA]

[*B'DAY* DELUXE EDITION / SINGLE]

Released: February 12, 2007 (single) / April 3, 2007 (album)
Writers: Ian Dench, Mikkel Eriksen, Amanda Ghost, Tor Erik Hermansen, Beyoncé Knowles
Producers: Eduardo Cabra, Beyoncé Knowles, Shakira, Stargate
Select Alternate Versions: Freemasons Remix Edit, Spanglish Version, Spanish Version

Imagine cheating on Beyoncé *and* Shakira. That's the scenario in "Beautiful Liar", in which the women discover that they're dating the same man. Instead of getting mad at each other, however, the women decide to become friends, comfort each other and jettison the two-timing cheater. "Beautiful Liar" was nominated for a Grammy, while the Spanish version ("Bello Embustero") received Latin Grammy nods.

"She's one of my favorite Latin singers, and I have nothing but respect for her," Beyoncé said. "She's so sweet, so sexy, so positive... We met three or four years ago at the MTV Video Music Awards, and we said, 'We have to do something together', and finally, we made it happen."[33]

Stargate's Mikkel Eriksen noted that he and Tor Erik Hermansen wrote the music for "Beautiful Liar" – which hewed towards R&B-pop with Mariachi horns, slinky Latin grooves and Arabic percussion and instruments such as oud and ney – long before the song was recorded. The duo played it for one of their managers [and a long-time Jay-Z colleague], Ty Ty Smith, who "loved the track and said that it'd be perfect for a duet between Shakira and Beyoncé."[34] Eriksen found this preposterous: "We were like, 'Yeah, right!' and laughing and shaking our heads and thinking it could not be done. But he was really devoted to that idea."[35]

Figuring out the lyrics and topline melody wasn't easy, so Smith called up Amanda Ghost, a solo artist who co-wrote James Blunt's smash "You're Beautiful" and was writing songs with Ian Dench, guitarist for electronic rock act EMF. Ghost and Dench travelled to New York City to hear more about the Beyoncé opportunity but weren't convinced. "Amanda sort of went, 'Well, I don't really write songs for other people,'" Dench recalls. "'I'm an artist. The James Blunt thing was a one-off.'"[36]

However, Dench shares that it ended up being an offer the songwriters couldn't refuse. Beyoncé and Jay-Z subsequently walked into the meeting room and reiterated that they wanted Ghost and Dench to write a song – and, in fact, had already booked a studio at 8 p.m. that night. Now galvanized, Dench and Ghost rose to the occasion and wrote "Beautiful Liar" in their hotel.

"It originally had a Spanish title and different lyrics, but then Tor said, 'You have that line "beautiful liar" in one of the verses'," Eriksen shares. "Why not use that as a feature?' So that became the punchline. We presented it to Beyoncé, who loved it and added her own twist to the lyrics."[37]

The pair weren't able to record "Beautiful Liar" in the studio at the same time because Shakira was on tour, but Beyoncé was thrilled with the results. "I think it's so great because it's about a guy who's kind of playing both of us, and instead of us arguing over the guy we say, 'Forget him. Let's stick together. He's a beautiful liar,'" she said. "I think it's a wonderful message for women."[38] For Stargate's Eriksen, "Beautiful Liar" is also a testament to perseverance. "It illustrates for us the importance of having dedicated people around who believe in your ideas and your music and push it forward to make it happen."[39]

Opposite: When Beyoncé and Shakira collaborated, magic happened in the form of the Grammy-nominated "Beautiful Liar."

WELCOME TO HOLLYWOOD

[*B'DAY* DELUXE EDITION]

Released: April 3, 2007
Writers: Shawn Carter, Beyoncé Knowles, Ne-Yo, Reggie Perry
Producers: Beyoncé Knowles, Reggie Perry

As with "Dangerously in Love 2", the *B'Day* cut "Welcome to Hollywood" is an update of sorts to a previously released tune: Jay-Z's "Hollywood" from his 2006 album *Kingdom Come*, which also features Beyoncé. Unsurprisingly, her solo update is seamless; among other things, both songs share the same musical track, a brisk combination of Neptunes-esque disco-funk and keening R&B. But on "Welcome to Hollywood", Jay-Z's rapping verses are excised and he merely adds background vocals; instead, Beyoncé takes centre stage singing about the insidious ways in which Hollywood deceives people seeking fame and fortune. Appropriately, "Welcome to Hollywood" ends with Beyoncé referencing a flurry of celebrities who fell prey to the dark side of celebrity: actors James Dean, John Belushi and River Phoenix, as well as musicians Janis Joplin, Jimi Hendrix and Jim Morrison. The song ends up as a cautionary tale, warning that Hollywood's shiny exterior might not be what it seems.

FLAWS AND ALL

[*B'DAY* DELUXE EDITION]

Released: April 3, 2007
Writers: Beyoncé Knowles, Solange Knowles, Ne-Yo, Shea Taylor
Producers: Beyoncé Knowles and Shea Taylor

A standout track from the *B'Day* era, "Flaws and All" is a tribute to the beauty of unconditional love. The narrator admits she can be difficult: not a morning person, occasionally moody and nasty, and emotionally unpredictable or unavailable. But she's grateful that her significant other accepts her *and* her imperfections. In a nod to the timeless feel of the song's lyrics, "Flaws and All" contains a sample of record-player static alongside a classic mélange of acoustic guitar, piano and jazzy drums.

Ne-Yo started writing "Flaws and All" while in the studio working on potential music for Britney Spears. "Ty Ty [Smith, the Jay-Z colleague] comes into the studio every other day just listening to what I'm doing," he says. "Every other song he's like, 'Yo, let me get a copy of that.' Mind you, if I'm doing it for somebody specifically, you're not supposed to give away a copy." A week later, however, Ne-Yo says he received some surprising news from Ty Ty. "[He said] 'Yeah, so that "Flaws and All" shit? Don't put that in the Britney pack. Beyoncé's taking that.'"[40]

"Flaws and All" also appeared on the 2007 soundtrack of Tyler Perry's *Why Did I Get Married?* and had a modern resurgence thanks to its showstopping inclusion on the *Renaissance World Tour*. Backed by a horn section and her live band, Beyoncé performed like she was the glam headliner at a 1960s nightclub, transforming the song into a nod of appreciation towards loyal fans who have stuck with her all these years.

Above and opposite: Beyoncé's star kept rising during this era, with a high-profile role in the movie *Dreamgirls* (above, at the Cannes Film Festival) and a performance at the 50th Annual Grammy Awards (pictured on the red carpet with "Flaws and All" co-writer Ne-Yo, opposite).

WORLD WIDE WOMAN

[*B'DAY* DELUXE EDITION]

Released: April 3, 2007
Writers: Angela Beyincé, LaShawn Daniels, Sean Garrett, Beyoncé Knowles, Makeba Riddick
Producers: Rodney Jerkins and Beyoncé Knowles

For his songs on *B'Day*, producer Rodney Jerkins enlisted a cadre of songwriting collaborators. "I brought basically five writers to work on different ideas," he says. "You either make the cut or you don't... We do a lot of songs when it's an artist of that magnitude, like Beyoncé. You're not sending her one song; you're sending her 20 ideas."[41] On "World Wide Woman", winning ideas came from LaShawn Daniels, who had won a Grammy for co-writing Destiny's Child's "Say My Name", as well as *B'Day* principal writers Angela Beyincé, Sean Garrett and Makeba Riddick.

Together, they came up with an imaginative song that borrows the concept of the expansive "world wide web" (a now-antiquated phrase that refers to the internet) to praise a "world wide woman". Accordingly, the lyrics weave in technical references (i.e., logging on, uploading, an ethernet cable, a URL) to describe this woman's power: much like the internet, she can take a man anywhere *and* be anything he wants her to be. This clever conceit unwittingly creates a second meaning: the "world wide woman" is also a glamorous, worldly figure. Fittingly, the music is '90s R&B that's a showcase for Beyoncé's growing power as a vocalist.

IF

[*B'DAY* DELUXE EDITION]

Released: April 3, 2007
Writers: Mikkel Eriksen, Tor Erik Hermansen, Beyoncé Knowles, Ne-Yo
Producers: Beyoncé Knowles and Stargate

"If" ended up on *B'Day: Deluxe Edition* after "Still in Love (Kissing You)" was removed from the album over a copyright infringement lawsuit (see opposite). In a testament to Beyoncé's deep bench of songs in the *B'Day* era, she had a seamless replacement: the string-swept ballad "If".

The song's protagonist is at a crossroads. She's distressed because her boyfriend is ignoring her; however, she's simultaneously being pursued by another man who is treating her much better. She's tempted to give in to these advances – but she reveals to her boyfriend that if he does let her go, then it's a sign he wasn't that into her in the first place.

To songwriter Makeba Riddick, these complicated scenarios were all part of Beyoncé's greatness as a songwriter. "Her concepts were so incredible," she said. "I never saw an artist have so much of her own vision and know exactly what they want to say. She would say, 'I have this crazy idea for this song, check out this situation.' We would be talking, bugging out – three hours later, then comes the song."[42]

AMOR GITANO (ALEJANDRO FERNÁNDEZ FEATURING BEYONCÉ)

[*B'DAY* DELUXE EDITION]

Released: February 12, 2007 (single) / April 3, 2007 (album)
Writers: Reyli Barba, Jaime Flores, Beyoncé Knowles
Producers: Beyoncé Knowles and Rudy Pérez

For *B'Day: Deluxe Edition,* Beyoncé recorded Spanish-language versions of multiple hits, including "Listen", "Irreplaceable" and "Beautiful Liar". "I wanted to do the Spanish versions because four or five years ago, Destiny's Child did a duet with Alejandro Sanz ['Quisiera Ser']," she said. "Our Latin fans were so excited, they were like, 'When are you going to do more?'"[43] Beyoncé also teamed up with Latin music superstar Alejandro Fernández for "Amor Gitano", a flamenco-pop original song that doubled as the theme song of the telenovela *Zorro: La Espada y La Rosa (The Sword and the Rose).*

The collaboration came about due to a smart business arrangement. Kevin Lawrie, the president of Sony BMG Latin, had been working with other executives to find a song for *Zorro.* As it so happens, Reyli Barba's song came up as something that might work for Fernández – and Lawrie called Beyoncé's dad, Mathew Knowles, to gauge her potential involvement.[44] "When they suggested it, I liked the idea," Fernández said. "I thought it was spectacular. So we went, I gave her the song and she liked it.... We recorded it in one day. She seemed like a fine lady to me, very humble, with a great voice and beautiful."[45] The feeling was mutual. "When I was asked to record with him, I immediately said 'yes'," Beyoncé said. "He is extremely talented."[46] The combination was dynamite: "Amor Gitano" hit No. 1 in Spain.

STILL IN LOVE (KISSING YOU)

[*B'DAY* DELUXE EDITION]

Released: April 3, 2007
Writers: Timothy Atack, Beyoncé Knowles, Des'ree Weekes
Producers: Nellee Hooper and Beyoncé Knowles

In the mid-1990s, the British singer Des'ree earned an international hit with an inspirational song called "You Gotta Be". Not long after, she appeared in Baz Luhrmann's hit 1996 film *Romeo + Juliet* performing a soulful piano ballad called "Kissing You" during a pivotal scene when the star-crossed lovers meet at a party. The love song sparkles like a fairy tale, between romantic lyrics gushing about a partner and dramatic strings.

Beyoncé was an avowed fan of "Kissing You" and recorded a faithful version of the tune under the title "Still in Love (Kissing You)" for *B'Day: Deluxe Edition.* "I've always loved that song," she said. "It gives you this emotion – I don't care who you are, you just feel it. And it meant a lot for me to do this."[47]

Unfortunately, her take ended up causing controversy in the form of a copyright infringement lawsuit. In a nutshell, Des'ree's publishers claimed that they had allowed the cover if it was released under the same title – and when the version on *B'Day: Deluxe Edition* emerged under the slightly different name, they retracted their permission. (The publisher also claimed they hadn't given Beyoncé clearance to release a music video for the song, which was also scheduled to happen.) In the end, *B'Day: Deluxe Edition* was pulled from stores and reissued with "If" in the place of "Still in Love (Kissing You)".[48]

Opposite and above: Beyoncé expanded her sound during the *B'Day* era by collaborating with Latin music superstar Alejandro Fernández (opposite) and covering Des'ree (above).

BACK UP

[*B'DAY* CIRCUIT CITY EDITION]

Released: September 5, 2006
Writers: Angela Beyincé, Anesha Birchett, Antea Birchett, LaShawn Daniels, Fred Jerkins III, Rodney Jerkins, Beyoncé Knowles, Delisha Thomas
Producers: Rodney "Darkchild" Jerkins and Beyoncé Knowles

As it turns out, "Creole" wasn't the only *B'Day*-era song inspired by New Orleans music. So does the club jam "Back Up", which boasts brisk horns and swerving grooves influenced by not just New Orleans bounce but also Houston hip-hop. "We were doing a lot of ideas around that [New Orleans inspiration], and the horns, but at the same time, we wanted to give that urban street edge," says producer Rodney Jerkins. "So we tried to get that combination. That's really where ['Back Up'] started from, from that inspiration that she gave us."[49] Jerkins had a front row seat in the studio to Beyoncé recording "Back Up", meaning he was witness to a gravity-defying vocal performance that was tenacious, celebratory and diva-powerful. "She gave us direction, and she had like four or five studios going at one time, but then she only sings what she likes," he says. "'Back Up' was one of those records."[50]

LOST YO MIND

[*B'DAY* INTERNATIONAL iTUNES STORE EDITIONS]

Released: September 1, 2006
Writers: Sean Garrett, Beyoncé Knowles, Swizz Beatz
Producers: Sean Garrett, Beyoncé Knowles, Swizz Beatz

One of the more under-the-radar tracks from the *B'Day* era is "Lost Yo Mind", which was available only in certain territories. The obscurity is a shame, as Beyoncé portrays a scorned woman absolutely incensed by her boyfriend's infidelity. She keeps finding belongings that aren't hers (for example, an expensive purse or earrings) and sarcastically tells her soon-to-be-ex he must've lost his mind when he cheated. As the protagonist, Beyoncé captures the stages of rage with one of her most fiery vocal performances of the era; as the song progresses, she expresses regret for supporting her partner, calls out his lies and finally tells him off spectacularly. The music matches her urgency by incorporating shrill whistles, handclaps, cheerleader-like chants and synth-led production.

MY FIRST TIME

[*B'DAY* BEST BUY DELUXE EDITION / *LIVE AT WEMBLEY*]

Released: September 5, 2006
Writers: Chad Hugo, Beyoncé Knowles, Pharrell Williams
Producers: The Neptunes

Beyoncé's *Live at Wembley* DVD came with a bonus CD of studio recordings that included multiple remixes, a cover song (Rose Royce's "Wishing on a Star") and several studio tracks. A leftover from the *Dangerously in Love* sessions, the early '90s R&B throwback "My First Time" features a narrator ready to give in and make herself totally vulnerable to her partner. She stresses that she's not scared because her beau makes her feel safe and respected – but does remind him to take things slow.

Opposite: To herald the launch of the Emporio Armani Diamonds perfume, Beyoncé covered "Diamonds Are A Girl's Best Friend."

DIAMONDS ARE A GIRL'S BEST FRIEND

[ADVERT]

Released: 2007
Songwriter: Leo Robin
Composer: Jule Styne

In 2007, Giorgio Armani released a fragrance called Emporio Armani Diamonds. To promote the perfume, the legendary fashion designer enlisted Beyoncé. "He saw me perform [at a charitable benefit], and immediately was like, 'That's the girl for Diamonds,' because the fragrance represents strength and sexiness and a woman that's independent and that can buy her own diamonds," she said. "And that's what I represent. So it's a perfect collaboration."[51]

As part of the marketing campaign, Beyoncé starred in a glamorous black-and-white ad and covered "Diamonds Are a Girl's Best Friend". Carol Channing debuted the classic song in 1949 in the original Broadway production *Gentlemen Prefer Blondes* – and Marilyn Monroe made the song famous in the musical's 1953 film adaptation. Beyoncé honours the song's legacy by belting out the lyrics atop brassy big band music with retro flair.

DREAMGIRLS

"WE'RE LIKE THE SUPREMES OF THE '90S AND A YOUNGER EN VOGUE," BEYONCÉ ONCE SAID WHEN DESCRIBING DESTINY'S CHILD. "OUR STYLE OF MUSIC AND OUR STYLE IN GENERAL IS DIFFERENT THAN ANY OTHER. WE WANT TO BE IN A CLASS BY OURSELVES."[52] IT'S SAFE TO SAY THIS WISH CAME TRUE: DESTINY'S CHILD CARRIED ON THE LEGACY OF MOTOWN GIRL GROUPS LIKE THE SUPREMES AND BECAME A DOMINANT POP AND R&B FORCE IN THE LATE 1990S AND EARLY 2000S. AND WHEN BEYONCÉ STEPPED OUT AS A SOLO ACT, SHE GAINED SUPERSTAR SUCCESS THAT WAS COMPARABLE TO THAT OF HEAD SUPREME, DIANA ROSS.

This background and experience made Beyoncé perfectly suited to star as Deena Jones in 2006's *Dreamgirls*, a movie adaptation of the 1981 Broadway musical. Often perceived as a fictionalized version of The Supremes' story, the musical follows the triumphs and struggles of an ambitious, talented girl group, The Dreams. Romantic complexities abound, and major career and interpersonal conflicts arise when powerhouse vocalist Effie is forced out of The Dreams, thrusting Deena into the spotlight.

Dreamgirls ran for more than 1,500 performances on Broadway before closing in August 1985. It also won six Tony Awards and produced a major hit with Jennifer Holliday's rendition of Effie's signature tune "And I Am Telling You I'm Not Going". But incredibly enough, a *Dreamgirls* film took 25 years to get to the finish line; over the years, Whitney Houston, Ms. Lauryn Hill and Kelly Price were all floated as potential stars for a movie version. It took the vision and determination of director and writer Bill Condon, who previously found much success adapting

Below and opposite: "We're like the Supremes of the '90s and a younger En Vogue," Beyoncé once said when describing Destiny's Child, making her the perfect star for the movie adaptation of the 1981 Broadway musical *Dreamgirls*.

the musical *Chicago* for the silver screen, to finally put *Dreamgirls* in production.

As it happens, Beyoncé always felt a special kinship with *Dreamgirls* and Deena Jones, starting with the fact that she was born in 1981, the same year the musical premiered. "The first time I met my choreographer, I was 15," she recalled. "He said, 'Deena Jones, Dreamgirl.' And I was like, 'What is that?' And he said, 'Go get the soundtrack.' When I heard they were doing this movie, I was like, 'Okay, this is finally the part that I know is made for me.' I just knew that I was supposed to be Deena."[53]

Beyoncé stressed that she wasn't simply given the part; she had to audition for the film like everyone else. She starred alongside Jennifer Hudson, then an up-and-coming singer who had been an *American Idol* finalist, as Effie. Jamie Foxx, meanwhile, portrays Curtis Taylor Jr., a shady record executive who Deena later marries. Other big names in the cast included Danny Glover, Eddie Murphy, John Lithgow and Anika Noni Rose.

Beyoncé admitted she and Hudson were "scared" as production began. "We were all nervous," she said. "You know, [we were working with] legendary actors. They have Oscars and we grew up watching them and it was amazing to be in the presence of greatness. They brought out great things in me."[54] As always, Beyoncé gave her all while playing Deena, working with an acting coach, losing 20 pounds, and "doing emotional diaries and crying" every day. "I thought about some of my toughest moments in my life, and brought out a lot of emotion that I don't have to think about."[55] To inform Deena's musical approach, she also studied performance tapes of Diana Ross.[56]

The hard work paid off, as Beyoncé put her own stamp on the musical's familiar songs. "Dreamgirls" – a sparkling '60s girl group homage that introduced The Dreams and also featured Hudson and Rose – was stellar. She also dueted with Jamie Foxx on the wistful R&B ballad "When I First Saw You", trading off tender lines tinged with regret and resignation, and gives fierce disco-diva on the uptempo version of "One Night Only". Unique to the film, there was also a new song, "Listen" [*see* page 91] that served as a pivotal moment for both Beyoncé *and* Deena.

Beyoncé was careful to note that she was playing a character in the film. "Initially, I was afraid audiences would think this is my life story," she said. "But I don't see myself at all in this performance, which is exactly what I wanted. My own vocal style isn't nearly as laid back as Deena's, and it was amazingly difficult for me to sing so restrained and poised and still deliver all that soul. Every blink had to be perfect."[57]

She had good reason to stress the fictional nature of her role. As it turns out, the film's story seemed to lean in even more to the story of The Supremes (and their label, Motown Records); the movie even took place in Detroit, Motown's homebase, rather than Chicago. This caused controversy: in early 2007, DreamWorks Pictures even took out full-page ads in trade magazines *Variety* and the *Hollywood Reporter* apologizing to Motown founder Berry Gordy Jr. and noting, "*Dreamgirls* is a work of fiction. It is also an homage to Motown."[58]

But *Dreamgirls* was a box office hit, grossing more than $103 million in the US, and racked up a ton of awards and nominations. Hudson won an Oscar for Best Performance by an Actress in a Supporting Role, while Beyoncé was nominated for a Golden Globe for Best Performance by an Actress in a Motion Picture – Musical or Comedy. "I've done movies before, but I've never been able to call myself an actor until this film," Beyoncé said. "Now I can say it with confidence."[59]

Doing *Dreamgirls* also had a major impact on *B'Day*, as Beyoncé went directly into the studio to make the album after filming the movie, channelling her experience into sophisticated new music. "Deena was a woman, and her dreams became her husband's dreams and her whole life," Beyoncé said. "She didn't do what she wanted to do. She didn't know who she was, she didn't know her voice, and eventually she does find her voice. She knows where she wants to go in life. And I *was* Deena for six months."[60]

Opposite and below: Often perceived as a fictionalized version of The Supremes' story, *Dreamgirls* follows the triumphs and struggles of an ambitious, talented girl group, The Dreams. Beyoncé portrays Deena Jones.

ENCORE FOR THE FANS

[ALBUM TRACK]

Released: September 5, 2006
Writer: Beyoncé Knowles

On some versions of *B'Day*, Beyoncé introduces the *Dreamgirls* song "Listen" with a brief spoken-word interlude that thanks fans and explains how portraying Deena in the movie affected her songwriting. "I'm very content in my life, but Deena felt like she was trapped," she says. "She was married, [and] was in this relationship for so long. It was all the things I wanted to say while I was doing the movie, all the things I wanted the character to say."[61]

However, Beyoncé turned this very specific experience into universal songs and sentiments, she continued. "[On *B'Day*] I'm speaking for every woman that's kind of been in a relationship for a long time, and it's supposed to empower women to have the extra boost to say all the things that they feel in their hearts. It's really a strong album, and it really makes women feel like they're powerful. It makes you want to get your power back."[62]

Below and opposite: *Dreamgirls* was a box office hit and led to Beyoncé being nominated for a Golden Globe for Best Performance by an Actress in a Motion Picture – Musical or Comedy.

LISTEN

[SOUNDTRACK / SINGLE]

Released: October 2006 (single) / December 5, 2006 (soundtrack album)
Writers: Scott Cutler, Beyoncé Knowles, Henry Krieger, Anne Preven
Producers: The Underdogs
Select Alternate Versions: Spanish version ("Oye")

In the first act of *Dreamgirls*, Deena's one-time bandmate Effie famously takes the spotlight with the jaw-dropping "And I Am Telling You I'm Not Going". For the film adaptation, director/screenwriter Bill Condon wanted an equally big song for the second act.[63] Cue the Beyoncé-helmed majestic power ballad "Listen".

One of four new songs in the movie – all with music by Henry Krieger, the composer of the original musical's songs – "Listen" tells a story of resilience. Tired of being underestimated and misled (and of having her hopes and dreams ignored or diminished) Beyoncé-as-Deena pushes back on her controlling husband, Curtis Taylor Jr. (played by Jamie Foxx) and gives him an ultimatum: let me soar.

Vocally, the song is also about rediscovering your spark. Beyoncé's voice grows more determined and powerful as "Listen" progresses, matching the song's gradual crescendo to melodramatic orchestral flourishes and squealing electric guitar. At the end of the song, Beyoncé asserts Deena's independence with a sustained, triumphant high note.

"Listen" was nominated for an Oscar and a Golden Globe in the Best Original Song categories. "Even though it takes place in the '70s, this is a song that you can play on the radio and that my generation of fans can relate to today," Beyoncé said. "And it has soul, which is really the legacy of Motown."[64]

09 I AM ... SASHA FIERCE

DUALITIES ABOUND ON BEYONCÉ'S THIRD FULL-LENGTH, *I AM ... SASHA FIERCE*, WHICH WAS INSPIRED BY HER PORTRAYAL OF ETTA JAMES IN THE MOVIE *CADILLAC RECORDS*. SHE DIVIDED THE DOUBLE ALBUM INTO TWO HALVES, WHICH REPRESENTED THE TWO SIDES OF HER PERSONALITY: INTROSPECTIVE SOUL-POP AND R&B FOR HER OFFSTAGE LIFE ("IF I WERE A BOY", "HALO"), AND EMPOWERING GENRE-BUSTING FOR HER ONSTAGE PERSONA SASHA FIERCE (THE RETRO-FABULOUS "SINGLE LADIES (PUT A RING ON IT)", SOUTHERN HIP-HOP ANTHEM "DIVA"). *I AM ... SASHA FIERCE* WAS A SENSATION, WINNING A GRAMMY FOR BEST CONTEMPORARY R&B ALBUM.

CADILLAC RECORDS

WHEN DARNELL MARTIN WROTE THE SCRIPT FOR *CADILLAC RECORDS* – A 2008 HISTORICAL DRAMA FILM THAT PROFILES LEONARD CHESS AND ARTISTS WHO RECORDED FOR HIS LEGENDARY CHICAGO RECORD LABEL, CHESS RECORDS – SHE ENVISIONED BEYONCÉ PORTRAYING THE PIONEERING, GENRE-BLURRING R&B VOCALIST ETTA JAMES.

When Beyoncé finally read the script, she had all sorts of feelings. "I said, 'I have to do this movie,' but I was terrified," Beyoncé admitted. "Was I really ready?"[1]

As it turns out, she most certainly was. Drawing on resources like James' autobiography, Beyoncé conducted meticulous research for the role. She also didn't shy away from digging into the rougher aspects of the musician's life, including her heroin addiction.

"I was surprised at how much Beyoncé threw the glamour out the window so easily and so joyfully, and embraced the unattractiveness of being strung out," said Martin, who also directed *Cadillac Records*. "She was really excited about getting that raw. She really wanted to dig in and get real."[2]

For Beyoncé, there was never any question that she was going to be as honest as she could with her portrayal. "I'm obviously playing a character, and I felt that story needed to be told," she said. "It gave me an opportunity to challenge myself and show, even myself, what I can do as an actor. I've never been so proud of something I've done."[3]

Being in the film also gave Beyoncé the opportunity to cover multiple songs popularized by James, including her signature song, "At Last" [*see* page 96]. From a vocal standpoint, Beyoncé's ability to channel James was nothing short of astounding; these performances were loving homages, not rote imitations.

On the smoldering "I'd Rather Go Blind", Beyoncé's voice possesses a rougher edge and conversational intonation, capturing the song's anguish. She dips into her lower register for "All I Could Do Was Cry", a grief-stricken song from the perspective of a woman watching the man she loves marry someone else; her delivery is full of pain and sorrow. And on "Trust in Me", Beyoncé is persuasive and seductive as she works to convince someone she loves that her aim is true.

"I always loved her voice, but now knowing what she's been through, she's one of my heroes," Beyoncé said. "I'm not sure if she thought [I would be good] as her. I'm very, very nervous." Luckily, however, James reportedly gave Beyoncé a vote of confidence for the film: "I actually spoke with her and she told me, 'I loved you from the first time you sung.'" [4]

Cadillac Records sadly underperformed at the box office, earning just around $9 million worldwide. But there was a silver lining: doing the movie had a profound impact on Beyoncé's solo career and led her to *I Am ... Sasha Fierce*. "I realized that Etta James was so unapologetic, bold and strong, that playing her was a big risk for me," Beyoncé says. "It gave me the confidence and the push to challenge myself a little more with my music."[5]

Opposite: Beyoncé portrayed Etta James in the movie *Cadillac Records*, a deeply challenging role that led her to *I Am ... Sasha Fierce*.

AT LAST

[SOUNDTRACK / SINGLE]

Released: November 3, 2008 (single) / December 2, 2008 (album)
Writers: Mack Gordon and Harry Warren

When Beyoncé filmed the *Cadillac Records* scene where she performs "At Last", it was a powerful experience. "It was like Etta took over," she said. "It was like she was here."[6] Indeed, many people have attempted to cover "At Last" – which first appeared in the 1941 Sonja Henie-Milton Berle movie *Sun Valley Serenade* but rose to prominence with James' 1960 cover – but few have succeeded.

But Beyoncé's cover is just about impossible to top. Through her performance, she communicates the narrator's relief at finally finding a dream partner – while simultaneously conveying that the narrator is still processing the hard times she went through to find this happiness. Fittingly, Beyoncé luxuriates in the song's melodic contours, taking care not to oversing and instead letting the myriad emotions unfold at their own pace.

"'At Last'," Beyoncé says, is "just timeless. It sounds like something that was written right now. The music ... it does something to your soul. You can hear the pain. You can hear the passion. It takes you back to the '50s."[7]

Beyoncé's version of "At Last" won a Grammy Award for Best Traditional R&B Vocal Performance. But she received the thrill of a lifetime at the 2009 Neighborhood Inaugural Ball: she sang "At Last" for the first dance of Barack and Michelle Obama, the first Black president and First Lady in American history. Her performance that night acknowledged the couple's deep love for each other, but also poignantly recognized the historic nature of the Obama presidency.

ONCE IN A LIFETIME

[SOUNDTRACK]

Released: December 2, 2008
Writers: Ian Dench, James Dring, Amanda Ghost, Beyoncé Knowles, Scott McFarnon, Jody Street
Producers: Ian Dench, Amanda Ghost, Beyoncé Knowles, The Rural

In addition to singing multiple tunes popularized by Etta James, Beyoncé sang the original song "Once In a Lifetime" in *Cadillac Records*. An easygoing waltz with a decidedly contemporary vibe, the song combines swooning electronic flourishes with tasteful beats. In fact, it's the perfect song for a romantic slow dance – especially since the lyrics are from the perspective of a protagonist expressing the love she feels for someone special.

Co-writer Ian Dench recalls previewing "Once In a Lifetime" for one of Beyoncé's reps, Jay Brown, in Brown's hotel room near London's Hyde Park. "Scott [McFarnon, co-writer] got the guitar out, and I can remember looking across Hyde Park when he played," Dench says. "And he did *such* a beautiful performance of this song. [You could] see Jay Brown was like, 'Oh, we have to have this song.' And [Beyoncé] tried it, and it sounded great."[8]

"Once In a Lifetime" received a Grammy nomination in 2010 for Best Song Written for Motion Picture, Television or Other Visual Media, as well as a Golden Globe nod for Best Original Song – Motion Picture in 2008.

Opposite and below: Beyoncé sang "At Last" for the first dance of Barack and Michelle Obama, the first Black president and First Lady in American history, and for Etta James herself at the 2008 Fashion Rocks event.

IF I WERE A BOY

[SINGLE]

Released: October 13, 2008 (single) / November 18, 2008 (album)
Writers: Brittany Jean Carlson and Toby Gad
Producers: Toby Gad and Beyoncé Knowles
Select Alternate Versions: Spanish version, Maurice Joshua Mojo UK Remix

Beyoncé's third full-length album *I Am... Sasha Fierce* was a double album divided into two halves, to represent two sides of her personality – including her onstage persona Sasha Fierce, introduced by her full name for the first time. "*I Am* ..., is about who I am underneath all the makeup, underneath the lights, and underneath all the exciting star drama," Beyoncé explained. "And *Sasha Fierce* is the fun, more sensual, more aggressive, more outspoken side and more glamorous side that comes out when I'm working and when I'm on the stage."[9]

"If I Were a Boy" kicks off the album on an introspective note. The narrator muses about the prosaic things she wouldn't have to worry about if she swapped genders: her looks, what she ate, fairweather friends, unnecessary social drama. But as the song progresses, the narrator also envisions more meaningful takeaways, like positive lessons she'd take back to a relationship. The "If I Were a Boy" bridge reveals why: in a twist, the narrator comes back to the present and announces a permanent split from her partner, leading to a final chorus where she laments that he wasn't honest or attentive.

Driven by fluttering acoustic guitar, gentle synthesizers, finger-snaps and soft background vocals, "If I Were a Boy" could slip onto a 1990s soft-rock playlist. And Beyoncé gives a standout vocal performance full of nuance – for example, solemn as she imagines the possibilities of new insights, hopeful as she lays out how to be a better boyfriend, and anguished as things start to break down. At the end of the song, she doesn't sound accusatory; instead, she sounds sad and disappointed by the outcome.

Toby Gad – who had recently found global success co-writing Fergie's "Big Girls Don't Cry" – penned "If I Were a Boy" with Brittany Jean Carlson, herself a recording artist under the name BC Jean. In fact, the pair originally co-wrote the song during a marathon period of songwriting for Carlson's album. One day, Gad and Carlson were strolling through Times Square and she smelled some delicious pizza. "I said, 'I wish I were a boy', and he's like, 'Why would you say that? That's very weird to me,'" Carlson recalled. "I said, 'That pizza smells really good, and I'm trying not to eat carbs, and I wish I were a boy so I didn't care.'"[10]

Gad prodded her to keep brainstorming. "He was like, 'What else would you do if you were a boy?'" Carlson says. "And I was going through a really hard breakup with my first real love, so I said, 'I'd be a better man than my ex-boyfriend!'"[11] Right there in Times Square, he started recording her singing – and the pair headed back into the studio and tracked "If I Were a Boy" the same day. "I remember Toby looking at me and going, 'We just wrote a smash.' I thought he was crazy. I was like, 'Really?'"[12]

However, Gad was correct: "If I Were a Boy" reached No. 1 on pop charts around the world (including in the UK) and No. 3 on the *Billboard* Hot 100. And during live performances in this era, Beyoncé even mashed up the song with a ferocious take on Alanis Morissette's empowerment anthem "You Oughta Know", giving the narrator's lingering anger space to breathe.

Opposite and above: At the 52nd Annual Grammy Awards, Beyoncé performed "If I Were A Boy" and Alanis Morissette's "You Oughta Know."

HALO

[SINGLE]

Released: January 20, 2009 (single) / November 18, 2008 (album)
Writers: Evan Bogart, Beyoncé Knowles, Ryan Tedder
Producers: Beyoncé Knowles and Ryan Tedder
Select Alternate Versions: Dave Audé Club Remix

In spring 2008, OneRepublic frontman Ryan Tedder tore his Achilles tendon right before a show in Michigan, forcing his band to cancel or postpone several weeks of shows. He headed home to Los Angeles, ostensibly to rest and recuperate – or so his friend Evan Bogart thought.

"On his first day back in LA I was going to take over some food and hang out with him," recalls Bogart, a music industry veteran who has written hits for a variety of pop stars. "When I got there, he was like, 'Dude, we should write. We should write a song,' and I'm like, 'Well, you're not supposed to be writing. You're supposed to be in bed.'"[13]

A crutches-toting Tedder had other ideas. He and Bogart instead headed into the studio and spent the next three hours putting together "Halo", crystallizing a very clear vision the pair had for the song. "The idea was always, 'Let's write a song that embodies Ray LaMontagne,'" Bogart says, referencing the celebrated folk-rock artist. "He has a song called 'Shelter' which is beautiful .... And I said, 'We should write a Ray LaMontagne "Shelter" kind of song for Jay-Z and Beyoncé.'"[14]

Naturally, Beyoncé loved the song and made suggestions to the original that impressed Tedder. "She does stuff on any given song that, when you go from the demo to the final version, takes it to another level that you never would have thought of as the writer," he says.[15] On "Halo" that meant she dismantled and reconstructed the original bridge to her liking. "Basically, she came in, ditched that, edited it, did her vocal thing on it and now it's become one of my favorite parts of the song," Tedder says. "The whole melody, she wrote it spontaneously in the studio."[16]

"Halo" – the title comes from the "angelic chords" that Tedder came up with, Bogart says[17] – captures the heavenly feeling of finding your soulmate. The lyrics compare the all-encompassing love of a partner to something holy and sacred; in fact, this love is more like salvation. Musically, "Halo" is relatively straightforward, with stomp-and-clap beats, spiraling piano chords, needling synthesizers and occasional flashes of thundering percussion and regal strings. As with "If I Were a Boy", Beyoncé elevates the song with her vocals, drawing on her upbringing of singing in church for an affectionate, awestruck delivery.

"Halo" reached the top 5 in the UK and US and won a Grammy for Best Female Pop Vocal Performance. In the years since its release, it's become a favourite song to cover, with versions by Florence & The Machine and Ane Brun, as well as a popular, standout orchestral take that featured on Netflix's *Queen Charlotte: A Bridgerton Story*.

Left and opposite: Beyoncé performed "If I Were A Boy" at the 2008 MTV Europe Music Awards (left), but took home Best Female Pop Vocal Performance for "Halo" at the 52nd Annual Grammy Awards (opposite).

DISAPPEAR

[ALBUM TRACK]

Released: November 18, 2008
Writers: Hugo Chakrabongse, Ian Dench, Amanda Ghost, Beyoncé Knowles, Dave McCracken
Producers: Ian Dench, Amanda Ghost, Beyoncé Knowles, Dave McCracken

After the success of *B'Day*, Beyoncé decided to switch things up for *I Am ... Sasha Fierce*. She booked a relaxed studio schedule, recording three songs a day for several months; decided to forgo having high-profile artist features; and worked with an abundance of new producers and songwriters, in addition to past collaborators like Amanda Ghost and Ian Dench.

"We spent three weeks together in New York working on the new record and we had the most incredible time," says Ghost. "She has a complete, almost laser-like focus on what she is and what she can do."[18]

In the end, Beyoncé recorded a staggering 70 songs for what became a double album where each half possesses a different sound and feel. "One side has songs that are more mainstream," she said, "and another has my more traditional R&B songs for my fans who've been there the whole time."[19] *I Am ... Sasha Fierce* also drew on an expanded palette of influences, including some that might surprise people.

"Some of it sounds like Barbra Streisand, Karen Carpenter and The Beatles around the 1970s,"[20] Beyoncé shared, noting the Fab Four is an influence on "Disappear". That's most evident in the dainty acoustic guitar chords and sweet, sun-dappled organ. But the heartbroken song's theme transcends eras: the protagonist is despondent that she and her beloved have slipped away from each other – especially since she's realized the irreparable distance was her fault.

BROKEN-HEARTED GIRL

[SINGLE]

Released: August 28, 2009 (single) / November 18, 2008 (album)
Writers: Kenneth "Babyface" Edmonds, Mikkel Eriksen, Tor Erik Hermansen, Beyoncé Knowles
Producers: Beyoncé Knowles and Stargate
Select Alternate Versions: Catalyst Remix

The main character of "Broken-Hearted Girl" is feeling bereft over a love who turned out to be a disappointment – but she no longer wants to feel heartbroken. Although she has misgivings over how she's been treated, she remains faithful to her ex and wants a second chance at romance. To tease out the song's emotional tumult, Beyoncé reunited with Stargate, the Norwegian production duo who brought so much magic to "Irreplaceable" from *B'Day*.

"I suppose many of our songs are in minor keys," says the group's Mikkel Eriksen, noting "Broken-Hearted Girl" is in D-minor. "We probably lean towards more a moody, melodic expression. It's what comes most natural for us."[21] Originally, however, Eriksen says the song was "a classic, full R&B track" that they wrote with Babyface. "He came in and changed one chord and wrote the lyrics and then he added a falsetto voice that we recorded as a demo."[22]

Inspired, Stargate decided to use Babyface's vocal as a guide to re-do the music. "We changed the chords, everything," Eriksen says, "and this is where that four to the floor piano emerged."[23] The group kept things simple beyond that, layering on melodramatic strings and spiky synths so as not to overwhelm the pensive piano chords.

Opposite: Beyoncé's Sasha Fierce persona is in full effect at a 2009 performance in Rotterdam.

AVE MARIA

[ALBUM TRACK]

Released: November 18, 2008
Writers: Ian Dench, Mikkel Eriksen, Amanda Ghost, Tor Erik Hermansen, Beyoncé Knowles, Makeba Riddick
Producers: Beyoncé Knowles and Stargate

Beyoncé has always had a soft spot for the classic composition "Ave Maria". When she visited Egypt, she chose to sing that in the pyramids. "I've never heard acoustics so clear," she recalled. "My voice sounded so pure. It was inconceivable."[24] On another occasion, Beyoncé and her sometimes-collaborator Amanda Ghost also both got married the same weekend – and each woman walked down the aisle to "Ave Maria" at their respective weddings.

For songwriter Ian Dench, a light bulb went off upon hearing about this coincidence. "And I said, 'Well, in classic American hip-hop style, why don't we just take the riff and write a song around it?' And that's what we did. I just borrowed the feel of Schubert's 'Ave Maria'."[25] Dench and the other songwriters wrote new lyrics to the familiar arpeggiated chords, and paired them with a swaying, lullaby-like rhythm track and snapping-finger beats.

In Ghost's opinion, the new "Ave Maria" is deeply personal. "[Beyoncé] talks about being surrounded by friends but she's alone," the songwriter says, but then names another line that speaks to a couple realizing that at the end of the day, they have each other. "I think that's probably the most personal line on the whole album about her and Jay," Ghost continues, "because they are very real, and they're very much in love, and it must be pretty tough to have that love when you're incredibly famous."[26]

Opposite and below: Beyoncé wowed the crowd at the 2009 BET Awards by performing "Ave Maria" (below). She won six awards overall at the 52nd Annual Grammy Awards, including Song of the Year for "Single Ladies (Put a Ring on It)" (opposite).

SATELLITES

[ALBUM TRACK]

Released: November 18, 2008
Writers: Ian Dench, Amanda Ghost, Beyoncé Knowles, Dave McCracken
Producers: Ian Dench, Amanda Ghost, Beyoncé Knowles, Dave McCracken

When Beyoncé portrayed Etta James in *Cadillac Records*, the role had a profound influence on her musical approach on *I Am ... Sasha Fierce*. "I made a completely different record after playing Etta James," she says. "She has so much passion and so much pain and vulnerability in her voice, and I really respected the fact that she made whatever type of genre her own."[27]

Songwriter Amanda Ghost noticed the differences in Beyoncé almost immediately. "She came from [*Cadillac Records*] straight into the studio with me, and I was shocked by some of the songs that she wanted to do," Ghost says. "But I think she really was inspired by Etta James to express herself directly and honestly."[28]

That's certainly the case with the stripped-down "Satellites", which boasts a sparse arrangement with ornate acoustic guitar, cinematic strings and faint blushes of keyboards. Using concise language, Beyoncé rues the fact that she and her partner are like satellites who keep physically missing each other. As a result of this distance, the couple are each in their own separate worlds, when being together would be preferable.

Tellingly, the music swells in intensity near the song's end when Beyoncé sings about how painful it is to be apart – and how much she needs someone else. It's a touching moment that speaks to *I Am ... Sasha Fierce*'s vulnerability. "I write a lot of my songs for women," Beyoncé says. "A lot of the songs are about things that we need to hear. Things I wouldn't really say, or I wish I could say. I'm kind of a voice for a lot of young women."[29]

SAVE THE HERO

Released: November 18, 2008
Writers: Jim Jonsin, Beyoncé Knowles, Rico Love, Alexandra Tamposi
Producers: Jim Jonsin, Beyoncé Knowles, Rico Love

Today, Ali Tamposi is an in-demand pop songwriter who has penned hits for Kelly Clarkson, Camila Cabello and Justin Bieber. But back in the late 2000s, she was an aspiring artist trying to get her own singer-songwriter career off the ground. One of her most promising compositions was "Save the Hero", a regal piano ballad she worked on with producers Jim Jonsin and Rico Love.

"Everyone was excited about the song, and I remember Jim [Jonsin, producer] asking me if I'd be open to pitching it to other artists," she says. "I naïvely said only if it was for Beyoncé, Mariah Carey or Rihanna. I was shooting in the dark." Talk about manifesting; Love started working with Beyoncé around this time. "Shortly after," Tamposi says, "I heard she wanted to cut it."[30]

The deeply vulnerable "Save the Hero" voices a common (and relatable) struggle women often face: they take care of other people and are generous with their time and energy, but when *they* need something, they have nobody they can turn to or depend on. The song's protagonist longs for a support system, admitting that beneath their strong façade they feel desolate. "Lyrically, it's the best album I've ever had," Beyoncé said of *I Am ... Sasha Fierce*. "If a song didn't say anything or mean anything to me, I didn't put it on the record."[31]

SMASH INTO YOU

[*I AM ... SASHA FIERCE* DELUXE EDITION]

Released: November 18, 2008 (album)
Writers: Beyoncé Knowles, Terius "The-Dream" Nash, Christopher "Tricky" Stewart
Producers: The-Dream, Tricky Stewart, Beyoncé Knowles

"Smash Into You" almost wasn't a Beyoncé song. Instead, the earnest singer-songwriter Jon McLaughlin intended to cut the song for his 2008 album *OK Now* under a slightly different title: "Smack Into You". Title aside, "Smash Into You" is actually a tranquil, soaring ballad using running-related imagery to describe the euphoria of wanting to be with someone you love.

The-Dream started writing "Smash Into You" in February 2008, after a song he co-wrote, Rihanna's "Umbrella", lost the Song of the Year Grammy Award. "I got in my car, drove to Vegas immediately, and went straight to the studio," he said. "I was thinking, 'Okay, I see what you're saying. I have to write a complete, best song.' Even though 'Umbrella' changed a lot of things for me, it wasn't good enough."[32]

Before appearing on the deluxe edition of *I Am ... Sasha Fierce*, "Smash Into You" was also in the 2009 movie *Obsessed*. In the film, Beyoncé portrays the wife of Derek Charles (played by Idris Elba), a man who is being stalked and pursued by an ex-colleague named Lisa (Ali Larter).

Opposite and right: Beyoncé always brought her A-game to awards shows, like the Grammy Awards (opposite), or movies, like the little-remembered 2009 film *Obsessed* (right).

THAT'S WHY YOU'RE BEAUTIFUL

[*I AM ... SASHA FIERCE* DELUXE EDITION]

Released: November 18, 2008 (album)
Writers: James Fauntleroy, Andrew Hey, Beyoncé Knowles
Producers: Andrew Hey and Beyoncé Knowles

What if Beyoncé was focused on alternative rock in the 1990s instead of R&B and hip-hop? She might have released a track like the emo-rock-leaning "That's Why You're Beautiful", a languid, smouldering song with grungy guitars that ebb and flow between placid and bruising. Beyoncé stretches her voice over this dynamic soundscape, embracing a reflective tone and graceful flourishes – such as a call-and-response approach on the bridge – that add delicacy.

"That's Why You're Beautiful" was her first collaboration with James Fauntleroy, the decorated songwriter who she would go on to work with on *Beyoncé* and *The Carters*. It's a fantastic start: lyrically, the song is about keeping the faith that good things come to those who wait – in fact, being patient makes these things that much sweeter when they do arrive – and that beauty can come from unexpected places.

SINGLE LADIES (PUT A RING ON IT)

[SINGLE]

Released: October 8, 2008 (single) / November 18, 2008 (album)
Writers: Thaddis Harrell, Beyoncé Knowles, Terius "The-Dream" Nash, Christopher "Tricky" Stewart
Producers: Beyoncé Knowles, The-Dream, Tricky Stewart
Select Alternate Versions: Dave Audé Club Remix, Karmatronic Club Remix, Craig C's Master Blaster Club Remix

In early April 2008, Beyoncé secretly married her long-time boyfriend Jay-Z. Six months later, she released "Single Ladies (Put a Ring on It)", a song written from the perspective of a woman who's enjoying a carefree life because her ex *didn't* want to commit. She chides him for feeling jealous of her moving on with another guy – while reminding him that he blew his chance with her thanks to his noncommittal behaviour – and stresses that she deserves fidelity and stability. In the end, "Single Ladies (Put a Ring on It)" isn't necessarily about wanting to get hitched; instead, it's about asserting your value and demanding romantic respect.

Beyoncé knew the song would provoke interesting conversations. "I've always tried to pick songs and singles that were a part of pop culture, a part of things that people are passionate about and want to talk about and debate," she says. "'Single Ladies (Put a Ring on It)' is an uptempo song that's fun. But it's also something women go through every day."[33] "Single Ladies (Put a Ring on It)" co-producer/co-writer The-Dream also put himself in the shoes of women navigating challenging relationships. "I thought it was a subject that most women wanted to talk about because most of us men are scared as s--- to be bound to a commitment," he says.[34]

Musically, it also sounds like a rallying cry to women everywhere – fitting, as it kicks off the *Sasha Fierce* portion of the album. Beyoncé calls all single ladies to the front atop irresistible beats that resemble a galvanizing playground game chant. "I always believe that every artist has a groove to them," says Christopher "Tricky" Stewart, the man responsible for the vibrant rhythmic part. "That rhythm is what she responds to."[35] Unsurprisingly, "Single Ladies" was a massive hit – it reached No. 1 on multiple charts, including the *Billboard* Hot 100 – and received multiple honours, including Grammys for Song of the Year and Best R&B Song.

For the song's equally sensational black-and-white music video, Beyoncé took inspiration from Shirley MacLaine in *Sweet Charity* and "Mexican Breakfast", a 1969 dance performance by Bob Fosse's wife, Gwen Verdon, that aired on *The Ed Sullivan Show*. Wearing simple black leotards and heels, Beyoncé and two other dancers perform a tightly choreographed dance. "I thought, wow, despite all the technology we have now, wouldn't it be great to just strip it all down – without a bunch of different camera shots and cuts, without any hair and wardrobe changes – and make it all about the performance?"[36]

The music video won Video of the Year at multiple awards shows and ended up becoming a pop culture phenomenon; among other things, it was parodied on *Saturday Night Live* by Justin Timberlake and was referenced by then-US President Barack Obama. "Out of all my videos, it was the least expensive and took the least amount of time," she says. "And it ended up being the most iconic. I absolutely didn't expect that – I don't think anyone did. But I knew exactly what I wanted to do: keep it simple."[37]

Left and opposite: "Single Ladies (Put a Ring on It)" slayed when Beyoncé performed the song live, including at the 2008 American Music Awards (left) and 2009 MTV Video Music Awards (opposite).

RADIO

[ALBUM TRACK]

Released: November 18, 2008
Writers: Anton Bakholdin, Jim Jonsin, Beyoncé Knowles, Rico Love
Producer: Jim Jonsin

Popular music contains no shortage of love letters to the radio; for examples, see LL Cool J's boombox ode "I Can't Live Without My Radio" and the Ravyns' pop-rock anthem "Raised on the Radio". With "Radio", Beyoncé joins this club: the song chronicles her deep, abiding love for music – and how she developed this love thanks to the radio. In a subtle twist, the sizzling electro-pop tune *sounds* like contemporary radio music from the time, which was dominated by danceable hits with house-music vibes and neon-hued beats.

"['Radio'] basically talks about my childhood," Beyoncé says. "It just seems like a feel-good record but when you really listen to the lyrics, it's about me growing up. In my household, I didn't go to all of the parties and I didn't do all the things that a lot of the other teenage girls did because I was so in love with my radio and my music."[38]

Cleverly, the song personifies the radio as a romantic partner, using several apt comparisons as supporting evidence. The radio provides comfort and solace and is never disappointing; moreover, you can have tender moments with the radio like you would a significant other. And, cheekily, Beyoncé notes her dad never minded her and her radio being together in her bedroom with the door closed.

DIVA

[SINGLE]

Released: January 20, 2009 (single) / November 18, 2008 (album)
Writers: Shondrae Crawford, Sean Garrett, Beyoncé Knowles
Producers: Shondrae Crawford, Sean Garrett, Beyoncé Knowles
Select Alternate Versions: Karmatronic Club Remix

The word "diva" is often considered a pejorative term – an insult thrown at strong, confident women who stand up for themselves, know what they want and don't suffer fools gladly. But on the Southern hip-hop standout "Diva", Beyoncé calls out sexist double standards and reclaims the word as a badge of honour, noting that a diva is comparable to men being called hustlers.

In other words, a diva is unapologetically ambitious and successful – on the radio everywhere, making loads of money, doesn't need a man – and proud of what she's achieved. "Right now I hear all the girls talking about 'I'm a diva, I'm a diva,'" Beyoncé says. "So now they have their anthem."[39]

Given these themes, "Diva" just might be the most Sasha Fierce-coded song on the album – something reinforced with her forceful vocals, as well as the bouncy, stutter-step beats and bustling production. But when asked if it was the "women's equivalent" to Lil Wayne's 2008 hit "A Milli" – both songs were co-produced/co-written by Shondrae "Bangladesh" Crawford and share themes – Beyoncé said the song "wasn't consciously" meant to overlap.

"The track has a very similar feel," she explains. "It's just a lot of 808. It's definitely like, 'I'm the most gangster. I'm fronting,' but I'm doing it with the melody. That's kind of a classic Destiny's Child melody, rap-singing, something that we've been doing for years. Well, I'm not rapping. If it doesn't have a melody, I can't do it."[40]

Opposite: Beyoncé made a guest appearance with Jay-Z at Coachella in 2010.

NEVER MIND

SWEET DREAMS

[SINGLE]

Released: June 2, 2009 (single) / November 18, 2008 (album)
Writers: Richard Butler Jr., Jim Jonsin, Beyoncé Knowles, Wayne Wilkins
Producers: Jim Jonsin, Beyoncé Knowles, Rico Love, Wayne Wilkins
Select Alternate Versions: Harlan Pepper & AG III Remix

The adventurous "Sweet Dreams" is propelled by an explosive vocal hook and booming, early '80s synthesizers; the song resembles a lost indie sleaze classic in the best possible ways. When it came time to record "Sweet Dreams", co-producer/co-writer Rico Love says Beyoncé didn't have much time to ponder the song because travel delays made her six hours late to a studio session. But after Rico played her the tune, she wanted to record it immediately.

"She looked at her assistant and said, 'How much time do we have?'" he recalls, noting it was a mere 25 minutes. "She took her earrings off and took her high heels off, went into the booth and cut 'Sweet Dreams' in 15 minutes."[41] The session was so quick that Rico has a prominent presence on the track. "It's actually my background vocals in the hook," he says. "She liked the way it sounded so we kept it."[42]

Separately, Beyoncé explained why "Sweet Dreams" appealed to her so much. "It's very rare to find an uptempo song that means something, that's not just about going to a club or partying or being a sexy girl," she notes. "It's basically saying that this relationship is so wonderful that it kind of scares me. It's almost [too] good to be true – is it a sweet dream or a beautiful nightmare?"[43]

As it turns out, "Sweet Dreams" was originally titled "Beautiful Nightmare" – and the song leaked online in early 2008 under that name right after it was recorded. This early preview didn't hurt the song; it was a top 10 hit in both the US and UK.

VIDEO PHONE

[SINGLE]

Released: September 22, 2009 (single) / November 18, 2008 (album)
Writers: Angela Beyincé, Shondrae Crawford, Sean Garrett, Beyoncé Knowles
Producers: Shondrae Crawford, Sean Garrett, Beyoncé Knowles
Select Alternate Versions: Extended Remix with Lady Gaga, Instrumental, Gareth Wyn remix, Oli Collins & Fred Portelli remix

In some ways, the lyrics of "Video Phone" – a grimy song propelled by swerving grooves and crunk beats with an industrial edge – are charmingly antiquated. The narrator drops coy hints about making sexy videos, capitalizing on the then-novelty of filming on your cell phone. Make no mistake, however: she's in charge of these video shoots, and gives her man permission to film *and* watch later.

An extended remix of "Video Phone" with Lady Gaga appeared on the deluxe edition of *I Am ... Sasha Fierce*, preserving the music but tacking on a twangy Spaghetti Western intro. The remix came about after the pair saw each other in early October 2009 at *Billboard*'s Women in Music luncheon. "I always admired her work, so I had the idea at the [event] to put her on 'Video Phone'," Beyoncé said, adding Gaga agreed and went into the studio "on her only few days off" to write and record her part. "She was so, so sweet, and we really, really had a great chemistry."[44]

Gaga also had positive things to say about the collaboration. "I had kind of lost faith a little bit in meeting artists in the business – and then I met Beyoncé,"[45] she said, before adding of the video shoot the pair did together: "It wasn't about competition. It was about, like, 'Man let's give the world what they want. Let's do a real girl-power collaboration where we support one another.'"[46]

Opposite: Lady Gaga and Beyoncé are pictured together at Billboard's Women In Music event in 2009.

WHY DON'T YOU LOVE ME

[SINGLE]

Released: September 22, 2009 (UK promo single) / November 18, 2008 (album)
Writers: Angela Beyincé, Beyoncé Knowles, Solange Knowles, Jesse Rankins, Eddie Smith III, Jonathan Wells
Producers: The Bama Boyz and Beyoncé Knowles
Select Alternate Versions: Jump Smokers Club Remix, MK Ultras Remix – Radio Edit, Starsmith Remix – Radio Edit

At the end of the *B'Day Tour*, production team The Bama Boyz, who had previously collaborated with Beyoncé, decided to stay in England because they were having such a great time. While there, they started writing "Why Don't You Love Me", a disco spy noir song inspired by their moviegoing habits and preference for action films. "We were running around on like – this is kind of embarrassing – pretend missions in our head and we felt like we needed a theme song for it," recalls Bama Boyz member Jesse Rankins, noting the group felt like Jason Bourne or James Bond.[47]

Solange Knowles later asked The Bama Boyz to send over some musical ideas that might work for Beyoncé, and "Why Don't You Love Me" made the cut. "We had a lot of bangers that felt more like Beyoncé, but we actually put that one last on the CD because we figured 'This is not Beyoncé', but we knew Solange would like it," Rankins says. That was an understatement, he added: "Solange sent it back with a song written to it, and it was the 'Why Don't You Love Me' lyrics. The song was hot!"[48]

HELLO

[*I AM ... SASHA FIERCE* DELUXE EDITION]

Released: November 18, 2008 (album)
Writers: Evan Bogart, Beyoncé Knowles, Ramon Owen, David Quiñones
Producers: Beyoncé Knowles and REO

Beyoncé released multiple bonus tracks during the *I Am ... Sasha Fierce* album cycle. Exhibit A: the mighty piano ballad "Hello", which appeared on the album's deluxe edition. "This song is my favorite song to sing," Beyoncé said to preface the song live on the *I Am ... World Tour*. "It talks about meeting the man of your dreams for the very first time." Expressive and full of gratitude, "Hello" gushes about this man's generosity, charisma and loyalty, and thanks him for keeping her grounded and prioritizing family. Due to some nifty layering of vocals and harmonies, Beyoncé sounds like she's fronting an En Vogue-esque R&B girl group, while the song's syncopated rhythmic backdrop gives it "Halo"-esque heft.

Opposite and right: The I Am... World Tour stretched for nearly a year and found Beyoncé performing a marathon set that covered her solo career to date and Destiny's Child.

EGO

[SINGLE]

Released: May 19, 2009 (single) / November 18, 2008 (album)
Writers: Beyoncé Knowles, Harold Lilly, Elvis Williams
Producers: Blac Elvis, Beyoncé Knowles, Harold Lilly
Select Alternate Versions: Remix featuring Kanye West, OK DAC Remix, Slang "Big Ego" Club Mix

With its bold brass accents and retro R&B vibe, "Ego" is the kind of song you might have heard in an upscale nightclub. That was no accident; after all, Destiny's Child had roots in classic R&B and Beyoncé possesses deep affection for the genre. "I had to make sure I still had those grooves on the album," she said. "And this song is fun; it's not to be taken too serious. It's very 'Sasha Fierce', which is why it's on the *Sasha Fierce* disc."[49]

That's because of the double-entendre-packed lyrics that *seemingly* use someone having a big "Ego" as a euphemism for a man who is well-endowed. Not that Beyoncé admitted this at the time. "It talks about someone being very confident and having this swagger when they walk and when they talk, and that being one of the reasons why I'm attracted to them," she says. "And also saying he's not the only one, I have the swagger too."[50] When a separate interviewer asked Beyoncé if "Ego" was about Jay-Z, she noted, "I am attracted to someone who is strong and confident," but laughingly refused to elaborate further.[51]

Chrisette Michele was originally offered "Ego" for her second album, *Epiphany*, but decided to pass. "It was really scary for me to release my pen because I had written my first album myself," she says. "You don't know if they're going to be able to capture your voice the same way that you captured it yourself." She did like Beyoncé's version of "Ego", however: "Incredible. So hot."[52]

SCARED OF LONELY

[*I AM ... SASHA FIERCE* DELUXE EDITION]

Released: November 18, 2008
Writers: Richard Butler Jr., LaShawn Daniels, Rodney Jerkins, Crystal Johnson, Beyoncé Knowles, Solange Knowles
Producers: Darkchild and Beyoncé Knowles

One of the most laid-bare songs on *I Am ... Sasha Fierce*, "Scared of Lonely" is thematically related to "Save the Hero". The protagonist senses distance in her relationship and is doing everything she can to make things better. However, she fears that it's too late, which is also frightening: she's well aware that carrying the world on your shoulders is an isolating experience – and being alone is terrifying.

On "Scared of Lonely", Beyoncé worked with her sister, Solange, along with several collaborators who date back to her Destiny's Child days, namely LaShawn Daniels and Rodney Jerkins. And like "Bills, Bills, Bills", this song features a prominent harpsichord sound; this time around, the instrument adds urgency and melancholy as the track layers on nimble synthesizers, stomping rhythms and Beyoncé vocals that grow increasingly panicked as the song progresses.

POISON

[*I AM ... SASHA FIERCE: THE BONUS TRACKS*]

Released: November 23, 2009 (album)
Writers: Johntá Austin, Mikkel S. Eriksen, Tor Erik Hermansen, Beyoncé Knowles
Producers: Beyoncé Knowles and Stargate

In general, being in a relationship with someone toxic is a recipe for disaster, particularly where mental health is concerned. But "Poison" poses a terrible conundrum: what if that same person also possesses the *antidote* to any negative emotional effects? Even though the relationship is bad for you, and makes you feel like you're slowly being poisoned, you keep going back because your partner is so irresistible. (In short, the song is the perfect summary of an on-off relationship.) On "Poison," Beyoncé worked with Johntá Austin – who co-wrote Mariah Carey's smash 2005 single "We Belong Together", as well as songs by Jennifer Hudson and Mary J. Blige – along with Stargate; musically, the shuffling hip-hop track pairs well with the vocals, a classic Beyoncé lead that sounds tortured by the romantic dilemma.

HONESTY

[*I AM ... SASHA FIERCE* PLATINUM EDITION]

Released: October 20, 2009
Writer: Billy Joel
Producers: Beyoncé Knowles and Scott Storch

Honesty was a major theme of *I Am ... Sasha Fierce*, so it makes sense that Beyoncé would record a faithful cover of Billy Joel's 1978 track "Honesty" adorned by organ and light-touch orchestration. The song's origins were quite simple, Joel explained; he extemporized the lyrics to "Honesty" during one studio session with his band. "It was a recording day without a song," he recalled. "I said, 'Here's this idea I got. I don't have lyrics for it yet, but it goes like this.'" Joel took to the piano and played the verse and chorus parts. "I liked the melody the band liked the melody; the studio time was booked," he explains. "I said, 'You know what fits? "Honesty".' And I wrote the lyrics right there and then."[53] Joel's take was nominated for Song of the Year at the Grammy Awards, while Beyoncé's version became massively popular in South Korea.

Opposite and right: When Beyoncé walked the red carpet at the Oscars in 2009, she did so wearing a gorgeous black-and-gold dress designed by her mother for House of Dereon (opposite). She also exuded glam during this 2009 I Am... World Tour stop in Los Angeles (right).

LOVE IN THIS CLUB, PART II (USHER FEATURING BEYONCÉ AND LIL WAYNE)

[SINGLE]

Released: April 28, 2008 (single) / May 13, 2003 (album)
Writers: Thomas Bell, Dwayne Carter, Jr., Linda Creed, Darnell Dalton, Keri Hilson, Jamal Jones, Jay Jenkins, Beyoncé Knowles, Ryon Lovett, Usher Raymond IV, Lamar Taylor, Keith Thomas
Producer: Soundz

Usher's "Love in This Club" was a massive hit that reached No. 1 on the US pop and R&B/hip-hop charts. It's easy to hear why: the groove-heavy anthem sounded like an alluring prelude to a night out where anything was possible. "It s about meeting somebody for the first time, and you kinda wish nobody was there," said producer Polow da Don. "You're like, 'You're the one.' Lust at first sight."[54]

The song's remix, "Love in This Club, Part II", makes that wish come true; musically, it resembles the soundtrack of a private after-party for two. Buoyed by a sample of The Stylistics' soulful "You Are Everything" and '80s-influenced bubblegum-R&B beats, it sits squarely in the pantheon of red-hot Usher slow jams.

Lyrically, however, it's a lengthy response to the tantalizing requests of Part I. Beyoncé portrays a woman who isn't sure about hooking up with someone in this public space. For starters, she points out that they're both dating other people; additionally, the club is full of people *and* security might step in. The woman is attracted to the man, of course, but stresses that discretion is key.

"I wanted it to be something that would be a surprise, be a shock," Usher says. "Have shock value. That's what the remix is all about. 'Damn, did you hear the remix? It's crazier than the original. I like it more.'"[55] This version was also a success, reaching the top 20 of the *Billboard* Hot 100.

TELEPHONE (LADY GAGA FEATURING BEYONCÉ)

[SINGLE]

Released: January 26, 2010 (single) / November 23, 2009 (album)
Writers: LaShawn Daniels, Lazonate Franklin, Stefani Germanotta, Rodney "Darkchild" Jerkins, Beyoncé Knowles
Producers: Rodney "Darkchild" Jerkins and Beyoncé Knowles
Select Alternate Versions: Alphabeat Radio Edit, Crookers Vocal Club Remix, Kaskade Club Remix, Passion Pit Remix featuring Beyoncé

When Lady Gaga was dropped by her record label, she found herself sobbing on her grandmother's couch and watching TV. "A Destiny's Child video came on," she recalled. "I remember watching Beyoncé, thinking, 'Oh, she's a star. I want that. I want to be on MTV.'"[56] Just a few short years later, Gaga had her wish; in fact, she was on MTV *with* Beyoncé, acting in the Jonas Åkerlund-directed, Quentin Tarantino-inspired clip for the duo's Grammy-nominated duet "Telephone". (That's the actual Pussy Wagon from Tarantino's *Kill Bill* in the clip.)

A song originally written for Britney Spears circa *Circus*, "Telephone" is a dizzying electro-pop song with audacious Darkchild co-production, pastoral harp and cartoonish vocal effects. Thematically, "Telephone" referred to a "fear of suffocation, or fear of never being able to enjoy myself because I love my work so much," Gaga says, noting she has trouble going out and relaxing. "A whiskey and a half into it, I start [thinking] 'I gotta go back to work.' So that's my fear: the phone's ringing and my head's ringing."[57]

In keeping with the song's theme, Beyoncé and Gaga unite for a bridge where they say they're not answering their phones because they're out dancing. On her own, Beyoncé also chimes in with a verse in which she's exasperated that her man won't stop calling her while she's trying to get ready. Her solution? She decides not to pick up.

Opposite and above: Beyoncé strikes a pose with Usher in 2010 while attending Keep a Child Alive's Black Ball (opposite) and Lady Gaga in the "Telephone" music video.

SING A SONG

[SOUNDTRACK]

Released: May 1, 2009
Writer: Bob Boyle (lyrics)

Wow! Wow! Wubbzy! was a short-lived Nickelodeon animated children's series from the late 2000s, starring a cute main character named Wubbzy who resembled a block-like mouse. In 2009, the show aired a four-episode special called *Wubb Idol* that found Wubbzy encountering a music group called the Wubb Girlz; the lead singer, Shine, was voiced by Beyoncé. Naturally, she contributed music to the event: "Sing a Song", a girl group collaboration with her Wubb Girlz bandmates Tara Strong (Shimmer) and Grey DeLisle (Sparkle). The adorable, harmony-heavy tune addresses *where* you can sing (at a campfire, while showering) and how songs can make your life better (for example, being like art, healing a broken heart, curing your sadness). Above all, what matters is that you sing and let your voice be heard – a worthy message we can all agree with.

Right and opposite: Whether singing solo in Australia (right) or with collaborators – such as Faith Hill, Jamie Foxx, and Alicia Keys (opposite) – Beyoncé shines.

SEE ME NOW (KANYE WEST FEATURING BEYONCÉ AND CHARLIE WILSON)

[*MY BEAUTIFUL DARK TWISTED FANTASY* iTUNES STORE BONUS TRACK]

Released: August 11, 2010 (single) / November 22, 2010 (album)
Writers: Beyoncé Knowles, No I.D., Brenda Russell, Brian Russell, Kanye West
Producers: Lex Luger, No I.D., Kanye West
Select Alternate Versions: Album Version with Big Sean

When Kanye West premiered "See Me Now" during an August 2011 interview with the New York radio station Hot 97, the song was quite literally fresh from the studio. "Beyoncé finished those vocals at five a.m. this morning," West shared. "I couldn't be the only person this summer riding around with that."[58]

"See Me Now" ended up only as a bonus track on *My Beautiful Dark Twisted Fantasy*, but the meaning came through loud and clear. Built off a lilting sample of Brian and Brenda Russell's 1977 song "Think About You", the tune finds Kanye (rightfully) demanding to be recognized for his talent, and letting his haters and critics know that he's rich and successful. Poignantly, Kanye entrusts Beyoncé to sing lines about how his beloved mother Donda is looking down from heaven and is proud of him.

PUT IT IN A LOVE SONG (ALICIA KEYS FEATURING BEYONCÉ)

[ALBUM TRACK]

Released: January 19, 2010 (single) / December 11, 2009 (album)
Writers: Alicia Keys and Swizz Beatz
Producers: Alicia Keys and Swizz Beatz

Alicia Keys and Beyoncé were both just 14 years old when they signed to Columbia Records in the 1990s. Although the label relationship didn't quite work out for Keys the way it did for Beyoncé and Destiny's Child – in the end, Keys finally broke through in 2001 with *Songs in A Minor* on J Records – the women became friends.

More than a decade later, the duo managed to align their busy schedules and head into the studio. The result was an upbeat duet, "Put It in a Love Song", that boasts high-stepping, marching-band beats and an earworm-like chorus resembling a cheerleader chant. Cheerfully, both Knowles and Keys tell a man that he needs to prove his love through actions *and* be vocal about it – say, by writing a letter, texting or penning a song.

Keys postponed the release of her fourth studio album, *The Element of Freedom,* for two weeks so that "Put It in a Love Song" could make the final cut. "We had a lot of fun," she said of recording it. "It's nice that we just celebrate each other's careers, that's what the song is about, coming together to empower each other. This song was meant for us at this time."[59] For further proof of that chemistry and affection, look no further than the duo's electric live performance of the song on St. Patrick's Day 2010 at Madison Square Garden.

10 4

ON 4, BEYONCÉ WASN'T INTERESTED IN REINFORCING GENRE BOUNDARIES. INSTEAD, SHE WANTED TO GO BACK TO THE DAYS OF OLD-FASHIONED SONGWRITING AND CLASSIC INSTRUMENTAL FLOURISHES; TOUCHSTONES IN HER MIND INCLUDED RETRO SOUL AND R&B FROM THE '70S THROUGH THE '90S, AFROBEAT, HORNS AND ROCK 'N' ROLL. THE RESULTING ALBUM WAS ANOTHER ROUSING SUCCESS, WITH THE OLD-SCHOOL VIBES OF "LOVE ON TOP" AND GALVANIZING ELECTRO-R&B NUMBER "RUN THE WORLD (GIRLS)" LEADING THE WAY.

1+1

[PROMO SINGLE]

Released: May 25, 2011 (single) / June 28, 2011 (album)
Writers: Beyoncé Knowles, Terius "The-Dream" Nash, Christopher "Tricky" Stewart
Producers: Beyoncé Knowles, The-Dream, Tricky Stewart

The-Dream originally included "1+1" on his 2009 album *Love vs. Money*, but removed it at the behest of then-Def Jam president L.A. Reid. Incredibly, the producer then *forgot* about it. "It was just on the hard drive, just floating there amongst the rest of the seas of songs," he says. "Because that point was, if I wasn't going to sing it, I wasn't going to give it to anyone else because I didn't feel like anybody else could sing it."[1] But his friend Chaka Pilgrim suggested he play it for Beyoncé, which gave the tune new life. A smouldering power ballad dedicated to the healing power of unconditional love – and how a protective partner provides security in the face of turmoil – "1+1" is distinguished by a stunning, raw Beyoncé vocal performance. "[I] gave myself more freedom to really belt out some songs, and bring soul singing back," she said about *4*. "I used a lot of the brassiness and grittiness in my voice that people hear in my live performances, but not necessarily on my records."[2]

I CARE

[SINGLE]

Released: March 23, 2012 (single, Italy) / June 28, 2011 (album)
Writers: Jeff Bhasker, Chad Hugo, Beyoncé Knowles
Producers: Jeff Bhasker and Beyoncé Knowles

As a producer, Jeff Bhasker put his stamp on influential Kanye West albums such as *808s & Heartbreak* and *My Beautiful Dark Twisted Fantasy*. But Bhasker also possessed his own musical ambitions and originally earmarked the power ballad "I Care" for a solo album he was working on called *Born on the Fourth of July*. "My sound is maybe a little more pure version of it," he said, describing his take on the Beyoncé song.[3]

No matter what the approach, "I Care" exudes emotional devastation. The protagonist is deeply hurt by the behaviour of a cold-hearted, emotionally distant partner; in fact, she can't understand why he's so unconcerned by her pain. She tells him she still cares about him and their relationship, but it's unclear whether this pleading pierces his indifference. Musically, "I Care" traces the contours of this agony. After starting with solemn synth drone and minimal beats, it blooms to include gospel-like backing vocals and swirling keyboards before culminating in a wailing electric guitar solo. Beyoncé sings along to this solo, following the melody in an anguished, octave-jumping voice brimming with sadness.

Opposite: Beyoncé triumphantly headlined the Pyramid Stage on Sunday night at the 2011 Glastonbury Festival.

I MISS YOU

[ALBUM TRACK]

Released: June 28, 2011
Writers: Beyoncé Knowles, Frank Ocean, Shea Taylor
Producers: Beyoncé Knowles and Shea Taylor

One Sunday morning, Jay-Z decided to listen to the hip-hop collective Odd Future as he and Beyoncé drove to Brooklyn. Her ears perked up when she heard Frank Ocean on the music. "I noticed his tone, his arrangements, and his storytelling," she said. "I immediately reached out to him – literally the next morning. I asked him to fly to New York and work on my record."[4] The result is "I Miss You", a moody R&B ballad driven by synthesizer swells and perforated electronic beats. As the title implies, the narrator pines for an ex and fantasizes about getting back together. This comes with its own insecurities and complications; for example, would the relationship be the same the second time around? In the end, the "I Miss You" bridge and outro explain why we long for what we can't have: love is universal and we're powerless to resist it. "The album is definitely an evolution," Beyoncé said of *4*. "It's bolder than the music on my previous albums because I'm bolder. The more mature I become and the more life experiences I have, the more I have to talk about. I really focused on songs being classics, songs that would last, songs that I could sing when I'm 40 and when I'm 60."[5]

BEST THING I NEVER HAD

[SINGLE]

Released: June 1, 2011 (single) / June 28, 2011 (album)
Writers: Antonio Dixon, Kenny "Babyface" Edmonds, Larry Griffin, Jr., Beyoncé Knowles, Caleb McCampbell, Patrick "J. Que" Smith, Shea Taylor
Producers: Babyface, Antonio Dixon, Beyoncé Knowles, Caleb McCampbell, Symbolyc 1, Shea Taylor
Select Alternate Versions: Lars B Remix

With the benefit of hindsight, sometimes a breakup is for the best. That's the conclusion of the majestic power ballad "Best Thing I Never Had", on which stormy music ebbs and flows around a nostalgic piano line. The protagonist is downright relieved things didn't work out, and even taunts her ex for the regret he must be feeling that he fumbled the relationship. Beyoncé gives another fierce vocal performance full of conviction. Most notably, her voice breaks with righteous anger when she recounts the moment her ex *finally* showed his true colours.

Creating "Best Thing I Never Had" was an iterative process with many tweaks. (For example, one version of the song is an uptempo, late-'90s jam that sampled the drums from Slick Rick and Doug E. Fresh's "The Show".[6]) But originally, co-writer Patrick "J. Que" Smith was in Los Angeles and received a tantalizing offer: his friend Antonio (Tony) Dixon and Babyface were going to write some music for Beyoncé, and Smith was invited to take part. Despite being "super nervous", he dropped by the studio to write.[7]

Babyface then added his own transformative edits, Smith noted: "You know – a word here, a word there, a melody here, and all of a sudden the record had a completely new life."[8] And then at a later, separate session in New York City, Caleb McCampbell took further inspiration from the forceful piano on Vanessa Carlton's "A Thousand Miles" and added those striking keys to the song.[9] When it came time to record, Beyoncé came into the studio at 9 p.m., directly from an airplane, and put the finishing polish on it. "She loved it!" Smith said. "She jumped in the studio and knocked out three records that night."[10]

Opposite: Jay-Z and Beyoncé – the latter wearing an Emilio Pucci gown – cut stylish figures while attending the 2011 Met Gala, which had the theme "Alexander McQueen: Savage Beauty."

PARTY (FEATURING ANDRÉ 3000)

[SINGLE]

Released: August 30, 2011 (single) / June 28, 2011 (album)
Writers: Jeff Bhasker, Douglas Davis, Beyoncé Knowles, Dexter Mills, Ricky Walters, Kanye West
Producers: Jeff Bhasker, Beyoncé Knowles, Kanye West
Select Alternate Versions: Remix featuring J. Cole

In May 2010, Beyoncé commenced recording *4* at the New York City studio Roc The Mic. She first tracked the song "Party" to see how she'd get along with recording engineer Jordan "DJ Swivel" Young. "I pride myself on being a fast engineer, and I was able to execute all she wanted me to do in that first session," he says. "Thankfully, she liked the job, and the speed that I worked at, and we then started discussing the beginning of the record."[11] Their studio chemistry is evident on the Grammy-nominated "Party", a throwback electro-funk ballad with chill vibes and a sample of Doug E. Fresh and the Get Fresh Crew's 1985 song "La Di Da Di". Beyoncé compares having irresistible sexual and romantic chemistry with someone to the jubilant experience of a raging party. To enhance the festive feeling, Outkast's André 3000 contributes a tongue-twisting verse – "I've always felt Beyoncé was one of the best performers of our time, so to collaborate with her was an honor and a pleasure," he said[12] – and Kanye West adds production and a swaggering intro and outro. Beyoncé noted she wanted to work with West especially due to his song "Runaway", which affected her deeply. "The fact that he's belting out his pain, his confusion, and his anger, with no pre-written lyrics, was so moving."[13]

RATHER DIE YOUNG

[ALBUM TRACK]

Released: June 28, 2011 (album)
Writers: Jeff Bhasker, Beyoncé Knowles, Luke Steele
Producers: Jeff Bhasker, Beyoncé Knowles, Luke Steele

On *4*, Beyoncé wasn't interested in reinforcing genre boundaries. "Everything sounds the same on the radio," she said. "[This time] I tried to mix R&B from the '70s and the '90s with rock 'n' roll and a lot of horns to create something new and exciting. I wanted musical changes, bridges, vibrata, live instrumentation, and classic songwriting."[14] Accordingly, "Rather Die Young" – co-written by Luke Steele of dreamy electropop act Empire of the Sun – is a '70s soul homage featuring the talents of The Superpower Horns, a group that contributes trumpet and alto, tenor and baritone saxophone. Thematically, the song references one of history's notable tragedies. The first verse compares a love interest to the actor James Dean, who passed away in 1955 at age 24, to set up the song's premise: the narrator would rather die young than live without her beloved. "I really want people to think when they listen to my music," she said. "I want it to help them through their painful memories, their painful moments, and their most happy moments. I want it to be a conversation."[15]

START OVER

[ALBUM TRACK]

Released: June 28, 2011 (album)
Writers: Ester Dean, Beyoncé Knowles, Shea Taylor
Producers: Beyoncé Knowles and Shea Taylor

Much like how David Bowie retired his alter-ego Ziggy Stardust when he wanted a fresh start, Beyoncé announced she had killed her Sasha Fierce persona before releasing *4*. "I don't need Sasha Fierce anymore, because I've grown and I'm now able to merge the two," she said. "I want people to see me. I want people to see who I am."[16] Relatedly, Beyoncé also took a lengthy break from public superstardom before *4* to get back in touch with her private self. "For the first time in my life I was able to travel the world, hear different influences, see different types of dance and choreography and taste different types of food, she said."[17] The twin ideas of rejuvenation and rebirth inform "Start Over", an inspirational song about a couple trying to save a stagnant relationship that's become riddled with discord. In Beyoncé's eyes, the solution is a hard reset, because starting over is the best way to resurrect good love.

Opposite and right: During her 2011 Glastonbury Festival set, Beyoncé performed "Baby Boy" with special guest Tricky and covered songs by Kings of Leon ("Sex On Fire") and Prince ("The Beautiful Ones").

LOVE ON TOP

[SINGLE]

Released: January 10, 2012 (single) / June 28, 2011 (album)
Writers: Beyoncé Knowles, Terius "The-Dream" Nash, Shea Taylor
Producers: Beyoncé Knowles and Shea Taylor
Select Alternate Versions: DJ Escape & Tony Coluccio Remix

In a 2024 conversation with Beyoncé, the interviewer observes that in hindsight *4* was "deliberately anti-pop – or at least 'anti-trend' – in regard to what was happening in pop music at the time."[18] She disagreed slightly with the characterization, noting that she "respected pop", and clarified her mindset during this era.

"It was a time where everyone was doing pop/dance music, and R&B and soul were getting lost," she said. "It was popular and fun, but it wasn't my thing. It was not where I was going with my music career at that time. I was yearning for something deeper with more musicality."[19]

In practice, this meant she went crate-digging into the more vintage corners of her record collection, drawing inspiration from a cavalcade of soul, funk and R&B superstars: Earth, Wind & Fire, DeBarge, Jackson 5, New Edition, Prince, Lionel Richie and Teena Marie.[20] But it also meant she didn't concern herself with following trends; instead, she listened to her creative muse and her heart when crafting songs.

This all culminated with the ecstatic "Love on Top", a classic love song about what it's like to finally find someone who prioritizes you (and your needs) and brings happiness into your life. Beyoncé positively beams with joy as she sings about dancing with (and smooching) her beloved; her gospel-soul delivery and acumen with showstopping key changes at times conjures idols like Whitney Houston. Musically exuberant, "Love on Top" boasts crisp arrangements and rich instrumentation – strutting 1980s funk grooves, snappy drums and guitars and red-hot horns – that exude sophistication. But the lyrics notably don't include pop-culture references that could date the music, giving the song a timeless feel.

"Love on Top" reached the top 20 in both the US and UK and most deservedly won a Grammy for Best Traditional R&B Performance. But the song will forever be associated with Beyoncé's beyond-iconic 2011 MTV Video Music Awards performance where she announced she was pregnant with Blue Ivy. Wearing a sparkly magenta jacket and tailored pants, she began the performance by posing jauntily like Michael Jackson-circa-*Thriller* and announcing, "Tonight I want you to stand up on your feet. I want you to feel the love that's growing inside of me."

This segued into a dynamite version of the song in which Beyoncé commanded the stage with virtuosic vocals. But her casual intro comments merely foreshadowed how she ended the song: literally dropping her mic, unbuttoning her jacket, and laughing with utter joy as she showed off and rubbed her belly.

Left and opposite: Beyoncé was visibly pregnant while walking the red carpet in a Lanvin dress at the 2011 MTV Video Music Awards (left) – but saved her baby bump reveal during her performance of "Love On Top" that same night (opposite).

COUNTDOWN

[SINGLE]

Released: October 4, 2011 / June 28, 2011 (album)
Writers: Michael Bivins, Ester Dean, Julie Frost, Beyoncé Knowles, Cainon Lamb, Nathan Morris, Wanya Morris, Terius "The-Dream" Nash, Shea Taylor
Producers: Beyoncé Knowles and Shea Taylor
Select Alternate Versions: Isa Machine Remix, Olli Collins & Fred Portelli Remix, RedTop Radio Edit, Reggae Rewind Remix

Early in their career, Beyoncé and Destiny's Child toured with R&B superstars Boyz II Men. "They showed us how to treat an opening act," she said, "and I will never forget that."[21] Beyoncé wasn't kidding, as on "Countdown" she returned the favour in a big way: the song samples the countdown sung in the Boyz II Men song "Uhh Ahh" in context, with a narrator ticking off all the good things about life with her man.

The Boyz II Men part was plucked out by co-producer Cainon Lamb during a studio session. "I thought, 'Wow, that could be something. Just the countdown itself,'" he said. "Once the countdown was in the computer, I sped it up a little bit. I put the snare drum taps to it and I started a beat."[22] Lamb sent this instrumental to his publisher – who happened to have a meeting with Beyoncé the next day – and received good news almost immediately. "[My publisher said] 'I played a couple other songs I had and she wasn't really feeling them. When I played the beat that you sent me, you should have seen how she went crazy! She started dancing and bouncing up and down.'"[23] It's impossible not to react that way to the adventurous music, as "Countdown" is a stutter-stepping reggae and hip-hop hybrid marked by a peppy brass section, dizzying keyboards and steel drums.

END OF TIME

[SINGLE]

Released: April 23, 2012 (single) / June 28, 2011 (album)
Writers: Beyoncé Knowles, Terius "The-Dream" Nash, David Taylor, Shea Taylor
Producers: Beyoncé Knowles, The-Dream, Switch
Selected Remixes: JIMEK Remix, WAWA Extended

One of Beyoncé's early inspirations on *4* was the Afrobeat legend Fela Kuti. "I actually worked with the band from [Broadway musical] *Fela!* for a couple of days, just to get the feel for the soul and heart of his music; it's so sexy, and has a great groove you get lost in," she said, and added, "What I learned most from Fela was artistic freedom: he just felt the spirit."[24]

Fela's unfettered approach inspired the nimble bassline on "End of Time", a standout song espousing the joy of being with someone forever.[25] But the tune's musical density is also impressive. Touching on Afrobeat and Latin jazz, "End of Time" melds lovely vocal harmonies, marching band flair from The Superpower Horns, and a jittery rhythmic underbelly. "I listened closely to a lot of the rock musicians I saw at music festivals around the world, paying attention to their lyrics, melodies, and the mixture of their different instruments," she said in connection with the song. "The instrumentation was just so beautiful. I felt I needed some classics like that."[26]

Opposite and right: In 2013, Beyoncé headlined the Pepsi Super Bowl XLVII Halftime Show in New Orleans.

I WAS HERE

[ALBUM TRACK]

Released: June 28, 2011 (album)
Writer: Diane Warren
Producers: Kuk Harrell, Beyoncé Knowles, Brent Kutzle, Ryan Tedder

Award-winning songwriter Diane Warren has worked with icons such as Cher, Celine Dion, Lady Gaga and Taylor Swift. But when she wrote the windswept orchestrated ballad "I Was Here", she only wanted one vocalist to sing it: Beyoncé. Luckily, Warren's wish came true. Over the phone, Warren played Beyoncé a guitar-based version of the song; two days later, Beyoncé was in the studio cutting "I Was Here", having reportedly delayed mastering *4* so the tune could make the cut. "I said, 'Oh my God, I have to have this song,'" she said. "It was inspired by September 11. It's the tenth anniversary and I thought, 'Wow, this really completes my album.'"[27] Warren was understandably thrilled, especially with Beyoncé's vocal performance. "I've never had chills through my entire body like I had from hearing [her] sing this song," she said. "'I Was Here' came from my soul and became the song that was coming from hers." [28]

GIRLS

RUN THE WORLD (GIRLS)

[SINGLE]

Released: April 21, 2011 (single) / June 28, 2011 (album)
Writers: Beyoncé Knowles, Terius "The-Dream" Nash, Adidja Palmer, Wesley "Diplo" Pentz, David Taylor, Nick van de Wall
Producers: Beyoncé Knowles, Switch, The-Dream, Shea Taylor
Select Alternate Versions: Jochen Simms Club Remix, Kaskade Club Remix, Redtop Club Remix

What happened to the protagonist of Destiny's Child's "Independent Women, Part 1" who was proudly in charge of her own life and finances? She grew up to be the fashionable boss lady depicted in "Run the World (Girls)". This powerful narrator stresses that the world turns due to the visible *and* invisible labour done by women. And while she gives credit to men who respect her, she acknowledges that women have endless responsibilities – to graduate college, become a mom, be a savvy business leader and a tireless worker – and praises *their* superhuman strength and grit.

Unsurprisingly, "Run the World (Girls)" is rooted in real-life experience. At one point the narrator notes that no man can fade (meaning diminish) her light. However, she mentions this in context of needing a barber, creating a double meaning; it's also a clever pun referencing the hairstyle. (Given that Beyoncé's mom Tina ran a hair salon, it's a lovely, subtle nod to her work.) In addition, The-Dream, who co-wrote the song, says certain lines in "Run the World (Girls)" were inspired by the special relationship he had with his mom.

"My mother gave birth to me when she was 19," he said. "All her friends were there at the house talking about women problems – [problems] with men usually....But I was just preview to a lot of conversations and a lot of sensitive points from a woman's standpoint and point of view so I was able, without knowing, to keep that in me, to be able to deliver it through songs."[29]

Musically, "Run the World (Girls)" matches its fierce messaging by drawing heavily from Major Lazer's 2009 song "Pon de Floor", a baile and dancehall song based around spiralling rhythms and wriggling beats. "That song never really had a push," admitted Diplo, the DJ and producer who's also in Major Lazer. "It was a song we did, kind of like a funny kind of a joke song."[30] Perhaps that's one reason he tried to dissuade Beyoncé from using the song when she enquired about sampling it. "It was already in the clubs two years earlier and I told her that," Diplo said. "She said to me, 'No, but do people know this shit?' So I was like, 'Fine, go ahead.'"[31]

However, Beyoncé was delighted at how complex and adventurous the song sounded. "I just heard the track and loved that it was so different," she said. "It felt a bit African, a bit electronic and futuristic. It reminded me of what I love, which is mixing different cultures and eras – things that typically don't go together – to create a new sound. I can never be safe; I always try and go against the grain."[32]

"Run the World (Girls)" reached the top 40 in the US and, while not Beyoncé's biggest hit, it became one of her foundational empowerment songs. "I try to write songs that will bring out the best in all of us and keep us close together," she said. "I think about saying the things that women want to say but sometimes are not confident enough to say. I'm going to continue to write those songs that give women strength."[33]

Opposite and above: Beyoncé dominated the 2011 Billboard Music Awards with a galvanizing performance of "Run The World (Girls)."

DREAMING

[4 - JAPANESE EDITION]

Released: June 29, 2011
Writers: Antonio Dixon, Kenneth "Babyface" Edmonds, Beyoncé Knowles, Patrick "J. Que" Smith
Producers: Babyface, Antonio Dixon, Beyoncé Knowles

"Dreaming" is a sparkling '90s R&B ballad about the utter bliss of being with someone you love. Or is it? Upon close reading, it can be difficult to tell if the song's narrator has her perfect man – or is simply dreaming of him. Much like a dream itself, the lyrical perspective of "Dreaming" shapeshifts back and forth between different states: daydreaming and night dreaming, happiness and uncertainty, physical comfort and vivid imagination. On the one hand, the narrator mentions being able to stay with her partner whenever she wants and that being asleep is comforting because he's always there. But then she also says that *if* dreams are the only place she can be with her love, then that's where she'd rather stay. Perhaps that's the only solid thing in the song: her heart knows exactly what it wants.

LAY UP UNDER ME

[4 - DELUXE EDITION]

Released: June 28, 2011
Writers: Mikkel Eriksen, Sean Garrett, Tor Erik Hermansen, Beyoncé Knowles, Shea Taylor
Producers: Beyoncé Knowles and Shea Taylor

Songwriter/producer Sean Garrett originally recorded "Lay Up Under Me" for his 2008 solo album *Turbo 919*. Driven by his earnest croon, the song is a smooth, soulful love song where the protagonist beckons a lady to cancel her going-out plans; instead, he'd like her to stay inside with him and have a cozier kind of club night. On her version, Beyoncé preserves the general theme of the original – a couple celebrating each other with an intimate gathering at home – and sprinkles in references to her real-life relationship with Jay-Z; for example, she still feels a spark with him despite being together ten years. Musically, however, she takes a strikingly different approach to "Lay Up Under Me", incorporating extroverted horns and disco grooves that make the song feel like a champagne-popping confetti shower.

SCHOOLIN' LIFE

[4 - DELUXE EDITION]

Released: June 28, 2011
Writers: Beyoncé Knowles, Carlos McKinney, Terius "The-Dream" Nash
Producers: Beyoncé Knowles, The-Dream, Los Da Mystro

"Schoolin' Life" is one of the most distinctive songs of the *4* era. With its ultra-lacquered production, booming electronic beats and upbeat synthesizers, the tune sounds like it could've slipped onto top 40 radio stations in the late 1980s. When mixing the song, DJ Swivel absolutely "went for that '80s sound on the snares", he said. "They were originally very tight, so I added a gated reverb for the snap sound, a long, drawnout snap sound actually; and I also subbed in an additional kick underneath to add some real oomph to the bottom."[34]

Lyrically, "Schoolin' Life" is also a delight. In a brassy and confident voice, Beyoncé doles out sage life advice and gentle warnings to people of all ages and types (such as pretty, sexy, bitter). "This record was, of course, about the vocals – but a lot of it was about the production elements too," said DJ Swivel. "Everything had to be audible; there's some interesting percussion, and the hook had to feel nice and big."[35]

DANCE FOR YOU

[4 - DELUXE EDITION]

Released: June 28, 2011
Writers: Beyoncé Knowles, Terius "The-Dream" Nash, Christopher "Tricky" Stewart
Producers: Beyoncé Knowles, The-Dream, Tricky Stewart
Select Alternate Versions: Remix featuring T.I.

"'Dance for You' is about giving yourself fully to one person," Beyoncé said. "It's about being able to lose control with the person you're meant for."[36] In a voice that alternates between breathy and reverent, she expresses gratitude for her man – and outlines exactly how she's going to show her dedication, loyalty and attraction. Slow-motion, Prince-like beats and languorous grooves add to the seductive vibe, while a nuanced church organ that hums throughout the song signals respectful idolatry. "When I write, when I perform, and when I make music videos, I don't hold anything back," she said. "'Dance for You' is about that same passion; to be free and unrestrained."[37] Accordingly, the black-and-white music video for the song features Beyoncé channelling her best noir film chanteuse and paying tribute to the glamorous actress and singer Marlene Dietrich. "Both the melody and the lyrics make it one of my most intimate songs, so I wanted the video to have the same rawness," she said. "I wanted the video to have a classic feel; to be seductive but still keep the sense of mystery."[38]

Below: Medleys, covers, interpolations, and Destiny's Child – Beyoncé's setlist at her 2010 concert in Rio de Janeiro had it all.

MOVE YOUR BODY

[SINGLE]

Released: April 3, 2011
Writers: Angela Beyincé, Sean Garrett, Beyoncé Knowles, Solange Knowles, Makeba Riddick, Swizz Beatz
Producers: Sean Garrett, Beyoncé Knowles, Swizz Beatz
Select Alternate Versions: Spanish version ("Mueve el Cuerpo")

In early 2011, Beyoncé teamed up with the First Lady of the United States, Michelle Obama, to promote Let's Move!, a national initiative dedicated to addressing childhood obesity. Part of the campaign involved the development of a Let's Move! workout featuring various dance moves: running in place, high-stepping, faux jump roping and the Dougie. The intention was that junior high school students would all do this routine at the same time on a given day. Of course, every good workout needs an uptempo soundtrack – and Beyoncé delivered with a fire remake of *B'Day*'s "Get Me Bodied" called "Move Your Body". Produced by Swizz Beatz, the new version features new lyrics that describe the dance moves and get exercisers pumped up. "It's all about promoting the benefits of healthy eating and exercise," Beyoncé said. "But what we want to do is make it fun by doing something that we all love to do, and that's dance."[39]

LIFT OFF (JAY-Z AND KANYE WEST FEATURING BEYONCÉ)

[SINGLE]

Released: August 23, 2011
Writers: Jeff Bhasker, Shawn Carter, Mike Dean, Bruno Mars, Seal, Kanye West
Producers: Jeff Bhasker, Mike Dean, Don Jazzy, Q-Tip, Kanye West, Pharrell Williams
Select Alternate Versions: Instrumental Version

Talk about musical star power: not only was *Watch the Throne* a collaborative album between Jay-Z and Kanye West, but "Lift Off" had writing contributions from Bruno Mars and Seal, production from Q-Tip and Pharrell Williams, and a recurring soaring vocal hook from Beyoncé. Genre-wise, the song unsurprisingly defies easy categorization, as its rich production, cinematic synthesizers and occasional spurts of thundering drums create a grandiose sound.

Fittingly for the title, the song also references celestial star power; in fact, "Lift Off" weaves in multiple outer space references to illustrate that the careers of the song's principals are rocketing into the stratosphere. It's no accident that Beyoncé also kicks off and ends the song: her description of a triumphant mission to the moon and Mars emphasizes that such a journey is rare and special – a nod to her own singular creative path.

Right and opposite: Beyoncé's confidence had grown exponentially, as evidenced by her 2010 concert in Rio de Janeiro (right) and powerful Mary J. Blige collaboration "Love A Woman" (opposite).

LOVE A WOMAN (MARY J. BLIGE FEATURING BEYONCÉ)

[ALBUM TRACK]

Released: November 21, 2011
Writers: Mary J. Blige, Sean Garrett, Beyoncé Knowles, Menardini Timothee
Producers: BridgeTown, Sean Garrett, Team S. Dot

Written from the perspective of a wise woman, the lush R&B slow jam "Love a Woman" offers up helpful romance tips for men. Among other things, he should be attentive and respectful, pay his lady compliments, back up his words with actions and be a sensual, leisurely lover. Beyoncé originally recorded "Love a Woman" for *4*, but it didn't quite match the sound on the rest of the album. According to producer/writer Sean Garrett, there was also a sense that releasing the song as a duet with R&B powerhouse Mary J. Blige duet would make a *statement*. "Both these women are two iconic female figures in the world, and what would be better than putting those two on a record?" he says. "We felt it would be a really iconic move."[40] As a result, Beyoncé decided to pass "Love a Woman" on to Blige, who was unsurprisingly wowed. "I was like 'Is she really trying to give me this song? Because it's pretty amazing,'" Blige says. "They were like, 'Yes, but she wants to stay on it with you.' And I was like, 'Wow! Beyoncé? Thanks!' And you know I love and respect her to death so I wouldn't pass that chance up."[41]

11 BEYONCÉ

WELL BEFORE MANY OTHER ARTISTS, BEYONCÉ RECOGNIZED THAT MUSIC WAS BECOMING AN INCREASINGLY VISUAL MEDIUM. AS A RESULT, SHE FILMED ELABORATE MUSIC VIDEOS FOR EVERY SONG ON HER SELF-TITLED ALBUM, TAKING CARE TO DEVISE UNIQUE PREMISES AND THEMES FOR EACH. OF COURSE, THIS GAMBIT RESONATED SO MUCH BECAUSE THE MUSIC ON THIS RECORD WAS STRONG AND AMBITIOUS. WORKING WITH NEW COLLABORATORS, SUCH AS THE ENIGMATIC PRODUCER/SONGWRITER BOOTS, BEYONCÉ ESCHEWED CONVENTION IN FAVOUR OF ATMOSPHERE-RICH ALTERNATIVE R&B WITH ELECTRONIC FLOURISHES.

PRETTY HURTS

[SINGLE]

Released: June 10, 2014 (single) / December 13, 2013 (album)
Writers: Joshua Coleman, Sia Furler, Beyoncé Knowles
Producers: Ammo and Beyoncé Knowles
Select Alternate Versions: Instrumental, R3hab remix

With no advance warning, at the stroke of midnight on Friday the 13th in December, Beyoncé released her fifth full-length album. The self-titled visual record kicked off with an unexpected opening: actor Harvey Keitel, portraying a beauty pageant host, asking Beyoncé (a.k.a. "Ms. Third Ward") what she wants out of life. The answer? Happiness.

So began the audacious "Pretty Hurts", a slow-burning pop song with spiral synths and torchy vocals. Incredibly enough, had Katy Perry paid closer attention to her inbox, she might have recorded the song instead of Beyoncé. According to the pop artist Sia Furler – who wrote "Pretty Hurts" in her Los Angeles apartment and then recorded it with the songwriter and producer Ammo – Perry didn't respond to an email Furler sent with a copy of the song.[1]

Undeterred, the songwriter then sent "Pretty Hurts" to Rihanna's manager for consideration. The pop star's team had the tune for eight months but didn't pay to keep reserving the song. That meant it was on the market – paving the way for Beyoncé, who flipped for the track. "Sia is such a genius," she said. "The second I heard the song, I'm like, 'I have to sing this song, I don't care how hard I have to fight for this song, this is my song!'"[2] (Perry eventually realized she had been emailed the song, but admitted: "It was meant to be with Beyoncé, of course."[3])

"Pretty Hurts" uses the backdrop of a beauty pageant to illuminate the immense pressure women feel to look perfect. The lyrics address unrealistic beauty expectations (for example, conflicting diet advice) and observe that contestants are often only valued for their looks, not their smarts or personality. The end of the song poses even more difficult questions: at the end of the day, when you're not onstage and you're alone with your thoughts, are you satisfied?

Poignantly, "Pretty Hurts" is also gentle with people struggling with these internal conflicts. Throughout, the song stresses that if you're feeling dissatisfied with yourself, fixing your appearance isn't the answer. Instead, working on your inner self is the solution – because good looks are ephemeral, but a nourished soul can bring stability.

Beyoncé understood "Pretty Hurts" immediately, as a pageant "is the most humiliating, judgmental place you can be as a woman," she said. "I feel like sometimes the world is a big contest, we're all being judged. I wanted to capture how humiliating and insecure that makes you feel."[4]

The accompanying visual is also set in the beauty pageant world. Drawing on her acting background, Beyoncé plays a contestant struggling under the stress and pressure of competition; among other things, she's hiding an eating disorder. It's "a behind-the-scenes look into society's take on beauty and how it doesn't bring you happiness and it doesn't move you forward in life," Beyoncé said. "It's really finding yourself that brings you true happiness."[5]

Left and opposite: Beyoncé's 2013 self-titled full-length was a visual album, and she held a screening of it soon after release in New York City (left); as part of the Mrs. Carter Show World Tour, she headlined the Rock in Rio Festival.

GHOST / HAUNTED

[ALBUM TRACK]

Released: December 13, 2013
Writers: Jordan Asher and Beyoncé Knowles
Producers: Boots and Beyoncé Knowles

On this album, Beyoncé worked closely with a mysterious producer and songwriter named Boots, who had a publishing deal with Roc Nation (but little-to-no online footprint) and was cagey about revealing his real name. (Online sleuths had other plans; Boots was quickly identified as Jordan Asher, a musician who had made a name for himself in southern Florida fronting bands like Blonds.)

Beyoncé marked his first high-profile production work – and set the bar incredibly high. Take the gothic-industrial fantasia "Haunted", which was prefaced by the ethereal "Ghost" and described by Beyoncé as being about "temptation in this music industry and being exposed to this craziness."[6] "Ghost" occasionally resembles Sarah McLachlan but also finds Beyoncé reciting the lyrics as if she was in a trance; musically, Boots took cues from Aphex Twin's confrontational electronic atmospheres.

"[I] made the beat from a dreamlike, hypnotic place, because that's where it began for me," he says, adding that the lyrics originated as a "stream-of-consciousness" piece written at 5 a.m. after a dissatisfying record label meeting. "When she heard that [piece], her eyes widened, and she was immediately like, 'That's *exactly* what I feel like,'" Boots says. "She just started talking about her experiences in the record industry, people telling her what they think her sound should be."[7]

"Haunted", meanwhile, is reminiscent of Grace Jones' avant-garde club music and is just as disorienting, carrying over the ghost imagery from the other song to illustrate abstract discord within an otherwise solid relationship. According to Boots, Beyoncé's request for the track? "This shit has to knock harder than any rap album out there."[8]

DRUNK IN LOVE (FEATURING JAY-Z)

[SINGLE]

Released: December 17, 2013 (single) / December 13, 2013 (album)
Writers: Jordan Asher, Shawn Carter, Rasool Díaz, Noel Fisher, Jerome Harmon, Beyoncé Knowles, Timothy Mosley, Andre Proctor, Brian Soko
Producers: Beyoncé Knowles, Detail, The Order, Timbaland, Harmon, Boots
Select Alternate Versions: Remix featuring Jay-Z and Kanye West, Rico Love and Plies remix, Future remix, Harmonimix remix

To put together her self-titled album, Beyoncé decided to move her family and "all of the writers I respected" – including Shea Taylor, Hit-Boy and The-Dream – to a giant place in The Hamptons for an extended, immersive studio session. This process was for practical *and* creative reasons: she had given birth to Blue Ivy not long before and was easing into balancing motherhood and music.

"I was breastfeeding, cornrows in my hair, because I was spending so much time being a mother," she said. "I would take a few hours out of the day and record. In real life, I was this woman, this mother, trying to get my focus and my dreams and myself back. Recording this album was such an outlet for me to kind of escape and create whatever world and fantasy that definitely, at the time, was not happening."[9]

In the end, she recorded more than 80 songs, and the experience was "much freer than anything I'd done in the past," she said. "We really just tried to trust our instincts, embrace the moment, and

Opposite and above: Beyoncé closed out a very successful 2013 with a concert at the Barclays Center as part of the Mrs. Carter Show World Tour (opposite). At the 56th Annual Grammy Awards, Beyoncé and Jay-Z performed "Drunk In Love", which eventually won two Grammys, for Best R&B Song and Best R&B Performance (above).

keep it fun."[10] As an example, she cited the music video for "Drunk in Love": a gorgeous black-and-white clip filmed on a Miami beach featuring just her and Jay-Z. "It's beautiful in its simplicity," she said. "If you want something to feel real and urgent, you can't overthink it."[11]

Accordingly, when Beyoncé started choosing the songs that would make the album, she found herself leaning into songs that also "were more effortless for me, that stuck around, that I still loved as much as I loved a year ago when I recorded them."[12] The sensual "Drunk in Love" also fit this bill.

The title is a play on words, referencing feeling intoxicated by someone *and* the ways in which being buzzed magnifies lustful feelings. Musically, "Drunk in Love" possesses an unconventional arrangement that eschews massive hooks in favor of more subtle, yearning vocal peaks. Beyoncé simply luxuriates in the music as she describes exploring her own desires and enjoying hedonistic pleasures. (And her pronunciation of "surfboard" – like "surfboardt" or "surfbort" – in context of referencing a sex act spawned countless jokes and memes.)

The music captures the fuzziness of feeling drunk, with a slightly unfocused, twinkling synthesizer track matched with a heartbeat-like rhythmic pattern. The producer Detail "had this really hard beat and he had this song called 'Drunk', and I'm like, 'That's what I wanna sing,'" Beyoncé said with a laugh. "I kind of freestyled the verse, and Jay went in and he started flowing out his verse. We just kinda had a party."[13]

"Drunk in Love" reached No. 2 on the *Billboard* Hot 100 and won two Grammys, for Best R&B Song and Best R&B Performance. "It was so great, because it wasn't about any ego," she adds. "We weren't trying to make a hit record, we were just having fun and I think you can hear that in the record."[14]

BLOW / CHERRY

[ALBUM TRACK]

Released: December 13, 2013
Writers: James Fauntleroy, J. Harmon, Beyoncé Knowles, T. Mosley, Justin Timberlake, Pharrell Williams
Producers: Beyoncé Knowles and J-Roc
Select Alternate Versions: Monsieur Adi remix, Remix featuring Pharrell Williams

Buoyed by a frothy roller-disco groove, '70s R&B harmonies and soft-glow production, "Blow" bluntly and proudly celebrates the pleasures of oral sex; playful lyrical imagery even compares the act to eating a sugary pink Skittle with a sweet middle. "There is unbelievable power in ownership, and women should own their sexuality," Beyoncé said. "There is a double standard when it comes to sexuality that still persists. Men are free and women are not. That is crazy."[15]

"Cherry" – an interlude with choppy, Neptunes-esque production and '80s soul-funk flair – embraces this power. In a forthright tone, the narrator spells out in explicit terms what she wants her partner to do. She knows what feels good, what she wants – and has no qualms asking for it. "The old lessons of submissiveness and fragility made us victims," Beyoncé said. "Women are so much more than that. You can be a businesswoman, a mother, an artist, and a feminist – whatever you want to be – and still be a sexual being. It's not mutually exclusive."[16]

Beyoncé filmed the colourful, 1970s-themed "Blow" video in Houston at a skating rink called Funplex. The space holds special memories for her, as she went there on one of her first dates with her first boyfriend. "And now I got the whole Funplex that I rented out," she said with a laugh. "I thought I was balling."[17]

Opposite and above: Although Beyoncé and Jay-Z were nominated for Best Rap/Sung Collaboration for "Part II (On the Run)" at the 56th Annual Grammy Awards, they sadly didn't win (opposite). On the Mrs. Carter Show World Tour, Beyoncé mixed the Verve's "Bitter Sweet Symphony" into "If I Were a Boy"(right).

NO ANGEL

[ALBUM TRACK]

Released: December 13, 2013
Writers: James Fauntleroy, Beyoncé Knowles, Caroline Polachek
Producers: Boots, Beyoncé Knowles, Caroline Polachek

Caroline Polachek of the indie-pop band Chairlift co-wrote and co-produced "No Angel", landing the gig because of her bandmate Patrick Wimberly: the drummer played with Solange Knowles and helped her with a show at Manhattan's Museum of Modern Art. Through this work, Wimberly met Beyoncé, who happened to casually mention she "loved Chairlift and would love to get in the studio some time."[18]

Wasting no time, Wimberly and Polachek ended up spending a week in the studio working on potential Beyoncé songs. As they were finishing up, she "threw in [a track] I'd written on my laptop while we were touring in the UK. I had all the production, I was just missing a verse. I thought it could be a good album track for Chairlift, but it would be incredibly sexy if Beyoncé did it."[19]

Her instincts were sound. A dreamy chillwave track with futuristic synthesizers that shapeshift like the vivid Northern Lights, "No Angel" celebrates the sexiness and strength of a partner's flaws. Beyoncé's breathy delivery drips with longing *and* admiration.

Polachek couldn't have been more thrilled with how the song turned out. "Her groove was different – my vocals were jumpier, and hers were more like panting," she shares. "And in my version the synths detuned really quickly for a second; she did the same thing but with her voice. It sounds like the whole song melts. It's amazing."[20]

YONCÉ / PARTITION

[SINGLE]

Released: February 25, 2014 (single) / December 13, 2013 (album)
Writers: Mike Dean, Jerome Harmon, Beyoncé Knowles, Timothy Mosley, Terius "The-Dream" Nash, Justin Timberlake, Dwane Weir
Producers: Boots, Mike Dean, Jerome Harmon, Beyoncé Knowles, Timbaland, Justin Timberlake, Key Wayne

"Yoncé" is a spirited self-empowerment anthem on which Beyoncé relishes turning heads in the club and playfully boasts about her musical skills. The nickname came courtesy of The-Dream; however, she wasn't introducing another persona but instead revealing more about herself. "Yoncé is Beyoncé," she said. "Ms. Carter is Beyoncé. Sasha Fierce is Beyoncé. I'm finally at a place where I don't have to separate the two anymore. We're all one. It's all pieces of me; just different elements of a personality, of a woman, because we are complicated."[21]

Snaky rhythms and midnight-dark synthesizers wobble in the background, while the song's insistent drumbeat came from Justin Timberlake, who started pounding on buckets in the studio. "It was really organic," she said. "It reminded me of being in middle school during lunch breaks when you just start freestyling."[22]

Beyoncé also viewed "Partition" as a hip-hop throwback, as its spry, booming bass line and snaps reminded her of Too $hort and E-40. The music also made her flashback to being a teenager listening to music in her car – and remember when she first met Jay-Z and "he's trying to scoop me and thinks I'm the hottest thing in the world."[23]

The resulting lyrics are raunchy, depicting a wild sex romp in the back of a fancy car complete with torn clothing and body fluids. "I didn't need a pen and paper. It just kind of flew out of my mouth,"[24] she said, adding, "I was so embarrassed after I recorded the song, because I'm just talking shit. I'm like, 'I can't play this for my husband.' I still haven't played it for my mom. She's gonna be very mad at me."[25]

Opposite: At the 2015 Budweiser Made in America Festival in Philadelphia, Beyoncé performed both "Yoncé" and "Partition" as part of the set.

JEALOUS

[ALBUM TRACK]

Released: December 13, 2013
Writers: Lyrica Anderson, Jordan Asher, Rasool Díaz, Noel Fisher, Beyoncé Knowles, Andre Proctor, Brian Soko
Producers: Boots, Detail, HazeBanga, Hit-Boy, Beyoncé Knowles, The Order, Andre Proctor

The main character of "Jealous" pulls out all the stops to make a romantic meal for her man, but he never shows up. In response, she vows to make him jealous: she puts on her most confident outfit – yes, that means the freakum dress – goes out for the night and catches up with an ex. The post-chorus and bridge, meanwhile, serve as her inner monologue; among other things, she rues the toxic relationship dynamic but also asks that her actions not be judged. "Jealous" is "a song about being human," Beyoncé says. "We all get jealous. It doesn't matter who you are; at some point, it's just inevitable."[26]

Musically, the song is one of the poppiest moments on the album, with muffled trip-hop drums and sunrise-like synths leading into a keening background vocal. But Boots says the distorted garage-rock song "Roach Cock" by the Los Angeles musician Hanni El Khatib was also an influence. "[Beyoncé] said, 'I'm inspired by how this feels – can you bring a little bit of that to 'Jealous'?" he says. "I was *more* than happy. So there's this gnarly fuzz guitar ripping in the background."[27]

ROCKET

[ALBUM TRACK]

Released: December 13, 2013
Writers: James Fauntleroy, Jerome Harmon, Beyoncé Knowles, Timothy Mosley, Miguel Pimentel, Justin Timberlake
Producers: Jerome Harmon, Beyoncé Knowles, Timbaland

Beyoncé characterizes "Rocket" as "one of the most sensual songs" on the album, comparable to the first time she heard D'Angelo's 2000 neo-soul touchstone "Untitled (How Does It Feel)".[28] That's no understatement: a lush R&B slow jam co-written with Miguel and Justin Timberlake, "Rocket" traces the arc of a steamy sexual encounter, starting with the foreplay of a lap dance. "What I love about this song is it takes you through this journey," she said. "You know, you're flirting and you're talking all of your arrogant shit. Then you climax, and then you have your cigarette."[29]

From a musical standpoint, "Rocket" exemplifies her artistic maturity and sophistication. "This song actually is about singing from the heart," she said."[30] The accompanying black-and-white video, which finds the camera lingering on Beyoncé as she expresses desire, self-love and sexual agency, is also vulnerable and honest. "I feel like I've earned the right to be me and to express any and every side of myself," she said. [31]

Left: At the Mrs. Carter Show World Tour stop at the Staples Center on December 3, 2013, Beyoncé dedicated a cover of Dolly Parton's "I Will Always Love You" to the actor Paul Walker.

MINE (FEATURING DRAKE)

[ALBUM TRACK]

Released: December 13, 2013
Writers: Sidney "Omen" Brown, Aubrey Graham, Majid Jordan, Beyoncé Knowles, Noah "40" Shebib, Key Wane
Producers: Sidney "Omen" Brown, Majid Jordan, Noah "40" Shebib

In early 2013, Drake teamed up with sometimes-Beyoncé collaborator James Fauntleroy for the track "Girls Love Beyoncé", which interpolated Destiny's Child's "Say My Name". Later in the year, he joined forces with the real deal – Beyoncé herself – on the ambitious "Mine". The sprawling multi-part epic employs spacious arrangements with clipped beats and minimal programming. "I had fun with it," Drake said. "I always wanted to write for her. She never really sings that minimal ... We'll see where that goes."[32]

Beyoncé came back with deeply personal lyrics. Alongside sparse piano, she muses about tumultuous postpartum life and specifically references a potential separation. From there she reminisces about love and wanting to get married, which opens the door to Drake playing the part of a partner who tells his side of the story. Tellingly, he employs sharply distorted vocals on his parts, while Beyoncé has her say via clear, honeyed vocals; the contrast makes the personal differences between their perspectives more prominent. But by the end, they sing in unity, as they both want the same thing: each other.

XO

[SINGLE]

Released: December 16, 2013 (single) / December 13, 2013 (album)
Writers: Beyoncé Knowles, Terius "The-Dream" Nash, Ryan Tedder
Producers: HazeBanga, Hit-Boy, Beyoncé Knowles, Ryan Tedder, The-Dream

Beyoncé had a nasty sinus infection the day she recorded the buoyant pop song "XO" – and instead of fixing the song later, she left it as-is. "I recorded it in a few minutes just as a demo and decided to keep the vocals," she said, noting this wasn't out of the ordinary for other songs on the album as well. "I really loved the imperfections, so I kept the original demos."[33] Where "XO" was concerned, this vocal rawness amplified the urgency of the song's message: seize the day and make every moment in your life count.

"XO" starts with brief audio from the 1986 space shuttle *Challenger* disaster. After the inclusion drew criticism, Beyoncé clarified they used the snippet "in tribute to the unselfish work of the *Challenger* crew with hope that they will never be forgotten" and noted, "The song 'XO' was recorded with the sincerest intention to help heal those who have lost loved ones and to remind us that unexpected things happen, so love and appreciate every minute that you have with those who mean the most to you."[34]

Right: Beyoncé looked stunning as she performed "XO" at the BRIT Awards 2014.

***FLAWLESS (FEATURING CHIMAMANDA NGOZI ADICHIE)

[SINGLE]

Released: August 2, 2014 (single, remix featuring Nicki Minaj) / December 13, 2013 (album)
Writers: Chauncey Hollis, Beyoncé Knowles, Raymond Martin, Rashad Muhammad, Terius "The-Dream" Nash
Producers: Boots, HazeBanga, Hit-Boy, Beyoncé Knowles, Rey Reel Music
Select Alternate Versions: Remix featuring Nicki Minaj; Baddygirl 2 (M.I.A. remix), Lil Kim unofficial remix

As Beyoncé was putting together the album, she flashed back to the time her childhood group Girls Tyme appeared (and lost) on the TV talent show *Star Search*. It didn't even occur to her they would lose; in her mind, they would win and earn a record deal. "I was only nine years old – so at that time you don't realize that you can actually work super hard and give everything you have and lose," Beyoncé said. "It was the best message for me."[35]

She includes the group's *Star Search* intro in "***Flawless", which starts with "Bow Down" [*see* page 158] before segueing into a sample of a speech by the Nigerian author Chimamanda Ngozi Adichie that zeroes in on the inequalities baked into the way girls are raised. Beyoncé had discovered Adichie's wisdom while looking for videos on feminism on YouTube, observing, "Everything she said is exactly how I feel."[36] On the album, the sampled section closes with Adichie's definition of feminism, which was important to Beyoncé; in fact, she also included it on the *Mrs. Carter World Tour*.

Beyoncé followed this up with a section discussing what she learned from her own family and then encourages people to love themselves – in other words, growing from setbacks and preserving your inner spark. "Something about the aggression of 'Bow Down' and the attitude of 'Flawless' – the reality is, sometimes you lose," she said with a laugh. "And you're never too good to lose. You're never too big to lose. You're never too smart to lose. It happens – and it happens when it needs to happen. And you have to embrace those things."[37]

SUPERPOWER (FEATURING FRANK OCEAN)

[ALBUM TRACK]

Released: December 13, 2013
Writers: Beyoncé Knowles, Frank Ocean, Pharrell Williams
Producers: Boots and Pharrell Williams

At the start of "Superpower", Beyoncé marvels at how different she is on her own, as opposed to when she's with Jay-Z. But the song's title refers to the strength the couple draws from each other, and the way their bond has endured through life's curveballs and challenges. In fact, the true superpower is how unstoppable the couple is when they're together.

Fittingly, "Superpower" finds Beyoncé once again teaming up with a formidable musical collaborator, Frank Ocean. Together, they unfurl a Prince-esque R&B simmer dotted with solemn doo-wop harmonies and timpani rolls. The duo's voices are particularly beautiful together, with Ocean's velvety croon matching Beyoncé's gravitas-filled lower register. "His low octave is so beautiful," she says. "I love the way we sound together."[38]

The Jonas Åkerlund-directed "Superpower" visual is striking and timely. Beyoncé leads a group of scrappy warriors (which includes her Destiny's Child mates Kelly Rowland and Michelle Williams) into a fiery street battle against oppressive forces. In the end, as she and others stare down riot police, she clasps the hand of a partner. "Basically, the message is, love is the most powerful thing we have," she said. "And it doesn't matter if a war, if a riot is going on, when you are with the person you love, you can survive any and everything."[39]

Opposite: Nigerian writer Chimamanda Ngozi Adichie had a speech of hers sampled on "***Flawless."

Above: The Mrs. Carter Show World Tour featured Beyoncé's usual mix of jaw-dropping vocals and choreography.

HEAVEN

[ALBUM TRACK]

Released: December 13, 2013
Writers: Jordan Asher and Beyoncé Knowles
Producers: Boots and Beyoncé Knowles

Try not to cry while listening to "Heaven", a simple piano ballad that's one of Beyoncé's best and most moving songs. The verses prepare to say goodbye to someone special by reminiscing about good times; the choruses proclaim that heaven is calling; and the song ends with the Lord's Prayer said in Spanish.

The "Heaven" video is also a tearjerker, as it juxtaposes imagery of church mourning with Beyoncé and her dance captain, Ashley Everett, having adventures (getting tattoos) and reaching life milestones (marriage). "'Heaven' is about death and finding the strength and knowing that someone had an incredible life – and that giving you some type of closure," Beyoncé said.[40]

Many people assumed "Heaven" was about the miscarriage she mentioned in the documentary *Life Is But A Dream* [*see* page 155]. However, creative director Todd Tourso let it slip that "originally, her main inspiration for that song and that video was watching her mother lose one of her best friends".[41] And producer and co-writer Boots was mum on the origins, noting it's "about something different to everyone", and allowing that the song's goal was universal: "To ease the hearts and minds of anyone who have suffered from an unthinkable loss."[42]

BLUE (FEATURING BLUE IVY)

[ALBUM TRACK]

Released: December 13, 2013
Writers: Jordan Asher and Beyoncé Knowles
Producers: Boots and Beyoncé Knowles

Placing "Heaven" and "Blue" next to each other on *Beyoncé* feels like a lovely nod to the circle of life. The former addresses the heartbreaking end of a life, while the latter embraces the wonder and joy of being a mom to a new baby, Blue Ivy. Warm, intimate production – Beyoncé sounds like she's in the same room as her listeners – cushions beatific programming and a textured rhythmic track that touches on jazz, trap and trip-hop. Near the end of "Blue", producer Boots made sure to include found sounds of birds chirping outside the studio in addition to a recording of Blue Ivy herself babbling happily. "Blue was talking so much – from the moment that I met that kid until then, the amount she said tripled," he recalled. "People were watching her making connections; she started telling everyone that the two dinosaurs she was running around with were mommy and baby dinosaur. The birds were like a stamp for the song; I wanted to remember that day."[43]

Above and opposite: Beyoncé and Jay-Z had performed live together plenty of times before, but firmed up their collaborations with a joint co-headlining stadium tour, the On The Run Tour.

HEARTBEAT

[*LIFE IS BUT A DREAM* DOCUMENTARY]

Released: February 16, 2013
Writer: Beyoncé Knowles

In the 2013 documentary *Life Is But A Dream*, there's a raw scene in which Beyoncé quietly revealed she had a miscarriage several years before having daughter Blue Ivy. She recalled hearing the fetal heartbeat ("Which was the most beautiful music I ever heard in my life") and shared she had even chosen potential baby names. "I envisioned what my child would look like," she said. "I was feeling very maternal."[44]

However, during a doctor visit, they discovered her unborn baby suddenly and unexpectedly no longer had a heartbeat. Beyoncé coped with the wrenching news via music. "I went into the studio and wrote the saddest song I've ever written in my life," she said. "And it was the best form of therapy for me, because it was the saddest thing I've ever been through."

In the documentary, Beyoncé then shares a brief snippet of a stunning a cappella song called "Heartbeat". She sounds grief-stricken as she speaks directly to an unnamed subject, lamenting that love couldn't guarantee life for them both, but reassuring them that she tried her best. In the end, Beyoncé says she yearns to hear a heartbeat, as the life's been taken from her. The simple line has a devastating double meaning: not only does it seemingly reference her miscarriage, but it also implies that Beyoncé is emotionally bereft. To date, "Heartbeat" has never been officially released.

7/11

[SINGLE]

Released: November 25, 2014 (single) / November 24, 2014 (album)
Writers: Noel "Detail" Fisher, Bobby Johnson, Beyoncé Knowles, Sidney Swift
Producers: Detail, Derek Dixie, Bobby Johnson, Beyoncé Knowles, Sidney Swift
Select Alternate Versions: Remix with Diplo and Skrillex; Remix with French Montana; Detail Christmas Version featuring French Montana

Beyoncé reminds everyone that she's a ferocious rapper on the trap-influenced club cut "7/11", a track that originated with Germany-based producer Bobby Johnson. "The first thing that I do for almost all my stuff is [start] out with some sort of melody or melodic rhythm," he says, "and then I always record a little beatbox and try to get my first spark down."[45] (Incredibly enough, while Johnson didn't write the track specifically for Beyoncé, he recalled that he did have the drums of "Drunk in Love" in mind while creating it.)

With "7/11" specifically, Johnson took his time, putting space between working sessions to give the track the attention it deserved. "I put it back for a month, worked on it again, and then I put it away for an even longer time," he said. "I felt like I was stuck with it, and I felt like it had potential."[46] Johnson sent the track that became "7/11" to producer Detail – and, as it turns out, also to the Chicago rapper ACE B8gie, who used it for the song "Bird's Eye View" right before Beyoncé did. There were no hard feelings: "Thank u Beyoncé," ACE B8gie tweeted.

RING OFF

[SINGLE]

Released: November 28, 2014 (single) / November 24, 2014 (album)
Writers: Adam Amezaga, Stephen Bishop, Michael Caren, Mike Dean, Derek Dixie, Geoff Early, Charles Hinshaw, Chauncey "Hit-Boy" Hollis, Beyoncé Knowles, William Lobban-Bean, Sidney Swift
Producers: Michael Caren, Cook Classics, Mike Dean, Derek Dixie, Hit-Boy, Beyoncé Knowles, Ariel Rechtshaid,

Built around a lilting acoustic guitar lick sampled from Stephen Bishop's "On and On" and a soft-breeze reggae groove, "Ring Off" is an uplifting pep talk about the freedom that comes from divorce. The song comes from the perspective of a daughter who's watched her mother's self-esteem crumble in a tumultuous marriage where she's not respected or complimented. However, after she splits from her husband, her life gets markedly better; as it turns out, jettisoning an indifferent partner paves the way for a new relationship and happiness. The daughter swells with pride over her beautiful mama and, tellingly, notes that both of them are starting over with the divorce; the song's denouement even weaves in joyous references to Beyoncé's own song, "Love on Top". Although Beyoncé hasn't explicitly discussed the inspiration behind the song, "Ring Off" is widely considered to be about her parents' divorce, which was finalized in 2011.

STANDING ON THE SUN (REMIX)

[*BEYONCÉ* PLATINUM EDITION]

Released: November 24, 2014
Writers: Rasool Diaz, Noel "Detail" Fisher, Sia Furler, Beyoncé Knowles, Greg Kurstin, Andre Eric Proctor, Brian Soko
Producers: Beyoncé Knowles, Greg Kurstin, Pharrell Williams

The curious thing about including a remix of "Standing on the Sun" on the platinum edition of *Beyoncé*? Only a tantalizingly short clip of the original version had surfaced before, in an H&M summer swimwear campaign commercial in which Beyoncé starred. (The full take eventually leaked online in June 2013, but it was never officially released.) But good things come to those who wait: the remix of "Standing on the Sun" celebrates a sizzling romance with vibrant dancehall beats and sassier vocals. According to the dancehall artist Mr. Vegas, who's on the track, Beyoncé was the impetus for the redo – and wanted to keep the music deliberately raw through the final mixes. "She was very involved," he said. "She wanted to do this remix. She was giving us tips: 'No, no, I want a hardcore dancehall vibe.'"[47]

GROWN WOMAN

[*BEYONCÉ* VISUAL EDITION]

Released: December 13, 2023 (streaming services) / December 13, 2013 (visual album)
Writers: Chris Godbey, Jerome Harmon, Beyoncé Knowles, Garland Mosley, Timothy Mosley, Terius "The-Dream" Nash, Darryl Pearson, Kelly Sheehan
Producers: J-Roc and Timbaland

"Grown Woman" technically ushered in the *Beyoncé* era, as the song debuted months before the album in a Pepsi commercial that found modern-day Beyoncé interacting with her past selves. She then performed it during the *Mrs. Carter Show World Tour,* no doubt because the song's dizzying Timbaland beats were perfectly suited for the live stage. Sonically, the song is a brisk throwback to *4*: chants by Ismael Kouyate (who toured with the musical *Fela!*), insistent African rhythms and taut horns – as well as a kinetic Beyoncé vocal performance – give the song a triumphant vibe. However, the self-assured lyrics were very much *Beyoncé*. She lays out how hard she worked growing up – and how much she dreamed of success – and triumphantly notes that she's *made it.* Now that she's an adult, she commands respect, oozes confidence and has a firm grip on her future. The full version of "Grown Woman" initially only appeared on the visual edition of *Beyoncé*, but in 2023, the song finally landed on streaming services to commemorate *Beyoncé*'s 10th anniversary.

Opposite: Beyoncé replicated the iconic video dance for "Single Ladies (Put a Ring on It)" during her The Mrs. Carter Show World Tour.

Right: Beyoncé sported a black Givenchy dress at the 2014 Met Gala, which had the theme "Charles James: Beyond Fashion."

OTHER SONGS

J. COLE RELEASED THE WILDLY POPULAR MIXTAPE *FRIDAY NIGHT LIGHTS* IN 2010. AMONG THE HIGHLIGHTS WAS A THROWBACK SOUL/R&B SONG CALLED "HOME FOR THE HOLIDAYS", WHICH VERY QUIETLY FEATURED ADDITIONAL BACKGROUND VOCALS BY BEYONCÉ.

She teamed up with equally high-profile artists in subsequent years, as evidenced by her incredibly busy 2013. In addition to releasing a self-titled album, Beyoncé released multiple collaborations and non-album tracks. One of the highlights found her reuniting with André 3000 to cover Amy Winehouse's "Back to Black" for director Baz Luhrmann's take on *The Great Gatsby*. As is fitting for a Luhrmann film, their version of the song is unorthodox: sinister beats whirr underneath André 3000's low-key vocals until spy noir guitars usher in Beyoncé, who sounds like an enchanted torch singer.

Several months before "Bow Down" appeared ahead of "***Flawless" on *Beyoncé*, the song surfaced online via part of another song: "Bow Down/I Been On". In an interview, Beyoncé described waking up and heading into the studio with a "chant in my head" that felt different from other songs.

"It was aggressive, it was angry," she said. "It wasn't the Beyoncé that wakes up every morning. It was the Beyoncé that was angry. It was the Beyoncé that felt the need to defend herself. And if the song never comes out? Okay – I said it."[48] Upon playback, she did like the song and decided to just release it right away for free; years later, however, "I Been On" appeared officially on 2019's *Homecoming: The Live Album*.

In 2013, Beyoncé also voiced Queen Tara, a matriarch of the forest, in the animated film *Epic*. Along with this appearance came the uplifting, inspirational song "Rise Up", a co-write with Sia that was co-produced by Hit-Boy. Later in the year, fans who pre-ordered the DVD of her documentary *Life Is But a Dream* received an equally gorgeous ballad called "God Made You Beautiful", which celebrates the birth of Blue Ivy. Musically, it sounds like a beatific sunrise, between the steady drums and orchestrated musical swells.

During this era, Beyoncé also appeared with some of her most trusted collaborators, starting with (of course) Jay-Z. Building on her multiple features in the recent past (2007's "Pray", 2009's "Venus vs. Mars" and 2012's "Young Forever") she featured prominently on the *Magna Carta ... Holy Grail* highlight "Part II (On the Run)". A thematic descendent of "03 Bonnie and Clyde", the song was nominated for a Grammy for Best Rap/Sung Collaboration.

Beyoncé also teamed up with her frequent collaborator The-Dream for the stirring electro-trap tune "Turnt", alongside 2 Chainz. And Kelly Rowland also enlisted her Destiny's Child girls Beyoncé and Michelle Williams for "You Changed" on her solo album *Talk a Good Game*.

After making a name for himself with his work on Beyoncé's 2013 self-titled album, the producer/songwriter known as Boots almost immediately branched out on his own. His debut solo effort was a mixtape, 2014's *Winter Spring Summer Fall*, that featured Beyoncé adding guest vocals on the cosmic "Dreams". With its gauzy electronic production and spacious arrangement, the song has an apt title; Beyoncé also sounds otherworldly, her vocals echoing Boots' lovelorn sentiments with aching melisma.

Above and opposite: Playing stadiums suited Beyoncé, as her On The Run Tour staging and choreography was impressive.

That same year, Michelle Williams orchestrated another Destiny's Child mini-reunion, enlisting Beyoncé and Kelly Rowland as guest vocalists on the single "Say Yes". Given the upbeat tempo and this starpower, it's no surprise the tune became a massive hit, spending seven weeks at No. 1 on *Billboard*'s Hot Gospel Songs chart. In sonic contrast, Beyoncé also held her own alongside rapper Nicki Minaj on "Feeling Myself", a highlight of *The Pinkprint* dominated by a sparse, eerie synth line.

In 2015, Beyoncé celebrated her seventh wedding anniversary with Jay-Z by releasing a new song – the heartwarming piano ballad "Die With You" – exclusively via the streaming service TIDAL. That same year she also turned up on several songs on Coldplay's album *A Head Full of Dreams*. She casually contributed backing vocals on the life-affirming global hit "Hymn for the Weekend" and joined multiple other famous artists (including vocal goddess Merry Clayton and actress Annabelle Wallis) singing as part of a choir on the album-closer "Up&Up".

In the mid-2000s, Carla Marie Williams – a musician influenced by Alanis Morissette and Mary J. Blige – formed a writing collective called New Crowd. Although she, Jonathan Coffer and Arrow Benjamin wrote "Runnin' (Lose It All)" together on piano, the song "was from my perspective", Williams says. "I was at a very low point in my life, and I didn't know where else to go or what else to do at that time. So [the song] came from a personal place of searching."[49] As it happens, Beyoncé and the British producer Naughty Boy both recorded versions of the song – though Williams came up with a solution that suited everyone: "It was a bit of a tug of war who wanted it, and then we all ended up on it."[50] Released in 2015, "Runnin' (Lose It All)" ended up as a surging electronic dance number that became a top 5 hit in the UK.

Opposite: Beyoncé's love for performing live always shines through when she's onstage.

Below: The star made a memorable guest appearance during Coldplay's set at the Pepsi Super Bowl 50 Halftime Show.

12 LEMONADE

LEMONADE MARKED A SIGNIFICANT TURNING POINT IN BEYONCÉ'S ARTISTRY *AND* CAREER. MUSICALLY, IT WAS VIRTUOSIC IN THE WAY THE SONGS HOPSCOTCHED BETWEEN ROCK, FUNK, COUNTRY, GOSPEL, TRAP, BLUES AND REGGAE. THEMATICALLY, SONGS LIKE "FORMATION" AND "FREEDOM" POSSESSED A SOCIALLY CONSCIOUS POLITICAL BENT THAT WOULD SOON BECOME AN INTEGRAL PART OF HER WORK. AND NOT ONLY DID BEYONCÉ ONCE AGAIN RELEASE *LEMONADE* AS A VISUAL ALBUM, BUT THE ACCOMPANYING FILM HAD A STORY ARC AND ORGANIZING STRUCTURE THAT DEEPENED THE FULL-LENGTH'S THEMES AND CONCEPTS. OVER TIME, ITS INFLUENCE HAS ONLY CONTINUED TO GROW: IN JANUARY 2025, *ROLLING STONE* PLACED *LEMONADE* AT NO. 1 ON THEIR GREATEST ALBUM OF THE 21ST CENTURY SO FAR LIST.

PRAY YOU CATCH ME

[ALBUM TRACK]

Released: April 23, 2016
Writers: James Blake, Kevin Garrett, Beyoncé Knowles
Producers: Kevin Garrett, Beyoncé Knowles, Jeremy McDonald

"Pray You Catch Me" opens with a solemn, uneasy sound: Beyoncé singing along wordlessly to plucked beats, like she's warming up her voice. After fifteen seconds or so, the song starts adding filigreed layers of vocal harmonies; the resulting section resembles an entire ensemble of Beyoncés getting ready for a chorale performance. As it turns out, they actually were: the rest of "Pray You Catch Me" possesses a church-like atmosphere, with spare production giving space to a funereal organ, undulating strings, mournful piano and a main vocal melody that brims with weary sadness.

Co-writer/co-producer Kevin Garrett noted that "Pray You Catch Me" was "a collaborative effort" with Beyoncé. "It's an incredibly special song to me because of the way it was written, lyrics first and on a guitar," he says. "Once she added her voice and her honesty to the track, it really pushed everything over the top."[1] Garrett was circumspect about what inspired this honesty ("Our inspiration was coming from very personal places," he said, and added cryptically, "That inevitably finds its way."[2]) though the lyrics are desolate, depicting a couple on the outs. The narrator is trying to determine whether their partner's been cheating – and fervently want to get caught sneaking in their business, as if it'll be a relief they're not imagining the hints of infidelity.

HOLD UP

[SINGLE]

Released: August 16, 2016 (single) / April 23, 2016 (album)
Writers: Brian Chase, Uzoechi Emenike, Emile Haynie, Beyoncé Knowles, Ezra Koenig, Kelvin McConnell, Karen Orzolek, Thomas Wesley Pentz, Doc Pomus, Antonio Randolph, Sean Rhoden, Mort Schuman, Joshua Tillman, DeAndre Way, Nick Zinner
Producers: Diplo, Beyoncé Knowles, Ezra Koenig

"Hold Up" builds on the plot of "Pray You Catch Me", as the narrator is snooping through her partner's phone looking for evidence he's been unfaithful. But her sadness has given way to anger, as she reminds him of how well she treats him – and that he wouldn't be half as desirable to other women if it wasn't for her. In the end, she wonders what's the better option: being taken for granted – or being perceived as jealous or crazy?

Musically, "Hold Up" is atmospheric and reggae-tinged. A clipped rhythm sampled from Andy Williams' "Can't Get Used to Losing You" adds cinematic tension, while the occasional curveball (a dainty interpolation of Soulja Boy Tell'em's "Turn My Swag On" above blaring sirens) shatters the minimalist vibe.

"Hold Up" is also steeped in the indie rock world. Ezra Koenig from the popular band Vampire Weekend was in the studio with producer Diplo working on a song. Koenig crafted a hook from a silly social media post he made years before – he idly mused about changing a lyric in Yeah Yeah Yeah's "Maps" – and then added melodies and some other lyrics.[3]

Next, rakish troubadour Father John Misty put in his two cents. He was sent the song's hook and beat and then wrote the first verse. "After we recorded, I was like, 'We cannot send this to her. This is ridiculous,'" he recalled. "I just couldn't. My voice is not ... the song is not intended to be sold by me."[4] Beyoncé was convinced, however; so Father John Misty's contributions made the cut after all.

Opposite: Beyoncé performed a five-song set at the 2016 MTV Video Music Awards that included "Pray You Catch Me."

DON'T HURT YOURSELF (FEATURING JACK WHITE)

[ALBUM TRACK]

Released: April 23, 2016
Writers: John Bonham, Diana Gordon, John Paul Jones, Beyoncé Knowles, Jimmy Page, Robert Plant, Jack White
Producers: Derek Dixie, Beyoncé Knowles, Jack White

Lemonade's narrator is still (rightfully) angry on the raw, soul-garage highlight "Don't Hurt Yourself", which samples the smashing-trashcan drums from Led Zeppelin's "When The Levee Breaks". Once again, she tells her partner he's only hurting himself with his disrespectful behaviour; in fact, she stresses she'll be just fine without him. But "Don't Hurt Yourself" is also a warning shot: the narrator threatens to leave, saying she'll easily move on with someone else.

"Don't Hurt Yourself" is a collaboration with the rocker Jack White, who also contributes white-lighting vocals and bass guitar. "You know, I just talked to her and she said, 'I wanna be in a band with you,'" White said. "I said, 'Really? Well, I'd love to do something.' I've always loved her voice – I mean, I think she has the kind of soul singing voice of the days of Betty Davis or Aretha Franklin."[5]

The former – a cult North Carolina-based funk/R&B artist who recorded risqué-and-empowering albums in the 1960s and 1970s – absolutely influences Beyoncé's ragged, distorted vocals. In the song's most powerful moment, she sounds hoarse with rage and embarrassment while discovering another woman's scent on her partner's Louis Vuitton shirt – and then snarls she's going to destroy her partner's stuff.

In the end, White was "so amazed at what [Beyoncé] did" with the song. "She took just sort of a sketch of a lyrical outline and turned into the most bodacious, vicious, incredible song. I don't even know what you'd classify it as – soul, rock and roll, whatever. [It's] incredibly intense."[6]

Above: Beyoncé collaborated with rocker Jack White on "Don't Hurt Me"; here, she and White are joined by the electro duo Daft Punk at a 2015 event.

Opposite: Beyoncé won an incredible eight awards at the 2016 MTV Video Music Awards, including Video of the Year for "Formation."

SORRY

[SINGLE]

Released: May 3, 2016 (single) / April 23, 2016 (album)
Writers: Diana Gordon, Beyoncé Knowles, Sean Rhoden
Producers: Diana Gordon, HazeBanga, Hit-Boy, Beyoncé Knowles, MeLo-X, Stuart White
Select Alternate Versions: Original Demo

"Sorry" makes good on the threat of "Don't Hurt Yourself": double middle fingers waving, the protagonist has dumped her partner's cheating ass and is celebrating in the club with her friends. (And she's *not* sorry.) Now her *partner* is begging for forgiveness, although she's not interested in apologies; in fact, she tells him to stop disrupting her grinding because he's *persona non grata* to her. Beyoncé's dynamic vocals mirror her conflicted emotions; she can be breezily sarcastic, irritated, stoic and even wistful.

Notably, "Sorry" also features one of Beyoncé's most iconic characters: her man's other woman, who she derisively calls Becky with the good hair. Co-writer Diana Gordon says the line was partly inspired by the iconic Dolly Parton song subject Jolene. But Gordon also meant it metaphorically, as a descriptor for when someone is "dating a light-skinned black girl", she says. "'Good hair' is just what we say in the black community for women who have not-so-kinky hair. It's like, 'Oh, she got good hair. It's curly, it's wavy.' It's just a metaphor for the lighter skin colorism thing in the black community."[7]

From a musical standpoint, the electronic-speckled R&B track "Sorry" was "like creating a vibe in the studio," co-producer MeLo-X says, noting he was proud to have brought a dancehall influence. "We were just working on a lot of stuff and the idea came up pretty simple. It was just some cool keys, drum patterns, and we started putting down vocal ideas and lyric ideas."[8] Co-producer Hit-Boy added "all these different sounds and layers to it and made it come together fully," MeLo-X added. "We created that vibe together."[9]

6 INCH (FEATURING THE WEEKND)

[ALBUM TRACK]

Released: April 23, 2016
Writers: Burt Bacharach, Ahmad "Belly" Balshe, Boots, Hal David, Ben "Billions" Diehl, Beyoncé Knowles, Noah Lennox, Terius "The-Dream" Nash, Dave Fortner, Danny Schofield, Abel Tesfaye, Brian Weitz
Producers: Ben Billions, Boots, DannyBoyStyles, Derek Dixie, Beyoncé Knowles

For the final show of the *Formation World Tour* in October 2016, Beyoncé debuted a jaw-dropping live version of "6 Inch": she performed the song while suspended in the air, often upside down, surrounded by kaleidoscope-like visuals. The gravity-defying move matched the attitude displayed by the main character of "6 Inch": an ultra-confident, hard-working, money-rich woman who commands respect and attention in every room she's in.

Musically, the song fits in well with The Weeknd's late-night electro vibes, between a spooky sample of Isaac Hayes' 1969 rendition of the Burt Bacharach-Hal David classic "Walk On By"; The Weeknd's soulful croon; and rapper Belly's drawl. Beyoncé sings the hook in a seductive lower register, her voice slightly digitally manipulated with steely menace; in context with the music, she sounds like an omniscient truth-teller revealing the woman's unassailable power.

Producer Ben "Billions" Diehl and Belly started writing "6 Inch" in October 2013 with DannyBoyStyles – but originally the song was going to be with rapper French Montana. "We got the word back that [Beyoncé] liked it," Diehl said, "and we all were like, 'We should keep working together. I think we're on to something. We're gonna be good when this sh– comes out.'"[10] Like many Beyoncé songs, that release date was very much TBD; however, Diehl, who also worked with The Weeknd, wasn't in a rush. "It all worked out," he says. "We just had to be patient."[11]

DADDY LESSONS

[ALBUM TRACK]

Released: April 23, 2016
Writers: Kevin Cossom, Alex Delicata, Diana Gordon, Beyoncé Knowles
Producers: Alex Delicata, Derek Dixie, Beyoncé Knowles

The bursts of exuberant New Orleans second-line horns at the start of the country-influenced "Daddy Lessons" give way to stomping honky-tonk beats, yee-haws and hollers, and cautionary figures: a father who warns his daughter to stay away from men who act dishonest like him – and the daughter's partner, who perpetuates the dishonourable behaviour. "Daddy Lessons" coalesced at co-writer Kevin Cossom's Miami condo, where Cossom, Diana Gordon and Alex Delicata had gathered to write. "[Alex] played the guitar, wrote it and we pretty much pressed record on the laptop and sang it down – harmonies, stomping and clapping, and that was the vibe," Cossom says. "We probably did it a few times till we got it right."[12]

Gordon ended up penning the lyrics, though the themes addressed were "more of a fantasy for me" since she grew up without a father.[13] But she nailed the heartache, as "Daddy Lessons" resonated deeply with Beyoncé. "She was like, 'This is my life,'" Gordon recalled. "I told her, 'You know what, take it, do what you want with it.' She went and re-produced it, she changed some words, added the bridge, it's hers."[14]

LOVE DROUGHT

[ALBUM TRACK]

Released: April 23, 2016
Writers: Ingrid Burley, Mike Dean, Beyoncé Knowles
Producers: Mike Dean and Beyoncé Knowles

Contrary to popular belief, the ethereal electronica track "Love Drought" – a song about trying to mend fences with someone you care about deeply – wasn't written about potential infidelity on Jay-Z's part. Co-writer Ingrid Burley, a Houston-based songwriter who grew up with Beyoncé, says she penned it in about 30 minutes as a "metaphor about music" due to frustration with Beyoncé's record label Parkwood Entertainment. "Two of the people who were running the label at the time had lied to me and told me that Beyoncé wasn't currently listening to any new music."[15] However, a few days later, Burley headed to a Beyoncé writing camp in Los Angeles, where she heard some "very inspiring" music – and notes from an A&R person from Beyoncé on the tunes. "And I'm like, 'They just told me that she's not listening to any music,'" Burley said. "I was so pissed ... I was just thinking as I'm looping this beat, I couldn't get out of my head the fact that they just lied to me!"[16]

Opposite and right: At the 58th Annual Grammy Awards, Beyoncé presented the award for Record of the Year to Bruno Mars and Mark Ronson for "Uptown Funk" (opposite); at the 2016 Met Gala, Beyoncé arrived in a pearl-studded Givenchy latex gown, a fitting nod to the theme of "Manus x Machina: Fashion in the Age of Technology" (right).

SANDCASTLES

[ALBUM TRACK]

Released: April 23, 2016
Writers: Vincent Berry II, Beyoncé Knowles, Midian Mathers, Malik Yusef
Producers: Vincent Berry II and Beyoncé Knowles

The unadorned piano ballad "Sandcastles" is about picking up the pieces of a broken relationship. Beyoncé's voice frays at the edges as she sings about her deep, eternal longing for her once-estranged partner, because she's realized that leaving isn't what she wants. "Sandcastles" originated with songwriter Vincent Berry II and poet/actor Malik Yusef. The latter had come up with a song called "We Built Sandcastles That Washed Away" with a gospel influence – and when he heard the song, Berry was overcome with emotion and memories of a decade-long relationship. "I hadn't really healed," he said. "When he sang the words I just thought about her and it was all I needed to get the rest out."[17] Berry next introduced the song to Midian Mathers, who cried upon hearing it; after some additional work on the song, Mathers then pitched the song to an A&R executive working on the Beyoncé album who *also* cried when she heard it. Berry ended up becoming homeless during the time Beyoncé worked on the track, which made landing on *Lemonade* that much sweeter. "When the biggest artist in the world sings your song," Berry says, "it's really a defining moment for yourself that you know you're supposed to be doing what you're doing."[18]

FORWARD (FEATURING JAMES BLAKE)

[ALBUM TRACK]

Released: April 23, 2016
Writers: James Blake and Beyoncé Knowles
Producers: James Blake and Beyoncé Knowles

The ghostly "Forward" describes the tentative first steps a couple takes after reconciliation, when everything feels unfamiliar and they're trying to remember their routines. It's a time when emotions are tender and fragile, which James Blake conveys perfectly in a solemn voice full of gravitas. Beyoncé, meanwhile, matches his precarious tone with her own whispery background vocals.

When Blake landed in the studio to record "Forward", it was an intimate setting: just him and an engineer. The latter played him a song that "sounded like the start of something," he recalls, so naturally he decided to finish it. "I wrote something that was completely against the brief," Blake said. "I've never sung anybody else's lyrics. So I got my phone out and sang some of my own lyrics that were about something else and about somebody else."[19] Luckily, Blake's instincts for the song were sound, and Beyoncé went with it. "It fit somehow into the song and it fit into the album," Blake said. "And I'm just honored that they used it."[20]

Above: Beyoncé performed "Sandcastles" during the 59th Annual Grammy Awards in February 2017.

FREEDOM (FEATURING KENDRICK LAMAR)

[SINGLE]

Released: April 23, 2016
Writers: Arrow Benjamin, Jonathan Coffer, Kendrick Duckworth, Beyoncé Knowles, Alan Lomax, John Lomax, Sr., Frank Tirado, Carla Marie Williams
Producers: Jonny Coffer, Just Blaze, Beyoncé Knowles
Select Alternate Versions: Instrumental Version

Driven by a sample of the psychedelic organ and strident drums of Kaleidoscope's 1969 song "Let Me Try" – and featuring two samples from the Lomax Family Audio Recordings, including 1959's Reverend R.C. Crenshaw's "Collection Speech/Unidentified Lining Hymn" – the empowering "Freedom" is one of Beyoncé's most political tracks. Speaking to Black women especially, she advocates for self-determination – encouraging them to nourish their freedom, seek out deeper truths and relationships, and believe in themselves. Kendrick Lamar's feature augments these themes, alluding to the social scourge of police brutality and racial oppression and speaking truth to the power of protest and the support of Black women.

"Freedom" emerged after Beyoncé tapped Carla Marie Williams and writing partners Arrow Benjamin and Jonathan Coffer (the team behind 2015's "Runnin' (Lose It all)" [*see* page 161]) to work on music. Within a day of hearing a verse and chorus idea for "Freedom" from the trio, Beyoncé started working on lyrics. "She's a visionary herself, so she started helping us find the direction of the song," Williams said. "She wanted it to be a female anthem, and we wanted to address certain issues."[21]

Songwriting stretched out over months, Williams added, as they polished the second verse to perfection. "It wasn't just like, 'Yeah, take the song,'" she said. "We really crafted it all together."[22] "Freedom" was nominated for Best Rap/Sung Performance at the 2017 Grammy Awards and eventually became a galvanizing anthem for the Black Lives Matter movement. Several years later, "Freedom" also became the theme song for Kamala Harris's 2024 US Presidential campaign.

ALL NIGHT

[SINGLE]

Released: December 6, 2016 (single) / April 23, 2016 (album)
Writers: Henry Allen, André Benjamin, Patrick Brown, Jaramye Daniels, Diplo, Ilsey Juber, Akil King, Beyoncé Knowles, Antwan Patton, Theron Thomas, Timothy Thomas
Producers: Henry Allen, Diplo, Beyoncé Knowles

The denouement of *Lemonade*, "All Night" finds the now-wiser narrator describing how she reconciled with her partner. She finally discovered the real story behind his deception – a revelation that emphasized honesty is the backbone of love – and learns that her support and affection have healing qualities. But the narrator has also discovered that love and pain are connected, and she needed to experience emotional anguish and sorrow to get back to good with her partner. Bluesy guitar twanging, a sample of the warm horns from OutKast's "SpottieOttieDopaliscious" and swaying reggae grooves give "All Night" a delicate feel, which Beyoncé exacerbates with torchy vocals and brisk pre-chorus singing that mimics giving affection. "All Night" ends with shivering strings and Beyoncé declaring that she's missed her partner – as if she's closing the book on a tumultuous chapter and ready to begin again.

Above: Kendrick Lamar and Beyoncé performed "Freedom" together at the 2016 BET Awards.

FORMATION

[SINGLE]

Released: February 6, 2016 (single) / April 23, 2016 (album)
Writers: Aaquil Brown, Khalif Brown, Asheton Hogan,
Beyoncé Knowles, Michael Len Williams II
Producers: Beyoncé Knowles and Mike Will Made It

In February 2016, Beyoncé performed at the Super Bowl 50 Halftime Show with Coldplay and Bruno Mars. She chose to make a striking statement with her solo spotlight, performing the newly released single "Formation". Her dancers wore outfits that nodded to militant political group the Black Panther Party, moving in precise formation to a marching band driving the song's martial rhythms, while Beyoncé's jacket nodded to the military-referencing look Michael Jackson sported at his 1993 Super Bowl halftime performance.

The song itself is a declaration of Black pride, between the music – Beyoncé raps in a laid-back drawl over distinctly Southern trap beats, while New Orleans bounce icon Big Freedia appears on the track – and the lyrics. Building on the theme of her older B-side "Creole", Beyoncé honours her Alabama and Louisiana roots (and Black and Creole heritage) and expresses pride in how this shapes her identity; elsewhere, she notes she always has hot sauce in her purse, a Black Southern tradition.

Like many Beyoncé songs, "Formation" came together piece by piece. Producer PLUSS crafted a beat and passed it to another producer, Mike Will Made It. The latter played the track for rapper Swae Lee as they were "in the middle of the desert", driving to the 2014 Coachella Festival. "And we're just coming up – we just freestyle, you know? – and Swae Lee said, 'Okay, ladies, now let's get in formation,'" Will recalled, adding they recorded it as a voicenote. "I'm like, 'Dog, we got to do that "get in formation" shit.' That could be a hard song for the ladies. Some woman-empowerment shit."[23]

Swae Lee recorded this idea and Will sent it to Beyoncé. Flash forward a few months later: Will was supposed to meet up with NBA star LeBron James and friends in Los Angeles after a basketball game – but fell asleep. Luckily, LeBron and his agent Rich Paul were night owls; Will woke up, started hanging out with them, and happened to meet Jay-Z and Beyoncé. "Formation" came up and Beyoncé mentioned she liked it – so much so that she ended up writing verses and then spending a week with Will in the studio making the song.

Among other things, Beyoncé amplified the empowerment angle, calling on women to mobilize, get things done and otherwise slay all day. That includes herself; in fact, she boasts that she could be the Black Bill Gates. Will was impressed, noting Beyoncé "took this one little idea we came up with on the way to Coachella, put it in a pot, stirred it up, and came with this smash. She takes ideas and puts them with her own ideas, and makes this masterpiece."[24]

Both the Super Bowl appearance and an accompanying music video directed by Melina Matsoukas drew ire for imagery mistaken as being anti-police. In an interview, Beyoncé clarified her stance, noting, "Anyone who perceives my message as anti-police is completely mistaken. I have so much admiration and respect for officers and the families of officers who sacrifice themselves to keep us safe. But let's be clear: I am against police brutality and injustice. Those are two separate things."[25]

"Formation" was nominated for three Grammy Awards, including in the prestigious categories of Record of the Year and Song of the Year, and won for Best Music Video. It became an enduring rallying cry for the Black Lives Matter movement. And its placement as the last song on *Lemonade* was a deliberate move: in retrospect, "Formation" was a bridge to a new phase of her career, one rooted in political activism and advocacy for underrepresented Black artists.

Right: Beyoncé performed an incredible version of "Formation" at the Pepsi Super Bowl 50 Halftime Show.

PINK + WHITE (FRANK OCEAN FEATURING BEYONCÉ)

[ALBUM TRACK]

Released: August 20, 2016
Writers: Christopher Breaux and Pharrell Williams
Producers: Frank Ocean and Pharrell Williams

Unlike Beyoncé's other collaborations with Frank Ocean, her presence isn't very prominent on "Pink + White", a standout on Ocean's influential album *Blonde*. Instead, she contributes heavenly backing vocals to the misty-eyed R&B track, which layers a pensive, circular piano part over watercolour strings. Her beatific voice is a comforting presence, matching the wistful tone of lyrics that detail sweet, hazy memories of spending time with someone who's since passed away. Ocean remembers the small moments that make up their relationship (such as climbing trees and listening to Michael Jackson) and acknowledges the unrelenting passage of time – but in the end embraces the idea that what they experienced remains alive.

PERFECT DUET

[SINGLE]

Released: December 1, 2017 (single)
Writers: Beyoncé Knowles and Ed Sheeran
Producers: Will Hicks and Ed Sheeran

When writing the original version of "Perfect", Ed Sheeran had lofty goals. "It was like, 'I need to write the best love song of my career,'" he said.[26] Luckily, he had excellent inspiration all around, as parts of the song came together while he was hanging out at James Blunt's house in Ibiza listening to (among other things) "March Madness" by the rapper Future. Given the welcoming environment, Sheeran did a rather good job with the original version; "Perfect" ended up reaching No. 4 in the UK in early 2017.

But the song's commercial fortunes improved mightily when Beyoncé hopped on a gentler remix of the song; among other things it spent six weeks at No. 1 in the US and was the UK's Christmas No. 1 in 2017. The secret was her approach: she transformed the song by converting one of the verses so the lyrics came from a female perspective.

Sheeran asked Beyoncé to be on the track as a lark. "It's something I kinda did just to see whether she would say yes," he said. "I just wanted to see what would happen. I can't believe it, to be honest."[27] He was also surprised by their low-key recording session: just him and Beyoncé alone in a New York studio with an engineer.

Opposite and right: Beyoncé's appearance at the Pepsi Super Bowl 50 Halftime Show was stunning (opposite); she and Ed Sheeran performed together onstage at the 2015 Global Citizen Festival (right).

COACHELLA

BEYONCÉ IS NO STRANGER TO PRODUCING MAJOR LIVE SHOWS. SHE HEADLINED SUPER BOWL XLVII, HAS BEEN ON MULTIPLE STADIUM TOURS AND PUT ON A HALFTIME SHOW DUBBED BEYONCÉ BOWL ON CHRISTMAS DAY 2024 AT THE HOUSTON TEXANS FOOTBALL GAME. BUT WHEN SHE BECAME THE FIRST BLACK WOMAN TO HEADLINE COACHELLA OVER TWO WEEKENDS IN APRIL 2018, SHE PUT ON ONE OF THE MOST AUDACIOUS SETS IN THE HISTORY OF THE CALIFORNIA MUSIC FESTIVAL.

"I had a clear vision for Coachella," Beyoncé said. "I was so specific because I'd seen it, I'd heard it, and it was already written inside of me."[28]

Colloquially known as Beychella, the set featured well over 30 songs spanning her entire career, numerous song snippets and interludes, and guest appearances: Beyoncé and Solange joined forces for irrepressible synchronized dances during "Get Me Bodied", while Jay-Z came onstage for an exuberant version of "Déjà Vu". (On weekend two, she also collaborated with J Balvin on "Mi Gente".) For good measure, Destiny's Child also reunited for a brief set featuring "Lose My Breath", "Say My Name" and "Soldier".

However, the show's production was most impressive, between the choreography, musicianship and sheer joy on display. The concert centred on and championed Black history and culture. Historically Black colleges and universities (HBCUs) were in the spotlight throughout the entire set, notably with a massive marching band, drumlines, nods to Black Greek life and stepping. "She re-imagined her entire catalog through the lens of HBCU musical culture by allowing the HBCU band tradition to do what it does best: serve as a distiller of Black popular music," wrote the critic Fredara Mareva Hadley.[29]

She also paid enormous respect to historical figures. Beyoncé's outfits – including her show-opening Egyptian queen look – made multiple references to Nefertiti. "Drunk in Love" incorporated a sample of Nina Simone's "Lilac Wine", while a portion of Malcolm X's 1962 speech "Who Taught You To Hate Yourself?" played during the second act. And right before Destiny's Child, she played Chimamanda Ngozi Adichie's speech from "***Flawless".

Most poignantly of all, Beyoncé sang a beautiful version of the Black national anthem "Lift Every Voice and Sing" right after a galvanizing version of "Freedom". Accordingly, Beyoncé hoped that her Coachella set would encourage students to enroll in HBCUs, as well as foster curiosity. "She said that her hope is that after the show young people would research this culture and see how cool it is," Beyoncé's mom, Tina, wrote on social media, "and young people, Black and white, would listen to 'Lift Every Voice And Sing' and see how amazing the words are for us all and bridge the gap."[30]

Overall, however, the performance cemented Beyoncé's commitment to using her platform to create deeply meaningful art. "I told Beyoncé that I was afraid that the predominately white audience at Coachella would be confused by all of the Black culture and Black college culture, because it was something that they might not get," Tina also wrote, before sharing Beyoncé's response. "She said, 'At this point in my life and my career, I have a responsibility to do what's best for the world and not what is most popular.'"[31]

Above, opposite and overleaf: Beyoncé's 2018 Coachella headlining performance (a.k.a. Beychella) is widely considered one of the greatest festival sets of all time.

13 EVERYTHING IS LOVE

BEYONCE AND JAY-Z ARE A REGULAR PRESENCE ON EACH OTHER'S ALBUMS, BUT UNTIL SURPRISE-RELEASING *EVERYTHING IS LOVE* UNDER THE MONIKER THE CARTERS, THE COUPLE HAD NEVER RELEASED A FULL-LENGTH RECORD TOGETHER. THE COLLABORATION WAS CERTAINLY WORTH THE WAIT; THE ALBUM IS EVERYTHING YOU'D WANT FROM A JOINT BEYONCÉ AND JAY-Z RECORD. THE FORMER ONCE AGAIN PROVES WHAT A GREAT RAPPER SHE IS, AND SOUNDS LOOSER AND MORE UNFETTERED AS A VOCALIST. BY THE TIME THE ALBUM LANDS ON "LOVEHAPPY", IN WHICH THE COUPLE SHUT DOWN GOSSIPS AND DECLARE THAT THEIR MARRIAGE IS IN A GOOD PLACE, IT'S CLEAR BEYONCÉ AND JAY-Z HAVE BROUGHT OUT THE BEST IN EACH OTHER.

THE CARTERS

IF YOU TALLY UP ALL OF BEYONCÉ AND JAY-Z'S COLLABORATIONS AND FEATURES ON EACH OTHER'S ALBUMS, YOU'D HAVE A RATHER IMPRESSIVE COMPILATION. CURIOUSLY, HOWEVER, THE COUPLE TOOK THEIR TIME MAKING A FULL-LENGTH ALBUM TOGETHER. THAT ALL CHANGED ON 16 JUNE 2018: AT A LONDON CONCERT DURING THEIR *ON THE RUN II TOUR*, THE COUPLE PREMIERED A MUSIC VIDEO FOR A NEW SONG CALLED "APESHIT" – AND THEN FLASHED THE WORDS "ALBUM OUT NOW" IN GIGANTIC LETTERS ACROSS THE SCREEN.

The surprise album was *EVERYTHING IS LOVE*, a full-length record released by the couple under the name of The Carters, which was everything you'd want from a Beyoncé and Jay-Z collaboration. "SUMMER" is a hazy 60s soul throwback about a luxurious summer romance; the trap song "FRIENDS" is a rumination on the character of the people in their lives; and on "BLACK EFFECT" the couple exude Black pride and celebrate their individual success, as a psychedelic sample of "Broken Strings" by the Japanese group Flower Travellin' Band floats in the background.

Unsurprisingly, Beyoncé once again proves what a great rapper she is throughout, but as a vocalist she also sounds looser and more unfettered – as evidenced on "713", when she interpolates Dr. Dre and Snoop Dogg's "Still D.R.E.' with slightly different lyrics that shout out Houston. *EVERYTHING IS LOVE* also features samples by artists like Hiatus Kaiyote and Graham Central Station and interpolations of Common and Erykah Badu. And by the time the album lands on "LOVEHAPPY" – as the title implies, it's the couple shutting down any gossip and declaring that their marriage is in a good place – it's clear that Beyoncé and Jay-Z have brought out the best in each other.

EVERYTHING IS LOVE had a lengthy, global genesis that you can trace back to the era encompassing Beyoncé's 2016 album *Lemonade* and Jay-Z's equally personal 2017 album *4:44*. "We were using our art almost like a therapy session," Jay-Z said then. "And we started making music together."[1] However, he noted that Beyoncé finished off *Lemonade* before the collaborative album was done, "so her album came out as opposed to the joint album that we were working on."[2]

Still, when the couple got started on *EVERYTHING IS LOVE* in earnest, they were all-in and worked fast – Beyoncé especially. "She put her mind to the music and did her thing," said Dre, one half of the production duo Cool & Dre, who worked on the album. "If she had a melody idea, she came up with the words. If we had the words, she came up with the melody. She's a beast."[3]

For example, Dre played "SALUD!" for Jay-Z in Los Angeles. "Bey walked in during the middle of me recording the hook and loved it and listened to it about four or five times," Dre recalled. A week later, he was in Miami and received a call from Jay-Z congratulating him: Beyoncé had just recorded "SALUD!"[4] (She liked the song so much that it appeared on the version of the album released exclusively on her website.)

That excellent chemistry led to Cool & Dre heading to France, as Beyoncé and Jay-Z dug seriously into recording while at a stadium in Paris rehearsing for the *On the Run II Tour*. In fact, the couple even went so far as to transform owners' suites at the venue into recording studios, so they could work. "Two days in Paris turned out to be three weeks," Dre says. "It was a life-changing experience."[5]

Once the finish line was near, work on *EVERYTHING IS LOVE* accelerated. "We got to London and knocked out two to three tracks [within] ten days of finishing up the album," Dre said, while noting that the couple was perfecting things up until nearly the last minute. "An hour and a half before showtime [the day of the announcement], Bey and Jay were still cutting up vocals. Three hours later it was released to the world. There are no rules when it comes to those two."[6]

EVERYTHING IS LOVE debuted at No. 2 on the *Billboard* 200 and won a Grammy for Best Urban Contemporary Album. And while Beyoncé and Jay-Z have continued to collaborate, as of early 2025, a second Carters' album has yet to materialize.

Opposite: When Beyoncé and Jay-Z embarked on their On The Run II Tour, the couple took the opportunity to release a new album as The Carters, *EVERYTHING IS LOVE*.

THIS IS REAL LOVE

APESHIT

[SINGLE]

Released: June 16, 2018
Writers: Shawn Carter, Kiari Cephus, Beyoncé Knowles, Quavious Marshall, Pharrell Williams
Producers: The Carters, Stuart White, Pharrell Williams

One of the freshest-sounding tracks on the album, "APESHIT" is top-tier trap about the Carters' musical and material success. Beyoncé and Jay-Z trade off rapping about their lives with playful double entendres and lyrics with an edge; the latter drops a pointed reference about how the Grammys shut him out of a recent ceremony despite earning eight nominations. Quavo and Offset from the rap group Migos contribute their signature *skrt skrt* vocal trills throughout, which adds verve.

Perhaps unsurprisingly, Migos was originally going to record "APESHIT"; in fact, Quavo made this song and the Migos hit "Stir Fry" back to back while in the studio with Pharrell. "I told him I was going to use ['Stir Fry'] for the album," Quavo says. "I totally forgot about 'APESHIT' – I just forgot about it. [But] I knew he was going to do something with it and then he called me one day saying, 'It's out of here' and it definitely was."[7]

Beyoncé and Jay-Z filmed the "APESHIT" music video at the Louvre, in Paris, a location that allowed the couple to create iconic moments; for example, the clip ends with them standing reverently in front of the *Mona Lisa*. The museum capitalized on this increased interest by putting together a 90-minute guided tour featuring 17 pieces of art seen in the clip. At the end of 2018, the Louvre reported a 25 per cent boost in attendance for the year – an increase attributed to the power of the Carters.[8]

Opposite and above: Beyoncé performed "APESHIT" during the Global Citizen Festival: Mandela 100 at FNB Stadium on December 2, 2018 (opposite); she also added the song to the On The Run II Tour setlist (above).

14 THE LION KING

IN 2019, BEYONCÉ PORTRAYED THE LIONESS NALA IN A JON FAVREAU-DIRECTED REMAKE OF *THE LION KING*. NATURALLY, BEYONCÉ ALSO WROTE AND PERFORMED THE LEAD SINGLE FROM THE FILM'S SOUNDTRACK ("SPIRIT") AND EXECUTIVE-PRODUCED A COMPANION ALBUM WITH MUSIC INSPIRED BY THE FILM, *THE LION KING: THE GIFT*. DRIVEN BY THE TALENTS OF AN ALL-STAR ROSTER OF AFRICAN MUSICIANS AND PRODUCERS – AND FEATURING CONTRIBUTIONS FROM KENDRICK LAMAR, 070 SHAKE, JESSIE REYEZ AND BEYONCÉ HERSELF – THIS COLLECTION OF CINEMATIC HIP-HOP AND EBULLIENT AFROPOP REACHED A BROAD GLOBAL AUDIENCE.

THE LION KING: THE GIFT

AS A TEENAGER, DISNEY'S 1994 ANIMATED FILM *THE LION KING* HELD A SPECIAL PLACE IN BEYONCÉ'S HEART. "IT'S SO MUCH NOSTALGIA FOR ME," SHE SAYS. "AND IT'S THE FIRST DISNEY MOVIE THAT BROUGHT ME TO TEARS."[1] A QUARTER OF A CENTURY LATER, BEYONCÉ WAS GIVEN THE OPPORTUNITY TO BE PART OF THE FILM'S LEGACY BY BEING CAST AS THE LIONESS NALA IN A JON FAVREAU-DIRECTED 2019 REMAKE, *THE LION KING*.

In addition to voicing Nala, Beyoncé also wrote and performed the lead single from *The Lion King* soundtrack, "SPIRIT" [*see* page 192] and executive-produced *The Lion King: The Gift*, a companion album with music inspired by the film. In true Beyoncé form, she had a meticulous, ambitious vision for the latter. "This is sonic cinema," she said. "This is a new experience of storytelling. I wanted to do more than find a collection of songs that were inspired by the film. It is a mixture of genres and collaboration that isn't one sound."[2]

Rapper 070 Shake and evocative songwriter Jessie Reyez team up for "SCAR", which mashes together desolate piano, trap beats, distorted vocals and unsettling production. Beyoncé and Kendrick Lamar tap into a minimal hip-hop vibe on "NILE", while the former also explores cinematic atmospheres ("BIGGER", co-written by RAYE); orchestrated balladry ("OTHERSIDE"); and electro-folk with Afrobeats ("FIND YOUR WAY BACK") through solo tracks.

In between this music are interludes featuring actors in the movie, such as James Earl Jones, Childish Gambino and Alfre Woodard. "I wanted to put everyone on their own journey to link the storyline," Beyoncé said. "Each song was written to reflect the film's storytelling that gives the listener a chance to imagine their own imagery, while listening to a new contemporary interpretation."[3]

Above all, however, *The Lion King: The Gift* is "a love letter to Africa", Beyoncé continues. "And I wanted to make sure we found the best talent from Africa, and not just use some of the sounds and did my interpretation of it."[4] To that end, she sought out an impressive roster of African producers and artists.

Nigerian stars Yemi Alade, Tekno and Mr. Eazi teamed up with

Above and opposite: Beyoncé attended the European premiere of *The Lion King* at Odeon Luxe Leicester Square on July 14, 2019 (opposite) and ended up meeting Prince Harry, Duke of Sussex and Meghan Markle, Duchess of Sussex (above).

PANDORA
Disney
THE LION KING

THE
LION KING
WORLD PREMIERE

Ghanaian-American artist Lord Afrixana on the hypnotic Afropop highlight "DON'T JEALOUS ME". Burna Boy chimes in with the laid-back "JA ARA E", while the Malian icon Oumou Sangaré is a crucial voice on another standout, "MOOD 4 EVA", which brings together Beyoncé, Jay-Z and Childish Gambino.

Elsewhere on the album, Beyoncé worked with artists from South Africa (Busiswa, Moonchild Sanelly, DJ Lag) on "MY POWER", while "WATER" features the Cameroon musician Salatiel. And on "ALREADY", she and Major Lazer cook up a fiery dancehall-inspired track with the Ghanian artist Shatta Wale.

"ALREADY" was co-produced by the Ghanaian DJ and producer GuiltyBeatz, who appreciated the ways Beyoncé was introducing African music to a broader audience. "It's just been little things [previously]," he said, and cites Drake and Wizkid's "One Dance" as an example. "Now that Beyoncé released a whole album, this will open the gateway."[5] Fittingly, both GuiltyBeatz and the Nigerian-British producer P2J later worked on *RENAISSANCE*'s standout "MOVE".

Alongside *The Lion King: The Gift*, Beyoncé also spent more than a year working on a companion film and visual album, 2020's *Black Is King*. Collaborating with "a diverse group of very gifted directors and actors and creatives from all over the world," she

wrote, directed and starred in a production that "reimagine[s] the story of *The Lion King*".[6]

Beyoncé decided to make *Black Is King* after learning about the unfair treatment of Solomon Linda, a South African singer whose song "Mbube" was the source material for "The Lion Sleeps Tonight". Linda died in 1962, and it took his family decades to get him a co-writing credit and retroactive compensation. However, Beyoncé discovered that by the release of *The Lion King: The Gift*, Linda's family was no longer receiving any money from Disney for "Mbube" due to the song being out of copyright under South African law.

This fact "really angered her," said Beyoncé's mom Tina. "I remember that day, leaving that studio, and her saying, 'I'm gonna create a film [...] and I'm gonna tell the real story of what happened and show Africa in its regalness and its beauty."[7]

In a lovely full-circle moment, Beyoncé reprised her role of Nala in 2024's *Mufasa: The Lion King* – and Blue Ivy was cast as Princess Kiara, Nala's oldest daughter. On the red carpet and in behind-the-scenes footage, Beyoncé was bursting with pride to see Blue Ivy come into her own.

Opposite, above and left: Beyoncé attended the world premiere of *The Lion King* in 2019 in Hollywood at the Dolby Theatre, and even brought daughter Blue Ivy Carter to the event (opposite); at the European premiere Beyoncé poses with Sir Elton John (left).

SPIRIT

[SINGLE]

Released: July 10, 2019 (single) / July 11, 2019 (album)
Writers: Beyoncé Knowles, Timothy Lee McKenzie, Ilya Salmanzadeh
Producers: Ilya, Beyoncé Knowles, Labrinth

Composer Hans Zimmer was blown away when Beyoncé first played "SPIRIT" for him. "At the last moment, she comes to the room and basically shows us a diamond and goes, 'If you want it, you can have it,'" he said.[8] And while the song was initially intended to go over the film's closing credits, Zimmer – who composed the new *The Lion King* score – offered a much more prominent placement within the film, a scene when Simba goes home to fulfill his royal destiny. "I just thought, 'Hang on. We should try this at this different spot as opposed to the end title,'" he said. "If it's in the body of the movie and it's over a crucial scene, I think it will have much more resonance and weight."[9] Zimmer was right: a majestic vocalist singing in Swahili introduces an expansive, striving gospel song that finds Beyoncé drawing from the entire range of her voice, including her powerful upper register.

BROWN SKIN GIRL (BEYONCÉ, BLUE IVY CARTER, SAINT JHN AND WIZKID)

[SINGLE]

Released: July 23, 2019 (single) / July 11, 2019 (album)
Writers: Stacy Barthe, Shawn Carter, Richard Isong, Beyoncé Knowles, Adio Marchant, Anathi Bhongo Mnyango, Carlos St. John, Michael Uzowuru
Producers: Derek Dixie, Beyoncé Knowles, P2J

"BROWN SKIN GIRL" embodies the collaborative spirit on *The Lion King: The Gift*. Beyoncé enlists daughter Blue Ivy, the Nigerian vocalist Wizkid, and the Guyanese-American rapper SAINt JHN for an empowering song encouraging girls to be proud of their brown skin and other attributes, like their hair. To boost her message, Beyoncé praises the beauty and confidence of other famous dark-skinned women, like model Naomi Campbell, actress Lupita Nyong'o and her girl Kelly Rowland. Above a foundation of shimmying Afrobeats, Beyoncé underscores her point with vocals that go from conversational to firm.

"BROWN SKIN GIRL" won the Ashford & Simpson Songwriter's Award at the 2019 Soul Train Music Awards. But Beyoncé was even more proud of its real-life ripples. "When I see fathers singing 'Brown Skin Girl' to their daughters, to know that my daughter can have the same opportunities and feel confident and feel like she doesn't have to take her braids down, she can comb her Afro out, she can glisten in her brown skin," she said. "That's why I make music."[10]

Right and opposite: Beyoncé's costumes have only become more elaborate as her career's progressed, as evidenced by her looks at a January 2023 event where (among other songs) she performed "BROWN SKIN GIRL".

BLACK PARADE

[SINGLE]

Released: June 19, 2020 (single) / July 31, 2020 (album)
Writers: Denisia Andrews, Shawn Carter, Brittany Coney, Derek Dixie, Akil King, Beyoncé Knowles, Kimberly Krysiuk, Rickie Tice, Paramount on Parade
Producers: Derek Dixie and Beyoncé Knowles

During the spring and summer of 2020, protests against police brutality and racial injustice sprang up globally after police officers murdered George Floyd in Minneapolis and killed Breonna Taylor in Louisville, Kentucky. In response to their deaths, Beyoncé also took additional direct action. Via social media, she encouraged fans to contact organizations who were seeking justice for George Floyd and subsequently penned an open letter to Kentucky's attorney general asking for justice for Breonna Taylor.

Against this backdrop, Beyoncé deliberately released a new song, "BLACK PARADE", on Juneteenth (19 June), a day that commemorates when America abolished slavery. The song "exists to give a much-needed boost to a community that has been fighting for civil and equal rights in the world for centuries," said co-producer Derek Dixie.[11]

Accordingly, it's an anthem of Black pride where Beyoncé embraces her Southern roots and upbringing, as well as African heritage, with exquisite lyrical specificity. She references the Yoruba goddesses Oshun and Yemaya; highlights Black icons she admires, like Curtis Mayfield and Malcolm X; and encourages people to lift a raised fist, in a nod to Black Power.

The song won a Grammy Award for Best R&B Performance, giving Beyoncé the most Grammy wins of all time by a female artist or any vocalist. "As an artist, I believe it's my job and all of our jobs to reflect the times," she said while accepting the award. "It's been such a difficult time, so I wanted to uplift, encourage, celebrate all of the beautiful Black queens and kings that continue to inspire me and inspire the whole world."[12]

Above and opposite: Beyoncé always gets by with a little help from her friends during concerts (above); at Beychella – her 2018 Coachella headlining set – Beyoncé performed with guests such as J Balvin (opposite).

OTHER SONGS

POST-*LEMONADE*, BEYONCÉ CONSISTENTLY STAYED ON THE POP CHARTS THANKS TO HIGH-PROFILE COLLABORATIONS. HER BIGGEST HIT CAME IN 2017, WHEN SHE HOPPED ON A REMIX OF "MI GENTE" BY J BALVIN AND WILLY WILLIAM: THE TUNE REACHED NO. 3 ON THE *BILLBOARD* HOT 100 AND SPENT A WHOPPING 12 WEEKS AT NO. 1 ON THE HOT LATIN SONGS CHART.

"Mi Gente" – itself a remake of "Voodoo Song" by Willy William – was already a massive global hit in 2017. But Balvin wanted to extend its hot streak by commissioning some remixes for the song. Naturally, his top choice was Beyoncé – and, as it turns out, she was happy to oblige because (among other things) then-five-year-old Blue Ivy was a fan of the song. Beyoncé sang in flawless Spanish and English and (for good measure) ensured Blue Ivy had a chance to hop onto the song as well for a line.

In the song's aftermath, Beyoncé donated proceeds to charities helping with hurricane and earthquake relief – and she invited J Balvin onstage to perform the song with her at Coachella 2018. "The power of the music goes beyond any language and any strategy," he said. "I am beyond grateful to have the Queen B join us. It's a dream come true."[13]

Elsewhere, three of Beyoncé's other featured collaborations involved both DJ Khaled and Jay-Z. This started with 2017's "Shining", which includes a prominent sample of 2013's "Dionne" by Osunlade; that song in turn is built on a sample of Dionne Warwick's "Walk the Way You Talk". The following year, 2018's wary "Top Off", which also featured Future, reached the US top 40. And 2021's laid-back "Sorry Not Sorry" gathered Nas, James Fauntleroy and a somewhat-sneaky Bey appearance; she was credited as Harmonies on the Hive.

Eminem and Beyoncé also had a global hit with the 2017 duet "Walk on Water", a spare piano ballad driven by a Beyoncé-sung hook written by Skylar Grey. She also had a chance to stretch out on the moody 2021 Drake song "Can I", singing the titular phrase repeatedly.

Jay-Z and Beyoncé also struck gold again with 2018's "Family Feud": driven by a sample of a Clark Sisters' gospel song, the tune was nominated for a Grammy for Best Rap/Sung Performance. In 2021, she was one of the vocalists contributing to "Say Her Name (Hell You Talmbout)", a powerful Janelle Monáe-helmed song raising awareness for Black women who had died due to the police in the US.

And the following year, Beyoncé teamed up with the Isley Brothers for a lush remake of "Make Me Say It Again, Girl" that found great success on the US R&B charts; in fact, it hit No. 1 on the US Adult R&B Songs chart.

SAVAGE REMIX (MEGAN THEE STALLION FEATURING BEYONCÉ)

[SINGLE]

Released: April 29, 2020
Writers: Shawn Carter, Brittany Hazzard, Beyonce Knowles, Derrick Milano, Terius "The-Dream" Nash, Megan Pete, Bobby Session Jr., Jordan Thorpe
Producer: J. White Did It

Megan Thee Stallion's "Savage" was already one of the biggest hits of early 2020, thanks to a viral TikTok dance and lyrics in which the rapper lists off (and celebrates) all of her contradictions. "'Savage' is just like an extension of this real hot girl shit that I be talking about," Megan said, noting the lyrics are based on her own life. "I had to put it in a song."[14] And then, much to the Houston rapper's shock and disbelief, her idol Beyoncé decided she wanted to remix the song – and hopped on the track to spit bars, matching Megan line for line. "You grow up and you friggin' watch Destiny's Child, and you go to the [Houston] Rodeo to see them perform," Megan Thee Stallion said. "You don't grow up and think you're gonna meet Be-*yon*-cé!"[15] Proceeds from this new collaboration were donated to the Houston nonprofit Bread Of Life, which provided aid to families during the COVID-19 pandemic. The original song was sitting at No. 14 on the *Billboard* Hot 100 when the remix dropped, but Beyoncé's presence had a galvanizing effect: "Savage Remix" ended up ascending to No. 1 on the chart and won a Grammy for Best Rap Performance.

BEFORE I LET GO

[SINGLE]

Released: April 17, 2019
Songwriters: Frankie Beverly, Larry Blackmon, Tomi Jenkins, Beyoncé Knowles, Jerome Temple
Producer: Frankie Beverly, Tay Keith, Beyoncé Knowles

The credits for the 2019 documentary concert film, *Homecoming: A Film by Beyoncé*, show Beyoncé covering Maze featuring Frankie Beverly's 1981 R&B hit "Before I Let Go". Her version tones down the easygoing vibe of the original in favour of the marching band horns heard throughout her Coachella performance; in addition, she weaves in an upbeat sample of DJ Jubilee's New Orleans bounce classic "Get Ready, Ready!" and elements from Cameo's 1980s electro classic "Candy".

As it turns out, Beyoncé was sentimental about the song *and* Maze. She had fond memories of seeing the group at the Houston Livestock Show and Rodeo. "It was like the biggest family picnic," she said. "There was laughter and music everywhere and everyone dressed in their Texas finest."[16] (She herself had "pink cowboy boots that you'd think were glued to my feet."[17]) Years later, Beverly also recalled meeting Beyoncé at a Houston Rodeo show – and noted he loved her cover. "She didn't make a big deal out of doing this song, and that's just the way she works," he said. "I love the way she does her thing."[18]

Above and opposite: Houston, represent! Beyoncé and Megan Thee Stallion accept the Best Rap Performance award for "Savage" at the 63rd Annual Grammy Awards (above). During the Academy Awards, Beyoncé performed "Be Alive," a tune from 2021's *King Richard* nominated for Best Original Song (opposite).

BE ALIVE

[SINGLE]

Released: November 12, 2021
Writers: Dixson and Beyoncé Knowles
Producers: Dixson and Beyoncé Knowles

With its thumping beats and lattice-like vocal harmonies, "Be Alive" is a triumphant song bursting with pride over a family's hard-fought victory. It's an appropriate theme song for the 2021 film *King Richard,* which is about Richard Williams, father of the tennis legends Venus and Serena Williams. Will Smith, who portrays the family patriarch, said Beyoncé was moved to create "Be Alive" after an early viewing of the film.[19] She quickly co-wrote the song with a musician named Dixson, who said he took inspiration from his own family situation, like the fact that he grew up around strong women. After finishing the demo, Dixson was nervous to play the song for Beyoncé, but she loved it. "The reaction was so positive," he said. "I felt encouraged to keep digging and get it really right."[20] His hard work paid off: "Be Alive" received multiple prestigious nominations, including the Golden Globe for Best Original Song and an Oscar for Best Original Song, and eventually won a Hollywood Critics Association Award.

15 RENAISSANCE

WHEN BEYONCÉ RELEASED *RENAISSANCE*, SHE REVEALED THAT IT WAS THE FIRST INSTALLMENT OF A PLANNED THREE-ALBUM TRILOGY. SHE COULDN'T HAVE STARTED ON A HIGHER NOTE: A FULL-ON DANCE ALBUM BRIMMING WITH LIFE-AFFIRMING ELECTRONIC MUSIC THAT WAS BOTH RETRO AND FUTURISTIC, *RENAISSANCE* CELEBRATED HOUSE MUSIC'S BLACK AND QUEER ROOTS. BEYONCÉ WORKED WITH BLACK, QUEER AND TRANS MUSICIANS; SAMPLED AND INTERPOLATED CLUB MUSIC TOUCHSTONES; AND CENTRED THE VOICES, PERSPECTIVES AND CULTURE OF THE QUEER COMMUNITY. *RENAISSANCE* WAS A GLOBAL NO. 1 HIT – AND WHEN IT EARNED A GRAMMY FOR BEST DANCE/ELECTRONIC MUSIC ALBUM, BEYONCÉ HAD OFFICIALLY WON THE MOST GRAMMYS OF ANY ARTIST IN HISTORY.

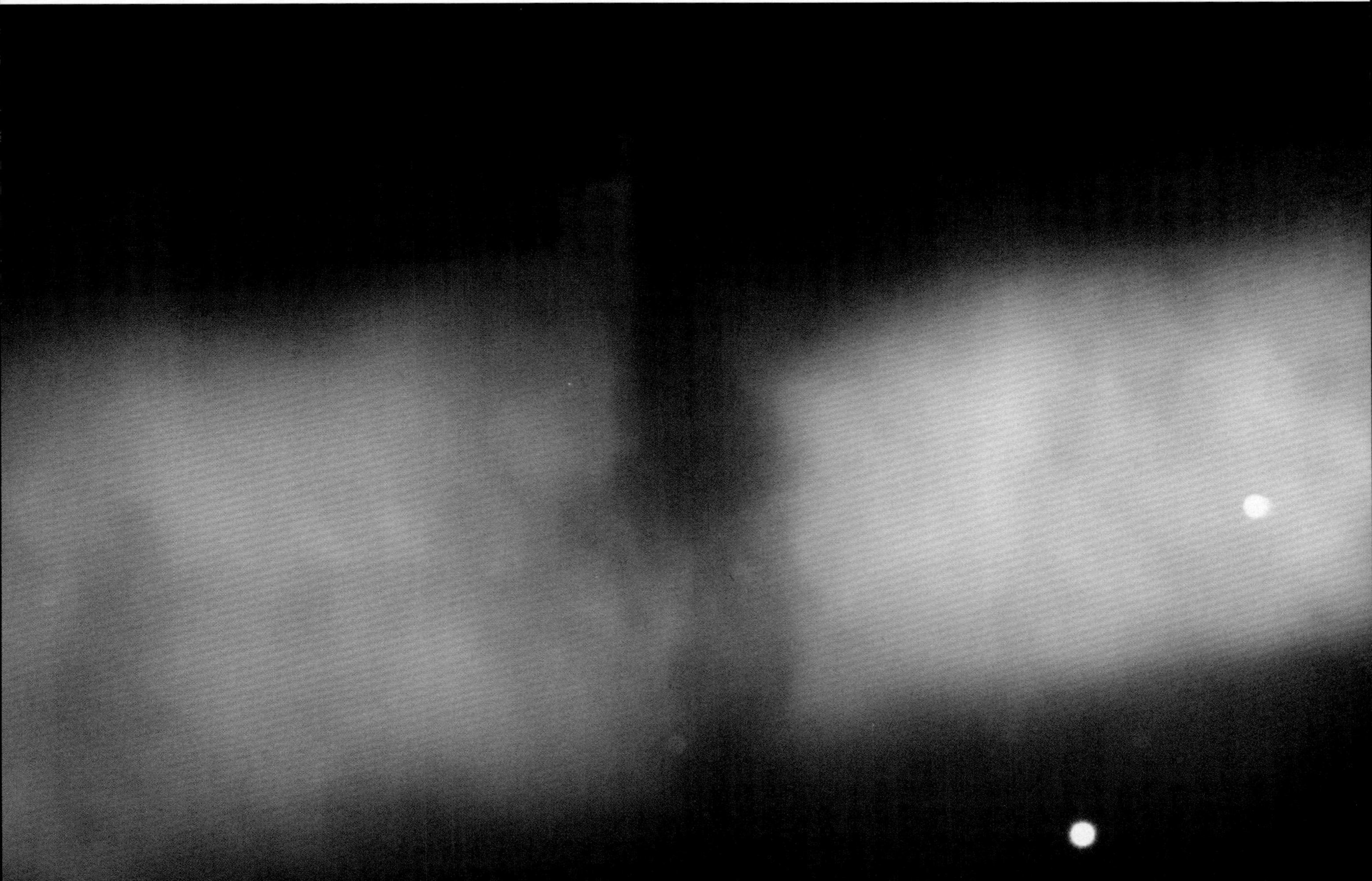

I'M THAT GIRL

[ALBUM TRACK]

Released: July 29, 2022 (album)
Writers: Michael Dean, Kelman Duran, Terius "The-Dream" Gesteelde-Diamant, Beyoncé Knowles, Andrea Summers, Tommy Wright III
Producers: Jameil Aossey, Mike Dean, Kelman Duran, Beyoncé Knowles, Symbolyc One, Stuart White

In a summer 2021 magazine cover essay, Beyoncé shared that she had been in the studio for a year and a half working on music. "I feel a renaissance emerging, and I want to be part of nurturing that escape in any way possible," she said.[1] Little did we know then that this quote was an Easter egg: this music would emerge a year later as *RENAISSANCE*, the first album in a planned three-album trilogy.

The reggaeton-influenced lead-off track, "I'M THAT GIRL" – a swaggering sonic mélange of dembow beats, Beyoncé's siren-like vocals and harmonies and surging synthesizers – clearly states that she derives her power and status from her own hard work and talent, *not* because of her marriage to Jay-Z or things like fancy jewellery. Moreover, Beyoncé isn't selfish with her platform; instead, she's secure enough to spread the wealth and love around and ensure other people in her orbit have a chance to benefit from her success.

"I'M THAT GIRL" demonstrates this idea in a rather poignant way: by prominently including an artist who died at a young age. A defiant declaration by the late Memphis rapper Princess Loko repeats underneath the surface like a news ticker; co-producer Kelman Duran sampled the snippet from Tommy Wright III's 1994 track "Still Pimpin".[2]

Opposite: Beyoncé rocked plenty of silver and glitter during the RENAISSANCE WORLD TOUR at MetLife Stadium on July 29, 2023.

COZY

[ALBUM TRACK]

Released: July 29, 2022
Writers: Nija Charles, Mike Dean, Terius "The-Dream" Gesteelde-Diamant, Dave Giles II, Curtis Alan Jones, Beyoncé Knowles, Christopher Lawrence Penny, Honey Redmond, Corece Smith, Luke Francis Matthew Solomon
Producers: Mike Dean, Honey Dijon, Beyoncé Knowles, Christopher Lawrence Penny, Luke Francis Matthew Solomon

Propelled by twirling geometric beats, the loose-limbed, throwback, house music anthem "COZY" praises anyone who's weathered challenging times and emerged on the other side stronger, more confident and comfortable in their skin. More specifically, Beyoncé revels in her Blackness and warns people not to disturb her peace – *or* the peace of anyone else who's embracing their true selves. Fittingly, the lyrics of "COZY" champion the expansive rainbow of Daniel Quasar's Pride Progress Flag, which was designed to be a more inclusive symbol for the LGBTQIA+ community.

Chicago house music legend Green Velvet co-wrote "COZY", as did the Grammy-winning trailblazing trans DJ and producer Honey Dijon. The latter also sampled the autobiographical 2020 video "B**ch, I'm Black" by TS Madison – specifically moments where Madison, a transgender actress and *RuPaul's Drag Race* judge, proclaims her Blackness. "When you listen to those lyrics, you know [Beyoncé] really sat and watched the whole video," she says. "So much of the lyrics, so much of the things she is talking about...if you know anything about my life and my story you know it runs parallel."[3]

Madison's take on "COZY" also aligns with *RENAISSANCE*'s inclusive themes. "My interpretation of it, it speaks specifically of Black trans women," she says. "It's a song about self-determination."[4] "COZY" reached No. 30 on the *Billboard* Hot 100, making Madison and Honey Dijon the first Black trans women to earn a top 40 hit on that chart.

ALIEN SUPERSTAR

[ALBUM TRACK]

Released: July 29, 2022
Writers: Denisia "@Blu_June" Andrews For @Novawav, Danielle Balbuena, Atia Boggs P/K/A Ink, David Debrandon Brown, S. Carter, Brittany "@Chi_Coney" Coney For @Novawav, Kim Cooper, Levar Coppin, Saliou Diagne, Mike Dean, Christopher Abbott Bernard Fairbrass, Richard Peter John Fairbrass, JDave Hamelin, John Michael Holiday, Leven Kali, Beyoncé Knowles, Robert Francis Anthony Manzoli, Timothy Lee McKenzie, Christopher Lawrence Penny, Peter Rauhofer, Honey Redmond, Luke Francis Matthew Solomon, Barbara Ann Teer, Rami Yacoub
Producers: Mike Dean, Honey Dijon, Terius "The-Dream" Gesteelde-Diamant, Beyoncé Knowles, Nova Wav, Chris Penny, Luke Solomon

R*ENAISSANCE*'s songs often felt like joyous sonic collages of dance and electronic music, as if each tune was its own crate-digging expedition. On "ALIEN SUPERSTAR", Beyoncé interpolated lyrics from Right Said Fred's "I'm Too Sexy"; included a warning message from Foremost Poets' late 1990s song "Moonraker"; and ends the song with a sample of Barbara Ann Teer's "Black Theater" recorded in 1973.

This collaging is a hallmark of Beyoncé's artistic process, says producer Lucky Daye. "She likes to take a lot of art and bring it into one thing. She understands [that] you take the whiteboard – you take all the colors and throw them on the board. And then you make the picture."[5] Daye worked on the futuristic discotheque-filler "ALIEN SUPERSTAR," which takes inspiration from '80s synth-funk and vintage house music; in fact, its cry of "unique!" is sampled from Danube Dance's early 1990s club cut of the same name. Lyrically, "ALIEN SUPERSTAR" is a twist on Beyoncé's empowerment anthems: she champions the unicorns who embrace their individuality (and every facet of their personality) and dare to be different.

Honey Dijon also co-produced "Alien Superstar", an experience that gave her a chance to highlight her Chicago house music roots, as she notes Beyoncé "wanted to make this a dance record and she wanted to go to the true source of Chicago house music." This exercise made her think of the artists who "laid the groundwork for me to be able to express that," like Frankie Knuckles, Ron Hardy and Derrick Carter. "For Beyoncé to acknowledge that was just so gratifying, and it made me proud."[6]

CUFF IT

[SINGLE]

Released: October 4, 2022 (US radio single) / July 29, 2022 (album)
Songwriters: Denisia "@Blu_June" Andrews For @Novawav, Mary Christine Brockert, Brittany "@Chi_Coney" Coney For @Novawav, Beyoncé Knowles, Allen McGrier, Terius "The-Dream" Gesteelde-Diamant, Morten Ristorp, Nile Rodgers, Raphael Saadiq
Producers: Beyoncé Knowles, Nova Wav, Rissi, Raphael Saadiq, The-Dream
Select Alternate Versions: A Cappella, Explicit Remix, Wetter Remix

The retro-fabulous "Cuff It" is a classic party song about downing a few drinks, letting the music (and perhaps other substances) take you higher, and getting ecstatic with your sweetheart. Buoyed by a sample of Teena Marie's 1988 R&B hit "Ooo La La La", the music is a sizzling slab of disco-funk with sleek grooves, piquant horns and strings, and honey-sweet harmonies.

Co-producer/co-songwriter Raphael Saadiq revealed that "Cuff It" was originally a demo earmarked for his R&B group Tony! Toni! Toné! However, he thought it might work better for Beyoncé. "She's one of those people where if she's feeling it, she's going 100 percent in," he noted. "I said, 'It's going to move people. It's going to work, I'm telling you.'"[7] Saadiq adds that he heard one of Beyoncé's frequent collaborators, The-Dream, "eventually found" the music he passed over and brought it to the forefront. "He was like, 'What is that?!'" Saadiq says. "I already knew it was one of them joints."[8]

"Cuff It" also features the unmistakable imprint of guitarist/producer Nile Rodgers, who said being asked to play on the tune "was the most organic thing that ever happened to me. I heard the song and I just said 'I wanna play on that. Right now.'"[9] Rodgers was so into the music and vibe that he nailed his part in one take. "I never even got, 'Well, Nile, maybe you should do this, maybe you should do that?'" he added. "It was just what I felt in my heart."[10] Given all this passion behind the song, it's no surprise "Cuff It" spent two weeks at No. 1 on *Billboard*'s R&B/Hip-Hop Airplay chart and nabbed a Grammy for Best R&B Song.

ENERGY (FEATURING BEAM)

[ALBUM TRACK]

Released: July 29, 2022
Writers: Denisia "@Blu_June" Andrews For @Novawav, Mary Christine Brockhert, Brittany "@Chi_Coney" Coney For @Novawav, Almando Cresso, Jordan Douglas, Terius "The-Dream" Gesteelde-Diamant, Beyoncé Knowles, Tizita Makuria, Allen Henry Mc Grier, Sonny Moore, Adam James Pigott, Freddie Ross, Tyshane Thompson
Producers: Al Cres, BEAM, Beyoncé Knowles, Nova Wav, Skrillex

The first part of *RENAISSANCE* pays tribute to 1970s disco LPs where artists mixed an entire side into one seamless track for maximum dancefloor grooves. Case in point: the end of "ENERGY" starts weaving in Big Freedia's "Explode", a crucial part of "BREAK MY SOUL", making the segue between the two tracks akin to a nonstop DJ mix. It's the perfect capper for the kaleidoscopic, Afrobeat-influenced song. Although clocking in at less than two minutes, "ENERGY" packs a punch, courtesy of bouncy, elastic beats and laid-back verses from the Grammy-nominated Jamaican rapper BEAM; the latter also contributes drums and production, as does EDM superstar Skrillex. Beyoncé herself gets into the upbeat vibe, singing a line interpolating Teena Marie's "Ooo La La La"; playfully embracing onomatopoeia by imitating a camera flash and sounding out an ellipsis; and making a sly reference to staying in line to vote out then-President Donald Trump. The original version of "ENERGY" interpolated Kelis' "Milkshake". However, the rapper wasn't contacted about the inclusion in advance and was upset to hear herself on the track; as a result, Beyoncé removed the reference.

Opposite: Beyoncé picked up a Grammy for Best R&B Song for "CUFF IT" in February 2023.

BREAK MY SOUL

[SINGLE]

Released: June 20, 2022 (single) / July 29, 2022 (album)
Writers: George Allen, S. Carter, Terius "The-Dream" Gesteelde-Diamant, Beyoncé Knowles, Fred Craig McFarlane, Adam James Pigott, Freddie Ross, Christopher A. Stewart
Producers: Terius "The-Dream" Gesteelde-Diamant, Jens Christian Isaken, Beyoncé Knowles, Christopher A. "Tricky" Stewart
Select Alternate Versions: Nita Aviance Club Mix, Honey Dijon Remix, The Queens Remix with Madonna, will.i.am Remix

When Beyoncé released *RENAISSANCE*, she issued a heartfelt message thanking everyone integral to the recording process. Among the people she acknowledged was her late Uncle Jonny, the "most fabulous gay man, who helped raise me and my sister"[11] who "was my godmother and the first person to expose me to a lot of the music and culture that serve as inspiration for this album."[12]

Several years before, Beyoncé also referenced her Uncle Jonny's bravery when she and Jay-Z received the Vanguard Award at the 2019 GLAAD Media Awards, which recognized the couple's LGBTQ allyship and support. "Witnessing his battle with HIV was one of the most painful experiences I've ever lived," she said. "I'm hopeful that his struggle served to open pathways for other young people to live more freely. LGBTQI rights are human rights."[13]

When creating *RENAISSANCE*, Beyoncé kept the memory of her uncle at the forefront of her music and lyrics. Look no further than the dancefloor anthem "Break My Soul", which celebrates resilience in the face of adversity (such as a stressful job) and the queer liberation at the heart of house music. The song's narrator rediscovers their sense of self by living life and seeking out happiness on their own terms. Throughout, Beyoncé defiantly repeats that "you" won't crush her soul; by leaving the subject of "you" open to interpretation, she makes the inner joy of "Break My Soul" universal.

Stacked piano and the galvanizing vocals from "Explode" by the New Orleans bounce artist Big Freedia keep the music revved up. But "Break My Soul" explodes thanks to its sample of the percolating electrobeats from Robin S.'s "Show Me Love". A global smash in the early 1990s, the dance hit reached the top 10 in both the US and UK pop charts and topped the American dance club charts.

Robin wasn't aware of the sample until after "BREAK MY SOUL" was released –her son discovered it when the song started trending – but she was thrilled and expressed her appreciation to Beyoncé. "Thank you so much for giving me my flowers while I'm still alive," she said. "I am honored and I'm excited to see what else can happen."[14]

"Break My Soul" spent two weeks at No. 1 on the *Billboard* Hot 100 and also topped the US dance and R&B charts on the way to winning a Grammy for Best Dance/Electronic Recording. A remix of the song mashed up with Madonna's "Vogue" also became a centerpiece of the *Renaissance World Tour*.

Beyoncé and her dancers strutted down the stage catwalk paying tribute to voguing, a style of dance that originated in Harlem within the Black and Latino queer communities. She then shouted out the Black peers and innovators who inspired her, including (to name a few) Grace Jones, Bessie Smith, Sister Rosetta Tharpe, Nina Simone, Roberta Flack, Ms. Lauryn Hill, Kelly Rowland and Solange.

The gesture fitted the humble gratitude Beyoncé expressed during this era. "Thank you to all of the pioneers who originate culture, to all of the fallen angels whose contributions have gone unrecognized for far too long," she wrote upon *RENAISSANCE*'s release. "This is a celebration for you."[15]

Left and opposite: Beyoncé opened the July 23, 2023, RENAISSANCE WORLD TOUR concert at MetLife Stadium wearing this beautiful black-and-white dress (left); a poster for her 2023 concert film *Renaissance: A Film by Beyoncé*.

RENAISSANCE
a film by beyoncé

CHURCH GIRL

[ALBUM TRACK]

Released: July 29, 2022
Writers: James Brown, Terius "The-Dream" Gesteelde-Diamant, Orville Erwin Hall, Beyoncé Knowles, Ralph Macdonald, Dion Lamont Norman, Derrick Robert Ordogne, Jimi Stephen Payton, Phillip Glen Price, William Salter, Elbernita Clark Terrell, Ernest "No I.D." Wilson
Producers: Terius "The-Dream" Gesteelde-Diamant, Beyoncé Knowles, No I.D., Stuart White

After a dance-heavy start, *RENAISSANCE* momentarily catches its breath with the intro to "CHURCH GIRL", which features a lush sample from gospel group the Clark Sisters. But from there, the song adopts more aggressive grooves that incorporate nods to jazz, funk, hip-hop and New Orleans bounce music – the perfect soundtrack for a song about reconciling sexual freedom and your faith. "CHURCH GIRL" began with a hang session between producer No I.D. and Jay-Z; the two had previously collaborated on the Grammy-nominated "Family Feud", which also featured Beyoncé. "I was at his house one day, and I had some equipment with me, and I just started making a beat," No I.D. recalled. "And he was rapping to it; it was for him."[16] No I.D. then "literally forgot about it" – until he received a phone call that Beyoncé was interested in the track instead. "Jay jokingly tells me, 'Man, she stole my beat. She was like, "Remember that idea in the computer that you didn't finish?"'"[17] Jay-Z's loss was clearly Beyoncé's gain.

PLASTIC OFF THE SOFA

[ALBUM TRACK]

Released: July 29, 2022
Writers: Sydney Bennett, Sabrina Claudio, Nick Green, Beyoncé Knowles, Patrick Paige II
Producers: Leven Kali, Beyoncé Knowles, Syd

RENAISSANCE cools things down even more with "PLASTIC OFF THE SOFA". A chill neo-soul/R&B number co-written and co-produced by Syd from Odd Future and the Internet, the song conjures both the halcyon days of Destiny's Child and Beyoncé's early solo career. In a breathy voice full of honeyed trills and tender flourishes, she reassures a partner (presumably Jay-Z) that her love runs deep because it's them against the world. Beyoncé shares how much she appreciates the sweet things he does (such as be a good listener, steal an extra kiss, freely expressing his emotions) and giggles after flirtatiously saying that she's the cool one in their relationship. In the end, Beyoncé affirms she finds solace in their family – and she still desires her boo. "PLASTIC OFF THE SOFA" won a Grammy for Best Traditional R&B Performance.

Opposite and below: The breadth and depth of the outfits Beyoncé wore on each date of the RENAISSANCE WORLD TOUR (opposite: London; below, Stockholm) was impressive.

VIRGO'S GROOVE

[SINGLE]

Released: June 2, 2023 (Italy single) / July 29, 2022 (album)
Writers: Denisia "@Blu_June" Andrews For @Novawav, Brittany "@Chi_Coney" Coney For @Novawav, Dustin Dab Bowie, Darius Dixson, Jocelyn Donald, Solomon Fagenson Cole, Leven Kali, Beyoncé Knowles, Daniel Memmi, Jesse Wilson
Producers: Terius "The-Dream" Gesteelde-Diamant, Leven Kali, Beyoncé Knowles

"Virgo's Groove" grew out of a Houston R&B-flavoured demo the Memphis songwriter Jozzy co-wrote called "Right Here, Right Now". Beyoncé "turned that s–t into a masterpiece," Jozzy said. "We had a great song, but the way she colored it ... it's crazy."[18] This didn't happen overnight, of course. Leven Kali – who worked on the track with his high school friends and tight musical collaborators Daniel Memmi and Solomon Cole – said it was a "two- to three-year process" getting the song finished. "It took a long time to really make it work in the context of the project as a whole."[19]

Luckily, Kali said the trio and Beyoncé's team were all on the same wavelength ("We were all thinking like: North Star, funk, positivity, love, dance and groovy music") and the chemistry he has with Memmi and Cole informed the song's harmonies and bassline. "When we all work together, we kind of come in with this fantasy of house, funk, R&B and jazz being fused together," Kali says. "The background vocals and the bassline is something that for me is like a signature."[20]

MOVE (FEATURING GRACE JONES AND TEMS)

[ALBUM TRACK]

Released: July 29, 2022 (album)
Writers: Denisia "@Blu_June" Andrews For @Novawav, Ronald Banful, Brittany "@Chi_Coney" Coney For @Novawav, Beyoncé Knowles, Ariowa Irosogie, Richard Isong, Temilade Openiyi
Producers: Terius "The-Dream" Gesteelde-Diamant, GuiltyBeatz, Beyoncé Knowles, Melo-X, P2J, Stuart White

A sleek, funky ode to women claiming their space on the dancefloor, "MOVE" is a summit of icons: the dancehall- and Afrobeat-influenced song features vocal contributions from the legendary musical iconoclast Grace Jones. Although she and Beyoncé had met before – they connected via Jones' brother's church – Jones had to be persuaded to collaborate. "I remember saying, 'Beyoncé, you know I don't usually do these kinds of things,'' she said. "I'm a born-alone, die-alone, sing-alone kind of girl."[21] Nevertheless, Jones' conditions for appearing on the track were reasonable: she wanted to sound like herself and not have her voice altered by Auto-Tune. To ensure this happened, she collaborated closely with the song's mixer. "I'd say, 'Okay, that part doesn't sound like me,' and 'This part sounds like me,'' Jones said. "I'd say, 'Don't do anything much, don't tweak my vocals.'"[22] If this wasn't exciting enough, "MOVE" features the Nigerian singer-songwriter Tems and producers P2J and GuiltyBeatz; the latter two also worked on 2019's *The Lion King: The Gift*.

Opposite and right: Beyoncé went for full-on disco glam at the September 2023 stop of the RENAISSANCE WORLD TOUR in Inglewood, California (opposite) and had a softer look during the ABC telecast of the Oscars in March 2022 (right).

HEATED

[ALBUM TRACK]

Released: July 29, 2022
Writers: Denisia "@Blu_June" Andrews For @Novawav, Brittany "@Chi_Coney" Coney For @Novawav, Aubrey Drake Graham, Beyoncé Knowles, Ricky Lawson, Oliver Rodigan, Matthew Samuels, Sean Seaton, Jahaan Sweet, Rupert Thomas, Jr.
Producers: Boi 1da For 1da Productions, Cadenza, Kelman Duran, Harry Edwards, Beyoncé Knowles, Neenyo, Jahaan Sweet, Sevn Thomas, Stuart White

In a sense, "HEATED" picks up where "MOVE" left off, with rousing Afrobeats paired to lyrics teeming with mentions of luxury brands (such as Hermès, Chanel, Tiffany) and declarations about needing to chill out. (Perhaps after the exuberant clubbing session of "MOVE"?) Fittingly, however, the song amps up the vocal sweetness, as a dreamy sample from Travis Garland's "Where To Land" bubbles under the surface, cushioning Beyoncé's honey-smooth vocals.

Beyoncé also lovingly references her Uncle Jonny throughout the song, including in the impressive outro: embracing the rapid-fire rhythmic delivery of a ballroom emcee, she unleashes a note-perfect stream-of-consciousness commentary that's jaw-dropping in its precision and ferocity.

Originally, one of the lines in "HEATED" featured the word "spaz", which is considered an ableist slur offensive to the disability community. After receiving criticism, Beyoncé changed the line, with a rep noting, "The word, not used intentionally in a harmful way, will be replaced."[23]

THIQUE

[ALBUM TRACK]

Released: July 29, 2022
Writers: Atia Boggs P/K/A Ink, Beyoncé Knowles, Julian Mason, Cherdericka Nichols, Jabbar Stevens
Producers: Hit-Boy, Ink, Beyoncé Knowles, LilJuMadeDaBeat, Stuart White

"THIQUE" is a spicy jam that starts with Beyoncé touting the ever-growing size of her wealth (and physical assets) above a trap-inspired seduction beat by Megan Thee Stallion collaborator LilJuMadeDaBeat. The verses, meanwhile, continue to revel in carnal pleasures and references to celebratory things (such as the 1980s' and 1990s' Atlanta spring break party Freaknik, the carefree vibe of Miami bass music, the high-end restaurant Mastro's) above a writhing house music beat.

"THIQUE" is an example of good things coming to those who wait; in fact, producer Hit-Boy revealed he been holding on to the beat for eight years before it surfaced in 2022. "That's the way the game goes sometimes," he said. "I've had a lot of ups and downs in the game and certain people will perceive like, 'Oh, where's Hit-Boy been? What's Hit-Boy been doing?'"[24] As it turns out, he and Beyoncé were playing three-dimensional chess, as the sexy "THIQUE" sounds perfect on *RENAISSANCE*. Lucky for us, Hit-Boy promises there might be more like this in his vault as well: "I'm sitting on stuff like 'THIQUE' that just hasn't materialized yet. Y'all don't even know how ahead I really am ... I've been holding on to legendary stuff, and there's plenty more."[25]

ALL UP IN YOUR MIND

[ALBUM TRACK]

Released: July 29, 2022
Writers: Jameil Aossey, Alexander Guy Cook, Mike Dean, Larry Griffin Jr., Beyoncé Knowles, Cherdericka Nichols, Jabbar Stevens, Michael Tucker
Producers: Jameil Aossey, BAH, BloodPop, A.G. Cook, Mike Dean, Terius "The-Dream" Gesteelde-Diamant, Beyoncé Knowles, S1A0

"THIQUE" ends with an ethereal R&B outro that luxuriates in the mental and physical connections between two people in love. That brief segment leads directly into "ALL UP IN YOUR MIND", which puts a twist on the mind-meld theme: possessive desire. The narrator is obsessed with someone else and is working to ingratiate herself into his world, claiming she'll do anything to get her way and make him crave her. "ALL UP IN YOUR MIND" is one of *RENAISSANCE*'s most striking musical moments. On previous albums, Beyoncé flirted with industrial music and Björk-like warped electronica, but here she goes full-on dark electro with corkscrew beats and grinding synthesizers. Her vocals occasionally display ragged edges that exacerbate the narrator's obsessive tendencies.

AMERICA HAS A PROBLEM

[SINGLE]

Released: May 19, 2023 (single, with Kendrick Lamar) / July 29, 2022 (album)
Writers: S. Carter, Mike Dean, Terius "The-Dream" Gesteelde-Diamant, Beyoncé Knowles, Tino Santron Mcintosh, Andrell D. Rogers
Producers: Mike Dean, Terius "The-Dream" Gesteelde-Diamant, Beyoncé Knowles
Select Alternate Versions: Kendrick Lamar remix

The title and icepick-spiky synth intro of "AMERICA HAS A PROBLEM" is a sample from Atlanta rapper Kilo Ali's early 1990s song "Cocaine". After this dramatic beginning, the song immediately kicks into a throwback Miami bass groove with sizzling hi-hats. It's an insistent backdrop for lyrics that equate the addictive nature of a drug like cocaine with the irresistible allure of love and sex. Nearly a year after *RENAISSANCE*'s release, Beyoncé issued a remix of "AMERICA HAS A PROBLEM" with Kendrick Lamar. The rapper contributes a savvy verse that not only finds him boasting that he's part of the Beyhive, but talks up his talent and wealth.

PURE/HONEY

[ALBUM TRACK]

Released: July 29, 2022 (album)
Writers: Denisia "@Blu_June" Andrews For @Novawav, Kevin Marquis Bellmon, Jerel Black, Brittany "@Chi_Coney" Coney For @Novawav, Michael D. Cox, Darius Dixson, Terius "The-Dream" Gesteelde-Diamant, Beyoncé Knowles, Count Maurice, Michael Pollack, Raphael Saadiq, Moi Renee, Andrew Richardson, Eric Snead, Michael Tucker
Producers: BloodPop, Mike Dean, Terius "The-Dream" Gesteelde-Diamant, Beyoncé Knowles, Nova Wav, Raphael Saadiq, Stuart White

Beyoncé's reverence for queer history, music and subcultures permeates *RENAISSANCE*, but is especially evident on this two-part highlight. The first half, "PURE", exudes confidence – atop strutting beats, the narrator relishes how good they look and move – while the disco-fied tease "HONEY" is a coy Prince doppelganger sonically reminiscent of Beyoncé's earlier song "Blow". On the *Renaissance World Tour*, Beyoncé made "PURE/HONEY" a showcase for ballroom culture. One by one, the tour's dancers each had a chance to step into the spotlight and show off their best moves in front of packed stadiums. Sample-wise, "PURE/HONEY" also elevates voices from the ballroom scene. Commentator Kevin Jz Prodigy "burst into tears" when he heard Beyoncé sampled his chant from the 2009 DJ MikeQ track "Feels Like". [26] Kevin Aviance was also appreciative that Beyoncé sampled elements from his "Cunty" for her song. "It's a love letter to my community, the Black gay community," Aviance said of his song, and adds, "When someone like Beyoncé [sees you] ... it's incredible."[27] And the tune ends with Beyoncé intertwining her voice with "Miss Honey" by Aviance's late friend Moi Renee.

Above: The RENAISSANCE WORLD TOUR traversed the globe in 2023, landing in stadiums in North America, Europe and the UK.

SUMMER RENAISSANCE

[ALBUM TRACK]

Released: July 29, 2022
Writers: Denisia "@Blu_June" Andrews For @Novawav, Peter Bellotte, Atia Boggs P/K/A Ink, Brittany "@Chi_Coney" Coney For @Novawav, Levar Coppin, Mike Dean, Saliou Diagne, Terius "The-Dream" Gesteelde-Diamant, Leven Kali, Beyoncé Knowles, Ricky Lawson, Giorgio Moroder, Donna Summer
Producers: Mike Dean, Terius "The-Dream" Gesteelde-Diamant, Leven Kali, Beyoncé Knowles, Nova Wav, Sol Was

The title "SUMMER RENAISSANCE" possesses multiple layers of meaning. It's first and foremost a literal descriptor of the July-released album. But it also refers to the song's source material – a throbbing sample and interpolation of Donna Summer's mighty disco anthem "I Feel Love" – and the ascendant legacy of the late disco icon.

The blocky, house music-inspired "SUMMER RENAISSANCE" helped usher in this resurgence, of course: droning synthesizers float through the mix like streaking comets as Beyoncé channels Summer's sexy, coquettish wails and gospel background for a forthright song about good loving. Cincinnati producer Sal Dali and Levar "LV" Coppin – a duo who had collaborated on an atmosphere-heavy, 1970s-replicating *Jacuzzi Spiritual Advisors* project – worked together to capture Beyoncé's desired approach. "We already knew coming in that she was trying to do a dance record and it was heavily disco-, Studio 54-influenced," Dali explains. "We wanted to encapsulate that as best as possible."[28]

Poignantly, Beyoncé had also referenced Donna Summer nearly 20 years before on "Naughty Girl", interpolating "Love to Love You Baby". The artistic growth she demonstrated between these two songs is striking – as is the beautiful way she spoke about *RENAISSANCE*. "My intention was to create a safe place, a place without judgment," Beyoncé said. "A place to be free of perfectionism and overthinking. A place to scream, release, feel freedom. It was a beautiful journey of exploration."[29]

DELRESTO (ECHOES) (BEYONCÉ AND TRAVIS SCOTT)

[SINGLE]

Released: July 28, 2023 (single and album)
Writers: James Blake, Mike Dean, Terius "The-Dream" Gesteelde-Diamant, Hit-Boy, Beyoncé Knowles, Allen Ritter, Travis Scott
Producers: Mike Dean, Hit-Boy, Beyoncé Knowles, Allen Ritter, Travis Scott

Talk about wish fulfillment. In late 2015, rapper Travis Scott expressed interest in someday working with Beyoncé. "You know, I'm from Houston, she's from Houston," he said. "I feel like we – we're definitely in due time to do some music."[30] Several years later, Tone Stith revealed that he wrote his 2018 single "Good Company", which featured Swae Lee and Quavo, with Travis Scott and Beyoncé in mind. "Somebody told me they were looking for a song," Stith noted, "but he [Swae] heard the track and was like, 'Let me do something with this'."[31] Five years later, Scott finally had his wish granted with "Delresto (Echoes)", a moody song from his studio album *Utopia* recorded with Beyoncé collaborators Hit-Boy, Mike Dean, James Blake and The-Dream. Given the participants, it's no surprise "Delresto (Echoes)" is atmospheric and even experimental, with shapeshifting electronic textures floating in the background as Beyoncé contorts her vocals in ghostly, hypnotic ways.

MY HOUSE

[PROMO SINGLE]

Released: December 1, 2023
Writers: Terius "The-Dream" Gesteelde-Diamant and Beyoncé Knowles
Producers: Terius "The-Dream" Gesteelde-Diamant and Beyoncé Knowles

According to The-Dream, it became clear in October 2023 – mere weeks before the premiere – that Beyoncé needed a new song for her concert film *Renaissance: A Film by Beyoncé*. He says they considered using a song that was already done, but thought better of it. "Then it was more so about, 'Hey, let's just do something from how we are feeling now. Man, let's just have a good time,'" he said.[32] The result is the triumphant "My House", which celebrates a core tenet of ballroom culture: supportive houses, which offer community to members in ways biological families often won't. The first part of the song is swaggering hip-hop that finds Beyoncé aggressively spitting bars, while the second part is slow-boiling house music that praises the revolutionary movement created by *RENAISSANCE*. "That's kind of the end of the story," The-Dream says. "'How do we wrap *RENAISSANCE* up in a way without also trying to compete with it or make something that's light-*RENAISSANCE*, because *RENAISSANCE* is a special thing?'"[33]

Left: Beyoncé performs onstage during the RENAISSANCE WORLD TOUR at the Tottenham Hotspur Stadium in London, England.

Above: A close-up of the poster for *Renaissance: A Film by Beyoncé*, her 2023 concert film.

16 COWBOY CARTER

INCREDIBLY ENOUGH, *COWBOY CARTER* — THE SECOND VOLUME IN BEYONCÉ'S PLANNED ALBUM TRILOGY — WAS SUPPOSED TO BE RELEASED BEFORE *RENAISSANCE*. BUT BEYONCÉ'S TIMING WAS ONCE AGAIN IMPECCABLE: RELEASED IN MARCH 2024, *COWBOY CARTER* KICKSTARTED A GLOBAL RESURGENCE IN COUNTRY/POP CROSSOVERS. BEYONCÉ TOOK MUSICAL INSPIRATION FROM WESTERN MOVIES (INCLUDING *URBAN COWBOY, SPACE COWBOYS, THE HARDER THEY FALL* AND *KILLERS OF THE FLOWER MOON*) AND OVERTLY (AND SUBTLY) ESTABLISHED THAT BLACK MUSICIANS WERE INSTRUMENTAL TO INNOVATIONS WITHIN CLASSICAL, COUNTRY, ROCK 'N' ROLL AND ROOTS MUSIC. *COWBOY CARTER* WAS THE FIRST ALBUM BY A BLACK WOMAN TO REACH NO. 1 ON *BILLBOARD*'S TOP COUNTRY ALBUMS CHART AND WON GRAMMYS FOR BEST COUNTRY ALBUM AND THE PRESTIGIOUS ALBUM OF THE YEAR — BEYONCÉ'S FIRST TIME WINNING THE LATTER AWARD.

AMERIICAN REQUIEM

[ALBUM TRACK]

Released: March 29, 2024
Writers: Jon Batiste, Atia Boggs, Shawn Carter, Derek Dixie, Darius Dixson, Tyler Johnson, Beyoncé Knowles, Camaron "Cam" Ochs, Michael Price, Raphael Saadiq, Stephen Stills, Khirye Tyler, Dan Walsh, Ernest Dion Wilson
Producers: Jon Batiste, Derek Dixie, Tyler Johnson, Beyoncé Knowles, No I.D., Camaron "Cam" Ochs, Khirye Tyler

If *COWBOY CARTER* has a mission statement, it's the psychedelic '70s soul epic "AMERIICAN REQUIEM". Sounding like a powerful country-gospel belter, Beyoncé calls for a reckoning with historical precedents. As she does on past songs, she proudly calls out her Southern roots in Alabama, Texas and Louisiana. But "AMERIICAN REQUIEM" alludes to the fact that her voice wasn't heard – and her authenticity was called into question – when she started dabbling in country music. It's not difficult to trace this back to real-life indignities: in late 2016, not long after an exuberant awards show collaboration with the Chicks [*see* page 221] that infuriated many in the country music world, the Grammys refused to include *Lemonade*'s "Daddy Lessons" in the nominations for country music categories. It was a quiet part spoken out loud: many people were not interested in hearing a Black woman playing country music – and didn't care about (or were even afraid of) what even a superstar like Beyoncé had to say.

Instead of becoming discouraged, Beyoncé decided to prove everyone wrong by making a country album *her* way. It's telling that within the song, Beyoncé says she alone is responsible for absolving the sins of the Founding Fathers; the implication is she's not relying on approval or support from the establishment, Nashville or otherwise. But on "AMERIICAN REQUIEM" she does align herself with allies, co-writing with artists like the country iconoclast Cam, R&B star Raphael Saadiq and genre-busting Jon Batiste, and interpolating the Stephen Stills-written Buffalo Springfield tune "For What It's Worth".

BLACKBIIRD (WITH BRITTNEY SPENCER, REYNA ROBERTS, TANNER ADELL AND TIERA KENNEDY)

[ALBUM TRACK]

Released: March 29, 2024
Writers: John Lennon and Paul McCartney
Producers: Beyoncé Knowles, Paul McCartney, Khiyre Tyler

As a young man, Paul McCartney learned about the story of the Little Rock Nine: a group of Black students enrolling at a previously segregated all-white public high school in Arkansas. Racism reared its ugly head; resistance to this integration was unnecessarily harsh and violent. In response, McCartney wrote The Beatles' folk-leaning "Blackbird".

"We would see what was going on and sympathize with the people going through those troubles," he once said before a show, "and it made me want to write a song that, if it ever got back to the people going through those troubles, it might just help them a little bit."[1]

On *COWBOY CARTER*, Beyoncé does a stunning, reverent version of the song (dubbed "BLACKBIIRD") that feels like a response to The Beatles – and an expression of gratitude. She enlists four Black country musicians – Brittney Spencer, Reyna Roberts, Tanner Adell and Tiera Kennedy – to contribute empathetic, delicate, multi-part harmonies and the occasional lead. "It was so beautiful," Kennedy said. "It feels like we were having a little Destiny's Child moment."[2]

With permission, Beyoncé used some of McCartney's original parts from The Beatles' recording (specifically acoustic guitar and his foot tapping) for her version[3]; in the mix, these are omnipresent next to the vocalists and newly recorded strings, a poignant (and pointed) bridging of eras. In the end, McCartney said Beyoncé did "a magnificent version" of "Blackbird" that "reinforces the civil rights message that inspired me to write the song in the first place."[4]

16 CARRIAGES

[SINGLE]

Released: February 11, 2024 (single) / March 29, 2024 (album)
Writers: Atia Boggs, Dave Hamelin, Beyoncé Knowles, Raphael Saadiq
Producers: Dave Hamelin, Ink, Beyoncé Knowles, Raphael Saadiq, Stuart White

In fall 2024, Beyoncé revealed that she began making *COWBOY CARTER* "almost five years ago", and noted, "Pay close attention to my age in the lyrics of '16 Carriages'".[5] (For the record, it's 38, so the timeline tracks.) An introspective gospel-country song rooted in classic storytelling, "16 CARRIAGES" jumps around to various eras in Beyoncé's life, referencing her as a teenager seeing her parents' rocky marriage and as a mom missing her kids while touring. These examples illustrate the sacrifices she's made being on the road chasing her dreams (long hours, homesickness, anxiety) but also her perseverance. After all, the title symbolizes tour equipment being hauled from town to town; Beyoncé mentions that these trucks carry her dreams *and* fears.

Pedal steel icon Robert Randolph appeared on the song and when he arrived in Los Angeles to record, he found a jaw-dropping scene: he says he was in the studio with a band that included Raphael Saadiq, Rhiannon Giddens, Khirye Tyler – and Beyoncé. "We were cutting," Randolph says. "We were getting down. It was, 'Let's try this,' then doing one or two takes. And [Beyoncé] sang with us, man. She sang it right there. You just follow her lead and go."[6]

In addition to Randolph's contributions, "16 CARRIAGES" incorporates solemn organ and resilient trumpet flares; these alternate to create a dynamic emotional pendulum. "She wanted to do something with some playing, with some country fire," Randolph says. "She said she liked the way I make my instrument sound like a singer."[7]

Opposite: In 2016, Beyoncé performed *Lemonade*'s "Daddy Lessons" with the Chicks at the CMA Awards in Nashville.

VICE PRESIDENT OF THE UNITED STATES
E PLURIBUS UNUM

PROTECTOR (WITH RUMI CARTER)

[ALBUM TRACK]

Released: March 29, 2024
Writers: Ryan Beatty, Beyoncé Knowles, Camaron "Cam" Ochs, Jack Rochon
Producers: Beyoncé Knowles and Jack Rochon

The stripped-down folk song "PROTECTOR" is a tender tune about the unconditional love between a mother and child. Beyoncé pledges to be there for her kid even when they're grown and can stand on their own; her compassion shines through via poetic imagery and gentle vocals, as well as keening guitar by blues-rocker Gary Clark Jr. Appropriately, the song also features Beyoncé's six-year-old daughter, Rumi, who pipes up and asks for a lullaby at the song's start. The celebrated country musician Cam co-wrote "PROTECTOR" along with several others on *COWBOY CARTER*. She heard the final version of the song while on a plane with her daughter Lucy, who was a toddler at the time, and was bowled over by its beauty and message. "I was so overwhelmed," she says. "I just remember thinking, all our parents have done this for us. They did it for us and now I'm doing it for her, and I just bawled my eyes out when I first heard that."[8]

SMOKE HOUR ★ WILLIE NELSON (WITH WILLIE NELSON) / SMOKE HOUR II (WITH WILLIE NELSON)

[ALBUM TRACK]

Released: March 29, 2024
Writers: Beyoncé Knowles, Leah Nardos Takele (both); Charles Anderson, Chuck Berry, Son House, Jesse Stone, Sister Rosetta Tharpe ("SMOKE HOUR ★ WILLIE NELSON"); Jeff "Gitty" Gitelman, Dave Hamelin ("SMOKE HOUR II")
Producers: Beyoncé Knowles (both); Dave Hamelin ("SMOKE HOUR II")

COWBOY CARTER contains multiple short songs and interludes that double as connective tissue for the album's themes and styles. For example, country legend Willie Nelson makes two memorable appearances, no doubt because Beyoncé is a long-time fan. She paid tribute to his iconic braids-and-bandanna look on a 2004 cover of the magazine *Texas Monthly* and appeared with him at a fall 2024 Kamala Harris presidential rally in Houston. Calling him "one of our national treasures," she noted: "You were so kind to me and the girls of Destiny's Child when we fanned out meeting you years ago. And you greeted me with the same kindness 20 years later!"[9]

On *COWBOY CARTER*, Nelson portrays a DJ for the fictional radio station KNTRY ("Radio Texas") who hosts a speciality show called Smoke Hour. His first appearance, "SMOKE HOUR ★ WILLIE NELSON", appropriately enough feels like someone scanning a radio dial; the song pointedly samples Black rock 'n' roll innovators like Son House, Chuck Berry and Sister Rosetta Tharpe. "SMOKE HOUR II", meanwhile, finds Nelson imparting wisdom about opening your mind (and ears) to someone introducing you to something good.

Opposite and above: Beyoncé introduced US Vice President Kamala Harris at an October 2024 campaign event in Houston. Also present at the event was Willie Nelson. Beyoncé is a long-time fan of the country legend; in fact, he guests on *Cowboy Carter*.

TEXAS HOLD 'EM

[SINGLE]

Released: February 11, 2024 (single) / March 29, 2024 (album)
Writers: Brian Bates, Elizabeth Lowell Boland, Megan Bülow, Nathan Ferraro, Raphael Saadiq, Beyoncé Knowles
Producers: Killah B, Nathan Ferraro, Beyoncé Knowles
Select Alternate Versions: Instrumental, A Cappella, Pony Up remix

In November 2016, Beyoncé dazzled at the Country Music Association Awards, teaming up with country trio the Chicks for a jubilant, horn-peppered version of *Lemonade*'s "Daddy Lessons" that was inspired by gospel, '70s soul, blues and (of course) classic country music. Beyoncé and the group harmonized like they had been performing together for years; in fact, the women even performed parts of the Chicks' own song "Long Time Gone" together for good measure. Unfortunately, reactions to Beyoncé's appearance were decidedly mixed: although she received plenty of enthusiastic praise, naysayers also hurled racist invective and criticized things like Beyoncé's political stances and country bona fides.

Flash-forward eight years, and Beyoncé announced the country-inspired album *COWBOY CARTER*. In the lead-up to the LP's release, it became obvious that she hadn't forgotten the chilly reception she received from certain corners in 2016. "[The album] was born out of an experience that I had years ago where I did not feel welcomed ... and it was very clear that I wasn't," she wrote upon the release of the *COWBOY CARTER* artwork. "I did a deeper dive into the history of Country music and studied our rich musical archive."[10]

The uptempo "TEXAS HOLD 'EM", one of two lead singles from *COWBOY CARTER,* exemplifies Beyoncé's meticulous research. Driven by honey-sweet harmonies, a stomping beat and fluid grooves, it unapologetically centres vintage country music signifiers while incorporating warm, modern production flourishes. Lyrically, "TEXAS HOLD 'EM" exhorts listeners to dance via tongue-twisting lyrics that touch on poker metaphors, saucy flirtations and passing references to liquor and dive bars. The vibe is inclusive and joyous: when Beyoncé celebrates country music, *everyone* is invited.

"TEXAS HOLD 'EM" also features viola and banjo from Rhiannon Giddens, a Pulitzer Prize-winning musician who's a fierce advocate for the Black musical and cultural roots of both the banjo and country music itself. "The beginning is a solo riff on my minstrel banjo – and my only hope is that it might lead a few more intrepid folks into the exciting history of the banjo," Giddens wrote on Instagram upon the release of "TEXAS HOLD 'EM", explaining her approach to the lively part.

"I used to say many times as soon as Beyoncé puts the banjo on a track my job is done," she added, a nod to previous interviews in which she discussed what it would take to raise awareness of country's Black roots. "Well, I didn't expect the banjo to be mine. And I know darn well my job isn't done, but today is a pretty good day."[11]

"TEXAS HOLD 'EM" immediately spawned several viral dances and reached No. 1 on pop charts in countries around the world, including the US *Billboard* Hot 100. But the song also topped *Billboard*'s Hot Country Songs chart, making Beyoncé the first Black woman ever to achieve this feat.

Opposite and above: At the NFL 2024 Christmas Day Halftime Show (a.k.a. the Beyoncé Bowl), Beyoncé wowed a hometown Houston crowd with tracks from *Cowboy Carter*.

BODYGUARD

[ALBUM TRACK]

Released: March 29, 2024
Writers: Ryan Beatty, Elizabeth Lowell Boland, Terius "The-Dream" Gesteelde-Diamant, Leven Kali, Beyoncé Knowles, Shawntoni Ajanae Nichols, Raphael Saadiq
Producers: Beyoncé Knowles and Raphael Saadiq

One of *COWBOY CARTER*'s standout tracks, "BODYGUARD" is written from the perspective of someone who wants to protect their significant other with the tenacity of (you guessed it) a bodyguard. This sets up a song with old-fashioned romantic imagery (a lipstick stain on a cigarette, a whiskey-fuelled makeout session) and a narrator swearing she'll swoop in and take control of any situation, whether it be driving in the car, a frightening mosh pit, or the gossip-filled tabloids.

"BODYGUARD" was co-written and co-produced by Raphael Saadiq; he also plays piano, keyboard, guitar and bass on the song. Unsurprisingly, he originally envisioned it as a solo song for himself. But during a review of some tracks stored in Saadiq's Dropbox, the intro of "BODYGUARD" caught Beyoncé's ear. "She was like, 'Go back, go back!'" Saadiq said. "And then what she added vocally was bars up from what I did. She sounded like Reba McEntire, felt like Aretha. She took what I did and completed it."[12] Adding to the sense of rose-coloured romance is Saadiq's guitars and drums, which possess a warm Laurel Canyon '70s rock vibe. The bouncy bassline, meanwhile, resembles Fleetwood Mac, which Saadiq admits was by design, "because I love those eras of music."[13]

Below and opposite: Stevie Wonder presented Beyoncé with the Innovator Award at the 2024 iHeartRadio Music Awards. "Whenever anyone asks me if there's anyone I could listen to for the rest of my life, it's always you," she told the icon. "'God bless you.'"

DOLLY P / JOLENE

[ALBUM TRACK]

Released: March 29, 2024
Writers: Dolly Parton (both); Beyoncé Knowles, Leah Nardos Takele ("DOLLY P"); Denisia "Blu June" Andrews, Brittany "Chi" Coney, Terius "The-Dream" Gesteelde-Diamant, Beyoncé Knowles (additional lyrics on "JOLENE")
Producers: Beyoncé Knowles, Jack Rochon (both); Nova Wav ("DOLLY P"); Denisia "Blu June" Andrews, Brittany "Chi" Coney, Terius "The-Dream" Gesteelde-Diamant, Khirye Tyler ("JOLENE")

Beyoncé is no stranger to Dolly Parton's catalogue. On *The Mrs. Carter Show World Tour*, she prefaced both "Halo" and "Heaven" with a cover of the Whitney Houston version of Parton's signature song, "I Will Always Love You". And so, when Beyoncé decided to make a country record, she specifically sought to cover another iconic Parton song: the temptation-heavy "Jolene".

Parton once described the song – which she wrote about two very different redheads she encountered – as "an innocent song all around, but [it] sounds like a dreadful one".[14] One inspiration was a young fan she met who wanted an autograph. "I said, 'Well, you're the prettiest little thing I ever saw,' she recalled. "So what is your name?'" The little girl answered: Jolene. "And I said, 'Jolene. Jolene. Jolene. Jolene,'" Parton continued. "I said, 'That is pretty. That sounds like a song. I'm going to write a song about that.'"[15]

The other redhead wasn't quite so innocuous: it was a bank teller who had "this terrible crush on my husband," she said. "And he just loved going to the bank because she paid him so much attention. It was kinda like a running joke between us – when I was saying, 'Hell, you're spending a lot of time at the bank. I don't believe we've got that kind of money.'"[16]

To preface "JOLENE" on *COWBOY CARTER*, Parton recorded an intro (dubbed "DOLLY P") in which she references the infamous Becky with the good hair from "Sorry". It's an apt lead-in to Beyoncé's version: the modern "JOLENE" protagonist is *very* territorial about her man despite being quite secure about their marriage and his fidelity. In fact, she's not pleading for Jolene to stay away from her man; she assures Jolene that she'll regret it if she comes near him. The unease is amplified by a stomping beat and the song's recognizable rootsy guitar line, distorted by a slight wobbling effect.

But as the song coasts to an end, a rapturous choir bursts into the mix, just as the narrator describes how she and her man have weathered ups and downs and now have secure roots. A chorus of male voices affirms this loyalty; Beyoncé echoes the same lyric back, only with flipped pronouns. The vaguely menacing vibe melts away, replaced by a feeling of calm.

Parton gave her stamp of approval to the new "JOLENE", saying she thought it was "very bold" of Beyoncé to do such a drastic update. "When they said she was gonna do 'Jolene', I expected it to be my regular one, but it wasn't. But I love what she did to it. And as a songwriter, you love the fact that people do your songs, no matter how they do them."[17]

DAUGHTER

[ALBUM TRACK]

Released: March 29, 2024
Writers: Shawn Carter, Derek Dixie, Terius "The-Dream" Gesteelde-Diamant, Beyoncé Knowles, Simon Mårtensson, Camaron "Cam" Ochs
Producers: Derek Dixie, Beyoncé Knowles, Simon Mårtensson, Camaron "Cam" Ochs

"DAUGHTER" is one of the most striking moments on *COWBOY CARTER*. The protagonist has come to the chilling realization that she has her father's temper. What results is a haunting murder ballad in which she wrestles with dark impulses (and a violent outburst) and fantasizes about seeking salvation in religious and spiritual traditions. Musically, "DAUGHTER" is also haunting. Beyoncé sounds wary as she sings a section of the Italian opera song "Caro Mio Ben" in the bridge, while elsewhere, churning acoustic guitar gives way to uneasy strings incorporating elements of a Tchaikovsky violin concerto. "DAUGHTER" also samples *Violin Concerto in D Major, Op. III No. 1: II. Adagio by* the composer and violinist Joseph Bologne, who was known as Chevalier de Saint-Georges. The son of a French plantation owner and an enslaved Black woman, he was a violinist and a prolific composer of things like string quartets, a harp concerto, *symphonie concertante* and operas.[18] "Black artists, and other artists of color, have been creating and mastering multiple genres, since forever," Beyoncé said. "This is why it was so important for me to sample [him]."[19] Calling the sampled piece "a testament to Chevalier's vision," she added: "I hope it inspires artists, as well as fans, to dig deeper and learn more about the Black musical innovators who came before us. Some of the most talented artists never achieve the mainstream praise they deserve, especially when they defy the norm."[20]

SPAGHETTII (WITH LINDA MARTELL AND SHABOOZEY)

[ALBUM TRACK]

Released: March 29, 2024
Writers: Shawn Carter, Collins Chibueze, Terius "The-Dream" Gesteelde-Diamant, Beyoncé Knowles, DJ Dede Mandrake, Khirye Tyler
Producers: Beyoncé Knowles, Swizz Beatz, Khirye Tyler

Linda Martell was a country music trailblazer. Born in South Carolina, she was the first Black woman to play the Grand Ole Opry and reached No. 22 on *Billboard*'s Hot Country Singles chart with 1969's "Color Him Father" – the most successful song by a Black female country artist on that chart (now known as Hot Country Songs) until Beyoncé reached No. 1 with "TEXAS HOLD 'EM" in 2024. Naturally, Beyoncé gave Martell her flowers on *COWBOY CARTER*. At the start of "SPAGHETTII", the pioneer serves as a voice of reason, criticizing genre definitions for being too narrow. The song – Beyoncé's take on outlaw country – lives up to this promise. An insistent beat sampled from the Brazilian funk act O Mandrake pulses behind her as she raps about being the best of the best – accept no substitutions.

The other guest on the track, Shaboozey, also knows a little something about not fitting into a neat pigeonhole. The Virginia-based artist combines country, trap, pop and folk – and spent a large portion of 2024 at No. 1 on the *Billboard* Hot 100 with the melancholy country hit "A Bar Song (Tipsy)", which interpolates J-Kwon's swerving 2004 hip-hop hit "Tipsy". In a subdued section influenced by *COWBOY CARTER*'s cinematic inspirations and Spaghetti Western noir, Shaboozey and Beyoncé are low-key fellow outsiders vowing to hold fast against law enforcement. The lyrics can be seen as a commentary on genre conformity or modern-day police brutality.

Opposite: The Beyoncé Bowl sadly didn't bring good luck for the hometown Houston Texans: the team lost to the Baltimore Ravens, 31-2.

ALLIIGATOR TEARS

[ALBUM TRACK]

Released: March 29, 2024
Writers: Terius "The-Dream" Gesteelde-Diamant, Beyoncé Knowles, Jack Siegel, Khirye Tyler
Producers: Terius "The-Dream" Gesteelde-Diamant, Beyoncé Knowles, Khirye Tyler

The simplest song on the record, "ALLIIGATOR TEARS" sounds like it was recorded around a campfire during a jam session. Honeysuckle-sweet acoustic guitar dances around rhythms that resemble handclaps and stomping feet. Vocally, Beyoncé sounds like she's in conspiratorial storytelling mode as she sighs about dealing with alligator tears. In one reading of the song, a romantic partner is turning on the fake waterworks to get their way – and it's working, going by the chorus where the protagonist notes they'll do anything (construct a dam to stop a river, switch religious faiths) if asked. Beyoncé isn't resentful of these requests, mind you; her voice softens and becomes more affectionate as she fondly notes that these tears can be restorative, and she still adores her partner. In another interpretation of the song, however, "ALLIIGATOR TEARS" refers to the overblown outrage about Beyoncé branching out into country music. She's tried to do everything people wanted her to do to fit in, to no avail. So she's decided that these alligator tears from her haters are only nourishing her soul and making her grow stronger – and reaffirming her commitment to country music.

JUST FOR FUN (WITH WILLIE JONES)

[ALBUM TRACK]

Released: March 29, 2024
Writers: Ryan Beatty, Jeff Gitty, Dave Hamelin, Beyoncé Knowles
Producers: Dave Hamelin, Beyoncé Knowles, Alex Vickery

The Carters' *Everything Is Love* demonstrated that Beyoncé didn't shy away from last-minute updates if it would improve an album. "JUST FOR FUN" continued that trend: country artist Willie Jones ended up jumping on the song at the end of February 2024, a mere month before *COWBOY CARTER* was released. "It was literally in the fourth quarter," he said, noting that producer Alex Vickery called him out of the blue about the request. "She's like, 'Are you sitting down?' I was like, 'Yeah.' And she's like, 'You know Beyoncé is working on a country album ... [and] she loves your voice.'"[21] Jones was gobsmacked – and flattered. "[Alex] was like, 'Can you come out here tomorrow?' I was like, 'Send the car.'"[22]

His smoky, sage-like voice was indeed the perfect flourish for the elegiac "JUST FOR FUN". The gospel-inspired song finds Beyoncé singing in a sober lower register about a restless protagonist whose brave, carefree façade hides despair and uncertainty. This nomadic soul is planning to leave town and head south, but first he is merely trying to make it through the dark night. He's searching for answers in this darkness – there's a lyric asking who provides light, symbolically meaning knowledge – and asserts he's praying to a female deity. Ponderous piano eventually gives way to a soaring choir, affirming the song's cautiously optimistic (if spiritual) bent.

Above: Beyoncé declared her love for country music with *Cowboy Carter*, which was released in March 2024.

Opposite: Beyoncé and Miley Cyrus became friends in 2008 after performing together at the Fashion Rocks concert, which benefited the charity Stand Up to Cancer.

II MOST WANTED (WITH MILEY CYRUS)

[SINGLE]

Released: April 12, 2024 (single) / March 29, 2024 (album)
Writers: Miley Cyrus, Andrew DeRoberts, Beyoncé Knowles, Michael Pollack, Ryan Tedder
Producers: Miley Cyrus, Shawn Everett, Beyoncé Knowles, Michael Pollack, Jonathan Rado

At a 2008 Stand Up to Cancer benefit, Miley Cyrus sang the all-star charity song "Just Stand Up!" onstage between Beyoncé and Rihanna. "They were these powerful, fully realized, grown women, and I'm pretty sure I had braces on the back of my teeth," Cyrus later recalled. "They were protective of me."[23] This show sparked a friendship between Miley and Beyoncé that eventually led to their collaboration on "II MOST WANTED".

Cyrus wrote the song several years before Beyoncé asked her about music. "I thought of it right away because it really encompasses our relationship," she said. "I told her, 'We don't have to get country; we are country. We've been country.'"[24] Accordingly, the lyrics have an us-against-the-world vibe – but rather than giving Thelma and Louise (or Bonnie and Clyde) the song is better interpreted as being about a sweet, enduring friendship. "I said, 'You know, between you being from Texas and me being from Tennessee, so much of us is going to be in this song,'" Cyrus says.[25] Fittingly, the women sound note-perfect harmonizing together; their voices intertwine like spun sugar with the occasional rock candy edge giving lovely texture.

Musically, "II MOST WANTED" is a meditative folk-pop song in the vein of Fleetwood Mac's "Landslide", with its topsy-turvy pedal steel, atmospheric vintage keyboards and seagulls-screaming guitar. An all-star cast of musicians backs Cyrus and Beyoncé, including decorated Americana veteran Sara Watkins (fiddle) and the War on Drugs' Adam Granduciel (guitar). Cyrus was thrilled with the results: "Getting to write a song, not just sing, for Beyoncé was a dream come true."[26]

LEVII'S JEANS [WITH POST MALONE]

[ALBUM TRACK]

Released: March 29, 2024
Writers: Shawn Carter, Terius "The-Dream" Gesteelde-Diamant, Beyoncé Knowles, Austin Post, Nile Rodgers
Producers: Terius "The-Dream" Gesteelde-Diamant and Beyoncé Knowles

Post Malone had a banner 2024, appearing on Taylor Swift's chart-topping hit "Fortnight" and releasing his own No. 1 country record, *F-1 Trillion*. But one of his other high-water marks was contributing sly (but earnest) vocals on Beyoncé's sassy, soulful "LEVII'S JEANS". Playing off one of the most common country music lyrical tropes – a great pair of blue jeans – Beyoncé crafts an ode to how empowering it feels to find a piece of denim that makes you feel sexy; in fact, the narrator flirtatiously tells her boyfriend he can be her jeans, so he'll be closer to her derriere. As the song progresses, the couple's romance heats up as they swap photos, exchange playful banter and open their hearts.

Beyoncé sent the "LEVII'S JEANS" music to Post Malone at his house in Utah. Then he texted with her as he worked on finishing the song.[27] Despite the distance, his preferred working approach didn't change much. "I feel like there's a lot of people set in their ways," he said. "I just want to make the song work in the best way for the song."[28] Here that means he gradually becomes more of a presence on the song and intertwines his voice with Beyoncé's voice, mirroring the song's increasing romantic intensity. Disco legend Nile Rodgers, who also played on *RENAISSANCE*'s "CUFF IT", also co-wrote and plays sweetly seductive guitar on the song.

In a testament to the song's success, by fall 2024, "LEVII'S JEANS" (and Beyoncé) were part of an actual campaign for Levi's.

Below: At the NFL 2024 Christmas Day Halftime Show (a.k.a. the Beyoncé Bowl), Post Malone made a guest appearance to sing "LEVII'S JEANS.".

MY ROSE / FLAMENCO

[ALBUM TRACK]

Released: March 29, 2024
Writers: Beyoncé Knowles and Shawntoni Ajanae Nichols (both)
Producers: Beyoncé Knowles and Mamii (both)

On *COWBOY CARTER*, Beyoncé collaborated on two tantalizingly short songs with the Indiana-born R&B artist Mamii. "This is the first set of songs out that I've been able to write and produce for someone other than myself," Mamii wrote on Instagram. "It's really a dream come true."[29] The fluttering "MY ROSE" is a harmony-rich ode to loving someone, flaws and all; the song feels like a dainty, pastel-coloured waltz. "FLAMENCO" possesses a similar stripped-down, harmony-driven vibe, but features a protagonist on the precipice of making a big decision. They aren't sure what to do, which is causing anxiety; instead, they're thinking about the aftermath and what regrets or should-have-beens might emerge.

THE LINDA MARTELL SHOW / YA YA

[ALBUM TRACK]

Released: March 29, 2024
Writers: Beyoncé Knowles (both); Leah Nardos Takele ("THE LINDA MARTELL SHOW"); Shawn Carter, Harry Edwards, Terius "The-Dream" Gesteelde-Diamant, Lee Hazlewood, Mike Love, Anaïs Marinho, Klara Mkhatshwa Munk-Hansen, Oliver Rodigan, Brian Wilson ("YA YA")
Producers: Beyoncé Knowles (both); Cadenza, Harry Edwards, Terius "The-Dream" Gesteelde-Diamant, Khirye Tyler ("YA YA")

With the brief interlude "THE LINDA MARTELL SHOW", the country pioneer pops up again to introduce "YA YA", noting that the song is singular because it spans multiple genres. It's truth in advertising: one of the highlights on *COWBOY CARTER*, the track is a classic Beyoncé sonic collage that critiques the American dream, honours the Chitlin' Circuit, celebrates getting your groove (and dance) on. "From the start of my career and on every album, I have always mixed genres," Beyoncé pointed out. "Whether it is R&B, dance, country, rap, zydeco, blues, opera, gospel, they have all influenced me in some way."[30]

Fittingly, "YA YA" notably incorporates multiple signifiers from Nancy Sinatra's classic kiss-off "These Boots Are Made for Walkin'" and interpolates the Beach Boys' influential pop song "Good Vibrations". But Beyoncé's most obvious influence on "YA YA" is her idol Tina Turner; specifically, Turner's days dominating the stage as part of a high-energy R&B-funk revue.

The decorated British artist Arlo Parks, a "massive fan" of Beyoncé, co-wrote the song and observed she found "something really interesting" writing with country music in mind. "I was listening to a lot of country music as research, to try and bring in that context," she said. "But also I think there was something inspiring about keeping it quite broad."[31] Echoing Martell's intro, Beyoncé clearly feels the same way: "I believe genres are traps that box us in and separate us," she notes. "I've experienced this for 25 years in the music industry. Black artists, and other artists of color, have been creating and mastering multiple genres, since forever."[32]

OH LOUISIANA / DESERT EAGLE

[ALBUM TRACK]

Released: March 29, 2024
Writers: Chuck Berry ("OH LOUISIANA"); Miranda Johnson, Beyoncé Knowles, Marcus Reddick, Jabbar Stevens ("DESERT EAGLE")
Producers: Beyoncé Knowles (both); Terius "The-Dream" Gesteelde-Diamant ("OH LOUISIANA"); BAH, Marcus Reddick ("DESERT EAGLE")

Despite being focused more on country music, *COWBOY CARTER* often flows tracks into one another much like the dance-oriented *RENAISSANCE*. Case in point: a 50-second snippet of Chuck Berry's psychelic-tinged 1971 song "OH LOUISIANA" segues right into a nasty-in-the-best-way funk jam "DESERT EAGLE". The contrast is striking. The vocals on Berry's original song are manipulated to sound almost child-like, as if the song is from the perspective of a young person reminiscing about their home. "DESERT EAGLE", meanwhile, describes in alluring detail some seductive carnal pleasures – and then just as quickly goes directly into the no-nonsense "RIIVERDANCE."

RIIVERDANCE

[ALBUM TRACK]

Released: March 29, 2024
Writers: Terius "The-Dream" Gesteelde-Diamant, Rachel Keen, Beyoncé Knowles, Mark Spears
Producers: Terius "The-Dream" Gesteelde-Diamant and Beyoncé Knowles

While writing the feminist anthem "9 to 5", Dolly Parton famously came up with a bustling beat by clicking her acrylic fingernails together. On the brisk "RIIVERDANCE", Beyoncé pays tribute to Dolly's iconic move and also uses her fingernails as percussion. "I didn't want some layers of instruments like strings, especially guitars, and organs perfectly in tune," Beyoncé said. "I kept some songs raw and leaned into folk. All the sounds were so organic and human, everyday things like the wind, snaps and even the sound of birds and chickens, the sounds of nature."[33]

As the title implies, the precise "RIIVERDANCE" takes influence from Irish dancing. A no-nonsense circular guitar loop spins through the song repeatedly as Beyoncé layers on spring-loaded beats and calls on people to bounce to dance (with no hands, please!). "The joy of creating music is that there are no rules," Beyoncé said. "The more I see the world evolving the more I felt a deeper connection to purity. With artificial intelligence and digital filters and programming, I wanted to go back to real instruments, and I used very old ones."[34] In the end, "RIIVERDANCE" only gets messy in the verses: these tell the story of a relationship where both parties know exactly how to wound each other, but yet find the other person irresistible.

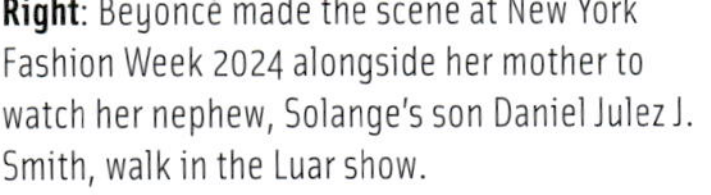

Right: Beyoncé made the scene at New York Fashion Week 2024 alongside her mother to watch her nephew, Solange's son Daniel Julez J. Smith, walk in the Luar show.

II HANDS II HEAVEN

[ALBUM TRACK]

Released: March 29, 2024
Writers: Ryan Beatty, Terius "The-Dream" Gesteelde-Diamant, Dave Hamelin, Beyoncé Knowles, Jack Rochon, Mark Spears
Producers: Dave Hamelin, Beyoncé Knowles, Jack Rochon

On the surface, "II HANDS II HEAVEN" might feel better suited for *RENAISSANCE*, as the song boasts a minimal musical foundation: shimmering electronica with bubbling beats, subtle key changes and strumming folk guitars. But "II HANDS II HEAVEN" is actually one of *COWBOY CARTER*'s most inward-looking songs – and despite the folktronica sound, its theme is a classic country trope: finding salvation, purpose and even yourself on the open road.

The narrator is wild and unbroken, in no small part because she's working through past-life heartaches. But she alludes to a life-changing trip to Marfa, Texas, a city known for its artistic community. Not long after, the song shifts into its part two: the narrator attaining emotional equilibrium thanks to healing love from someone else. "II HANDS II HEAVEN" gives listeners space to breathe and reflect – and an opportunity to let optimism creep in.

Right and opposite: In addition to Post Malone, guests at the Beyoncé Bowl included Tanner Adell, Brittney Spencer, Tiera Kennedy, Reyna Roberts and Shaboozey.

TYRANT (WITH DOLLY PARTON)

[ALBUM TRACK]

Released: March 29, 2024
Writers: Ezemdi Chikwendu, David Doman, Terius "The-Dream" Gesteelde-Diamant, Beyoncé Knowles, Camaron "Cam" Ochs, Dominik Redenczki; Leah Nardos Takele (additional lyrics)
Producers: D.A. Got That Dope, Dave Hamelin, Kuk Harrell, Beyoncé Knowles, Camaron "Cam" Ochs, Khirye Tyler

"TYRANT" starts off with a bang: Dolly Parton exhorting the album's namesake, Cowboy Carter, to get a juke joint going. From there, the tongue-twisting song grapples with the fallout from the actions of a mysterious figure called the Hangman, leading to lyrics exploring power dynamics, sexual conquests, seizing control and hints of criminal mischief.

Musically, "TYRANT" sails forward on an undulating groove, as Destiny's Child-esque backing harmonies from Brittney Spencer, Reyna Roberts and Tiera Kennedy add lift in the background. Producer David Doman (aka D.A. Got That Dope) provides the song's other prominent beat: a needling violin paired with drums.

Doman originally sent his bit to The-Dream's manager and discovered the music made *COWBOY CARTER* only a few weeks before the album hit stores. He was pleased with the outcome. "Immediately I was like, 'Oh, man, this is fire,'" he said, noting, "I'm really picky with songs that are done over my beats, and sometimes I don't love the outcome. But I really love this song."[35]

SWEET ★ HONEY ★ BUCKIIN' (WITH SHABOOZEY)

[ALBUM TRACK]

Released: March 29, 2024
Writers: Shawn Carter, Collins Chibueze, Hank Cochran, Terius "The-Dream" Gesteelde-Diamant, Harlan Howard, Beyoncé Knowles, Pharrell Williams
Producers: Beyoncé Knowles and Pharrell Williams

SWEET ★ HONEY ★ BUCKIIN'" begins with Beyoncé singing a dreamy interpolation of the Patsy Cline-popularized "I Fall to Pieces". It turns out to be the calm before the storm: with co-production from Pharrell Williams that merges quick-cut pop and hip-hop techniques with twangier sounds, the three-part epic quickly becomes a dizzying spin through gospel, country and Southern hip-hop. Shaboozey contributes a guest verse on "SWEET", a section with repetitive sounds that resemble a galloping horse; "HONEY" is languid R&B; and on the twangy "BUCKIIN'", which boasts vocals from Pharrell Williams, Beyoncé sings the title with such ferocity it sounds as if she's on a bucking bronco. In the end, "SWEET ★ HONEY ★ BUCKIIN'" breaks open genre boundaries in thrilling ways, which was one of Beyoncé's goals coming in. "When you are breaking down barriers, not everyone is ready and open for a shift," she admits. "But when I see Shaboozey tearing the charts up and all the beautiful female country singers flying to new heights, inspiring the world, that is exactly what motivates me."[36]

AMEN

[ALBUM TRACK]

Released: March 29, 2024
Writers: Danielle Balbuena, Derek Dixie, Darius Dixson, Ian Fitchuk, Dave Hamelin, Tyler Johnson, Beyoncé Knowles, Camaron "Cam" Ochs, Sean Solymar
Producers: 070 Shake, Derek Dixie, Ian Fitchuk, Dave Hamelin, Tyler Johnson, Beyoncé Knowles, Camaron "Cam" Ochs (Cam), Sean Solymar

As the title implies, "AMEN" feels like a final benediction. Beyoncé asks for mercy and pointedly tries to tell sceptics about things she's discovered, like the dishonesty of Confederate statues. But the lush, piano-dotted music sets up one of the album's most powerful moments. The choir we hear on *COWBOY CARTER*'s opening track, "AMERIICAN REQUIEM", creates a lovely full-circle moment by appearing prominently again on "AMEN". In another instance of symmetry, the lyrics of "AMEN" also offer a subtle but brilliant callback to the start of the album. In "AMERIICAN REQUIEM" she observes that *big* ideas are buried in America; in other words, the structural racism and oppression on which the country was founded are baked into our very existence. And Beyoncé is tasked to dismantle these things herself.

But on "AMEN" Beyoncé changes the words slightly, first singing instead that *old* ideas are buried; the insinuation is that we have the power to put these antiquated things to rest. She bolsters this assertion with the other lyrics in the outro: she tells us to pray for the past and the way things have always operated, as if these things are dying – and asserts that we the people have the power to cleanse the sins committed by past generations. Beyoncé isn't alone anymore in working for a more inclusive future; thanks to *COWBOY CARTER*, there's an entire movement behind her.

Left: The Beyoncé Bowl setlist included *Cowboy Carter* highlights such as "YA YA," "16 CARRIAGES" and "TEXAS HOLD 'EM."

NOTES

INTRODUCTION

1 Horan, Tom. "Beyoncé: dream girl." *The Telegraph*, November 8, 2008.
2 *Ibid.*
3 Goodman, Jessica. "Diana Gordon interview: The 'Becky with the good hair' scribe opens up about new music." *Entertainment Weekly*, August 2, 2016.
4 Tingen, Paul. "Stuart White: Recording & Mixing Beyoncé." *Sound on Sound*, October 2022.
5 Feeney, Nolan. "Beyoncé and JAY-Z Collaborators Cool & Dre Detail the Last-Minute Making of 'Everything Is Love.'" *Billboard*, June 18, 2018.

DESTINY'S CHILD

1 Arrillaga, Pauline. "Teen Rhythm and Blues Band Finds Fame With Major Album." *The Monitor* (McAllen, Texas), September 5, 1998.
2 Marks, Craig. "Producer Rob Fusari Dishes on Lady Gaga, Beyoncé." *Billboard*, February 24, 2010.
3 McClay, Caché. "Destiny's Child dropped classic album 'The Writing's on the Wall' 25 years ago: A look back." *USA Today*, July 25, 2024.
4 Flynn, Paul. "'Of course you can lose yourself." *The Guardian*, August 18, 2006.
5 *Ibid.*
6 No author. "Destiny's Child: Hot Young Divas Continue to Burn Up Music Charts." *Jet*, May 29, 2000.
7 Johnson Jr., Billy. "Kandi Burruss: Destiny's Child Didn't Like 'Bug A Boo' on First Listen." Yahoo! Music, February 15, 2015.
8 Taraborrelli, J. Randy. *Becoming Beyoncé: The Untold Story*. Grand Central Publishing, 2015.
9 No author. "Destiny's Child: Hot Young Divas Continue to Burn Up Music Charts." *Jet*, May 29, 2000.
10 Biakolo, Kovie. "Kandi Burruss Shares the Funny Story Behind Writing Destiny Child's 'Bills, Bills, Bills.'" *Glamour*, July 8, 2021.
11 Flynn, Paul. "'Of course you can lose yourself." *The Guardian*, August 18, 2006.
12 Compact disc liner notes, *Survivor*, 2001.
13 Taraborrelli, J. Randy. *Becoming Beyoncé: The Untold Story*. Grand Central Publishing, 2015.
14 Cumberbatch, Franklin, and Stas, Heather. "Destiny's Child: Three the Hard Way." MTV News interview, 2002.
15 *Ibid.*
16 Beyoncé stage speech, "4 Intimate Nights with Beyoncé" residency. Roseland Ballroom, August 2011.
17 *Ibid.*
18 *Billboard* staff. "Beyoncé Q&A: The *Billboard* Music Awards Millennium Artist Discusses Her Career and New Album." *Billboard*, May 11, 2011.
19 Norris, John. "Destiny's Child: Survivors." MTV News interview, 2001.
20 *Ibid.*
21 YouTube video. "Anthony Dent speaks on producing 'Survivor' for Beyoncé." Published January 20, 2011.
22 Beyoncé stage speech, "4 Intimate Nights with Beyoncé" residency.
23 Taraborrelli, J. Randy. *Becoming Beyoncé: The Untold Story*. Grand Central Publishing, 2015.
24 Vanhorn, Teri. "Aaliyah's Absence Felt At Lady Of Soul Awards." MTV News, August 29, 2001.
25 Cumberbatch, Franklin, and Stas, Heather. "Destiny's Child: Three the Hard Way." MTV News interview, 2002.
26 Van Horn, Teri. "Destiny's Child Put 'Stank' into Christmas on Holiday Album." MTV News, September 24, 2001.
27 *Ibid.*
28 Clark, Michael. "Destiny's Child to release first holiday album." *The Tribune* (Scranton, Pennsylvania), October 23, 2001.
29 Van Horn, Teri. "Destiny's Child Solo CDs Won't Compete With Group, Each Other." MTV News, December 11, 2000.
30 Nostro, Lauren. "Sean Garrett Tells All: The Stories Behind His Classic Records." *Complex*, November 22, 2012.
31 Moss, Corey. "Destiny's Child: Reunited And It Feels So Good." MTV News, November 8, 2004.
32 Moss, Corey. "Beyoncé Healing Fast Thanks To Serena Williams." MTV News, October 6, 2004.
33 *Ibid.*
34 Nostro, Lauren. "Sean Garrett Tells All: The Stories Behind His Classic Records." *Complex*, November 22, 2012.
35 Moss, Corey. "Beyoncé Salutes Jay-Z On Destiny's Child Track 'Soldier.'" MTV News, October 29, 2004.
36 Corner, Lewis. "Beyoncé wrote Destiny's Child track as plea to Kelly Rowland." Digital Spy, June 5, 2013.
37 Moss, Corey. "Destiny's Child: Reunited And It Feels So Good." MTV News, November 8, 2004.
38 *Ibid.*

BEYONCÉ – EARLY SOLO

1 Musto, Michael. "New Again: Missy Elliott." *Interview*, 1999.
2 Bracco, Lorraine, and Hodges, Suzanne. "New Again: Destiny's Child." *Interview*, August 2001.
3 *Ibid.*
4 Nord, Thomas. "'Hip-Hopera': Robert Townsend interprets '*Carmen*' for the MTV Crowd." *The Courier-Journal*, May 4, 2001.
5 Valdés, Mimi. "The Metamorphosis." *Vibe*, October 2002.
6 Dunn, Jancee. "A Date With Destiny." *Rolling Stone*, May 24, 2001.
7 Jacobs, Matthew. "'She Wanted to Be Fantastic' An oral history of Beyoncé in *Austin Powers in Goldmember*, a goofy anomaly in a now-rarefied pop career." *Vulture*, July 15, 2022.
8 Mottram, James. "Beyoncé Knowles: *Austin Powers in Goldmember*." BBC, July 17, 2002.
9 Jacobs, Matthew. "'She Wanted to Be Fantastic', An oral history of Beyoncé in *Austin Powers in Goldmember*, a goofy anomaly in a now-rarefied pop career." *Vulture*, July 15, 2022.
10 *Ibid.*
11 *Ibid.*
12 Lynskey, Dorian. "Missy Elliott – Beyoncé said: 'If I sound crazy, don't put this out!'" *The Guardian*, September 14, 2019.
13 Seymour, Craig. "50 Cent makes radio history 'In Da Club.'" *The Atlanta Journal-Constitution*, March 30, 2003.
14 Reid, Shaheem. "Beyoncé's First Solo Single Will Be A Club Banger." MTV News, April 4, 2003.

DANGEROUSLY IN LOVE

1 Garfield, Simon. "Uh-oh! Uh-oh! Uh-oh!" *The Guardian*, December 14, 2003.
2 D'Angelo, Joe. "Road to the Grammys: The Making of Beyoncé's 'Crazy in Love.'" MTV News, February 3, 2004.
3 Garfield, Simon. "Uh-oh! Uh-oh! Uh-oh!" *The Guardian*, December 14, 2003.
4 Beyoncé Interview. "About *Dangerously in Love* (Part 1)." Accessed via YouTube: https://www.youtube.com/watch?v=DsgTjYf0aW8.
5 Garfield, Simon. "Uh-oh! Uh-oh! Uh-oh!" *The Guardian*, December 14, 2003.
6 No author. "Beyoncé's debut album, *Dangerously in Love*." *Thread* online magazine (New Zealand), 2003.
7 Beyoncé interview. "The Making of *Dangerously in Love*." Accessed via YouTube: www.youtube.com/watch?v=Y3Z1v52PeQs.
8 Kaufman, Gil. "Jigga Who? Beyoncé Shares Fantasies With Sean Paul On 'Bonnie & Clyde' Sequel." MTV News, March 17, 2003.
9 Rouhani, Neena. "The Dancehall Album Heard 'Round the World: Sean Paul Talks 20 Years of 'Dutty Rock' & Announces New 'Scorcha' LP." *Billboard*, March 23, 2002.
10 Fekadu, Mesfin. "From 'Bad Boys' to "Baby Boy": Sean Paul on Collaborating With Will Smith and Beyoncé." *The Hollywood Reporter*, June 14, 2024.
11 Beyoncé Interview. "About *Dangerously in Love* (Part 1)." Accessed via YouTube: www.youtube.com/watch?v=DsgTjYf0aW8.
12 *Ibid.*
13 Richman, Simmy. "Shuggie Otis: 'It's a miracle – now I don't have the craving, my chops came back.'" *The Telegraph*, April 11, 2013.
14 Couric, Katie. "Beyoncé meets her destiny." NBC News, July 8, 2003.
15 Beyoncé interview. "The Making of *Dangerously in Love*." Accessed via YouTube: www.youtube.com/watch?v=Y3Z1v52PeQs.
16 *Ibid.*
17 *Ibid.*
18 Moss, Corey. "Beyoncé: Genuinely in Love." MTV News, June 27, 2003.
19 *Ibid.*
20 Menze, Jill. "How Beyoncé's 'Dangerously in Love' Became a Certified Classic." MySpace, June 19, 2014.
21 *Ibid.*
22 Beyoncé interview. "The Making of *Dangerously in Love*." Accessed via YouTube: www.youtube.com/watch?v=Y3Z1v52PeQs.
23 No author. "Beyoncé's debut album, Dangerously in Love." *Thread* online magazine (New Zealand), 2003.
24 Beyoncé interview. "The Making of *Dangerously in Love*." Accessed via YouTube: www.youtube.com/watch?v=Y3Z1v52PeQs.
25 Menze, Jill. "How Beyoncé's 'Dangerously in Love' Became a Certified Classic." MySpace, June 19, 2014.
26 Beyoncé interview. "About *Dangerously in Love* (Part 1)." Accessed via YouTube: www.youtube.com/watch?v=DsgTjYf0aW8.
27 Beyoncé interview. "The Making of *Dangerously in Love*." Accessed via YouTube: www.youtube.com/watch?v=Y3Z1v52PeQs.
28 Tyrangiel, Josh. "Destiny's Adult." *Time*, June 30, 2003.
29 No author. "Beyoncé's debut album, *Dangerously in Love*." *Thread* online magazine (New Zealand), 2003.
30 *Ibid.*
31 Richman, Simmy. "Shuggie Otis: 'It's a miracle – now I don't have the craving, my chops came back.'" *The Independent*, April 11, 2013.
32 Moss, Corey. "Beyoncé: Genuinely in Love." MTV News, June 27, 2003.
33 *Ibid.*
34 Tyrangiel, Josh. "Destiny's Adult." *Time*, June 30, 2003.
35 Kareem "Biggs" Burke interview, October 22, 2016. Instagram, @bet.
36 Reid, Shaheem. "Jay-Z Camp Refutes Toni Braxton's Tupac-Biting Claims." MTV News, October 9, 2002.
37 *Ibid.*
38 Video interview. "Beyoncé Clears Up Rumors & Talks Fighting Temptations Acting Role." BET's 106 & Park, 2003. Accessed via YouTube: youtube.com/watch?v=gOSBS2Bmdw4.
39 No author. "Beyoncé's debut album, *Dangerously in Love*." *Thread* online magazine (New Zealand), 2003.
40 BET's 106 & Park, 2003.
41 Petersen, George. "Rick Camp Travels With Beyoncé." *Mix*, May 1, 2004.
42 No author. "Beyoncé Knowles: Her quest for an Oscar." *The Independent*, March 7, 2006.

B'DAY

1 Video interview. "All Eyes on Beyoncé." MTV, 2006.
2 *Ibid.*
3 Hiatt, Brian. "Rodney Jerkins: How We Made Beyoncé's Greatest Song." *Rolling Stone*, August 1, 2022.
4 *Ibid.*

5 Reid, Shaheem. "Beyoncé Asks Women To Battle Over Her For Backing-Band Roles." MTV News, June 19, 2006.
6 Jeannine, Amber. "A Fashionable Life." *Essence*, September 2006.
7 Hiatt, Brian. "Rodney Jerkins: How We Made Beyoncé's Greatest Song." *Rolling Stone*, August 1, 2022.
8 Thompson, Paul. "Rema and Swizz Beatz on the Difference Between Flashy Possessions and Art." *Rolling Stone*, October 24, 2023.
9 *Ibid.*
10 Vineyard, Jennifer. "Beyoncé: Behind the B'Day videos." MTV News, April 2, 2007.
11 *Ibid.*
12 Reid, Shaheem. "All Eyes on Beyoncé." MTV News, 2006.
13 *Ibid.*
14 MTV News staff. "For The Record: Quick News On Eminem, Aaliyah, Panic! At The Disco, DMX, Beyoncé, Britney Spears & More." MTV News, August 25, 2006.
15 Conniff, Tamara. "Beyoncé's Little Secret." *Billboard,* June 24, 2006.
16 Vineyard, Jennifer. "Beyoncé: Behind the B'Day videos." MTV News, April 2, 2007.
17 *Ibid.*
18 Conniff, Tamara. "Beyoncé's Little Secret." *Billboard,* June 24, 2006.
19 Vineyard, Jennifer. "Beyoncé: Behind the B'Day videos." MTV News, April 2, 2007.
20 *Ibid.*
21 Jeannine, Amber. "A Fashionable Life." *Essence*, September 2006.
22 Feeney, Nolan. "Producer duo Stargate share the secrets behind their Rihanna, Katy Perry, and Beyoncé hits." *Entertainment Weekly*, April 9, 2018.
23 Morales. Wilson. "Stomp the Yard: An Interview with Ne-Yo." *Black Film Review*, January 11, 2007.
24 Kaufman, Gil. "Beyoncé's 'Irreplaceable' Could Have Gone Country: Behind The Grammys." MTV News, February 5, 2008.
25 Feeney, Nolan. "Producer duo Stargate share the secrets behind their Rihanna, Katy Perry, and Beyoncé hits." *Entertainment Weekly*, April 9, 2018.
26 Tingen, Paul. "The Stargate Writing & Production Team." *Sound on Sound*, May 2010.
27 Velasquez, Angelina. "Ne-Yo addresses the misogynistic origins of Beyoncé's smash record 'Irreplaceable.'" The Gloria Velez Podcast, as quoted on Revolt. August 5, 2023.
28 Video interview, 2006. Channel 4's 4music, London. Accessed via: www.youtube.com/watch?v=gXR5X0jEt0Q.
29 "Check On It" Making of the Video. Accessed via: https://www.youtube.com/watch?v=RIMzXg9FKgg.
30 *Ibid.*
31 *Ibid.*
32 Horowitz, Steven J. "5 Songwriters And Producers Explain Their Unreleased Beyoncé Collaborations." *The Fader*, March 3, 2016.
33 Vineyard, Jennifer. "Beyoncé: Behind the B'Day videos." MTV News, April 2, 2007.
34 Tingen, Paul. "The Stargate Writing & Production Team." *Sound on Sound*, May 2010.
35 *Ibid.*
36 Ian Dench interview. "The Weekly Show with David J. Maloney." June 3, 2021.
37 Tingen, Paul. "The Stargate Writing & Production Team." *Sound on Sound*, May 2010.
38 Moss, Corey. "Beyonce Turns Heads With *Sports Illustrated* Cover, Shakira Duet." MTV News, February 14, 2007.
39 Tingen, Paul. "The Stargate Writing & Production Team." *Sound on Sound*, May 2010.
40 Ne-Yo interview. "Ne-Yo Reveals How Britney Spears' Song's Ended Up with Beyoncé and Rihanna." Revolt, July 17, 2024.
41 Horowitz, Steven J. "5 Songwriters And Producers Explain Their Unreleased Beyoncé Collaborations." *The Fader*, March 3, 2016.
42 Reid, Shaheem. "All Eyes on Beyoncé." MTV News, 2006.
43 Vineyard, Jennifer. "Beyoncé: Behind the B'Day videos." MTV News, April 2, 2007.
44 Press release. "Beyoncé and Alejandro Fernandez Pair for Duet in Spanish." PR Newswire.
45 No author. "Staking New Ground." *Billboard*, July 7, 2007.
46 Burr, Ramiro. "Heir Apparent." *Billboard*, July 7, 2007.
47 Vineyard, Jennifer. "Beyoncé: Behind the B'Day videos." MTV News, April 2, 2007.
48 Vineyard, Jennifer. "Beyoncé's B'Day Over? Singer Pulls Deluxe Editions Due To Lawsuit," MTV News, April 24, 2007.
49 Horowitz, Steven J. "5 Songwriters And Producers Explain Their Unreleased Beyoncé Collaborations." *The Fader*, March 3, 2016.
50 *Ibid.*
51 Interview, MTV TRL Italy, December 17, 2007. Accessed via YouTube:
52 No author. "Destiny's Child: Hot Young Divas Continue to Burn Up Music Charts." *Jet*, May 29, 2000.
53 Video interview. Beyoncé, The *B'Day* documentary.
54 Reid, Shaheem. "All Eyes on Beyoncé." MTV News, 2006.
55 *Ibid.*
56 Ulmer, James. "After Conquering 'Chicago,' It's On to Motown." *New York Times*, September 10, 2006.
57 *Ibid.*
58 No author. "Producer apologizes to Motown over Dreamgirls." CBC, February 22, 2007.
59 Reid, Shaheem. "All Eyes on Beyoncé." MTV News, 2006.
60 *Ibid.*
61 No author. "Superstar Beyoncé Knowles talks about second album 'B'Day' and her life." *Associated Press* video interview, August 16, 2006.
62 *Ibid.*
63 Ulmer, James. "After Conquering 'Chicago,' It's On to Motown." *New York Times*, September 10, 2006.
64 *Ibid.*

I AM ... SASHA FIERCE

1 Light, Alan. "Pop Music's Dreamgirl Awakens Her Earthy Side." *The New York Times*, November 14, 2008.
2 *Ibid.*
3 Crosley, Hillary. "Worker B." *Billboard*, November 8, 2008.
4 Adler, Shawn, with reporting by Yasmine Richard. "Beyoncé, Etta James And 'Cadillac Records' Stars Come Out For Movie's Premiere." MTV News, November 25, 2008.
5 Crosley, Hillary. "Worker B." *Billboard*, November 8, 2008.
6 Video interview montage, "BEYONCÉ on ETTA JAMES — Diva on Diva." Clip from *Cadillac Records* – Behind the Scenes, 2008. Accessed via: youtube.com/watch?v=auYob8Yd2pA.
7 *Ibid*.
8 Ian Dench interview, The StageLeft Podcast, Episode 44. March 2, 2018.
9 Official Beyoncé biography, *I Am...Sasha Fierce*. Accessed via: ramentertainment.com/beyonce.
10 Danton, Eric. "A Girl's Pizza-Inspired Musing Produces A Smash Hit." *The Hartford Courant*, January 11, 2009.
11 *Ibid.*
12 *Ibid.*
13 No author. "Interview with Evan Bogart, songwriter for Beyoncé, Rihanna and Leona Lewis." *HitQuarters*, Feb 8, 2010.
14 *Ibid.*
15 Cragg, Michael. "Ryan Tedder: One Direction are so normal it almost turns you off." *The Guardian*, April 23, 2014.
16 *Ibid.*
17 No author. "Interview with Evan Bogart, songwriter for Beyoncé, Rihanna and Leona Lewis." *HitQuarters*, Feb 8, 2010.
18 Horan, Tom. "Beyoncé: dream girl." *The Telegraph*, November 8, 2008.
19 Crosley, Hillary. "Worker B." *Billboard*, November 8, 2008.
20 *Ibid.*
21 Tingen, Paul. "The Stargate Writing & Production Team." *Sound on Sound*, May 2010.
22 *Ibid.*
23 *Ibid.*
24 Knowles, Beyoncé. "Beyoncé Knowles' NYABJ Award-Winning ESSENCE Article: 'Eat, Play, Love.'" *Essence*, July 2011.
25 Ian Dench interview, The StageLeft Podcast, Episode 44. March 2, 2018.
26 Horan, Tom. "Beyoncé: dream girl." *The Telegraph*, November 8, 2008.
27 Video interview montage, "BEYONCÉ on ETTA JAMES — Diva on Diva." Clip from Hollywood.com, 2008. Accessed via: youtube.com/watch?v=auYob8Yd2pA.
28 Light, Alan. "Pop Music's Dreamgirl Awakens Her Earthy Side." *The New York Times*, November 14, 2008.
29 Horan, Tom. "Beyoncé: dream girl." *The Telegraph*, November 8, 2008.
30 LeDonne, Rob. "For 'Havana' & 'Youngblood' Co-Writer Ali Tamposi, A Career Surge After Sobriety." *Billboard*, October 29, 2018.
31 Official Beyoncé biography, *I Am...Sasha Fierce*. Accessed via: ramentertainment.com/beyonce.
32 The-Dream, verified annotation on Genius lyrics for "Smash into You." Accessed via: https://genius.com/5054977.
33 Mitchell, Gail. "Beyoncé: The *Billboard* Q&A." *Billboard*, October 2, 2009.
34 Herndon, Jessica. "INSIDE STORY: The Making of Beyoncé's 'Single Ladies.'" *People*, January 1, 2010.
35 *Ibid.*
36 Mitchell, Gail. "Beyonce: *The Billboard* Q&A." *Billboard*, October 2, 2009.
37 *Ibid.*
38 Official Beyoncé biography, *I Am...Sasha Fierce*. Accessed via: ramentertainment.com/beyonce.
39 Video interview. "Behind The Scenes: *I Am ... Sasha Fierce*." Accessed via: www.youtube.com/watch?v=hCKu7f4F8kA.
40 "Inside the Mind of Beyoncé/Sasha Fierce." MySpace interview. Accessed via: youtube.com/watch?v=Ke9iKnDxcZQ.
41 Video interview. "Rico Love Talks About Making 'Sweet Dreams' w/ Beyoncé." Playback I VH1, May 29, 2015.
42 Reid, Shaheem. "Usher, Beyoncé Collaborator Rico Love Talks 'Organic' Songwriting Process." MTV News, April 8, 2010.
43 Video interview. "Behind The Scenes: *I Am ... Sasha Fierce*." Accessed via: www.youtube.com/watch?v=hCKu7f4F8kA.
44 Video interview. "Beyoncé: Behind The Scenes of Video Phone – Part 2 (featuring Lady Gaga)."
45 Vena, Jocelyn. "Lady Gaga On Beyoncé: 'She Is A Real, Real Woman.'" MTV News, November 4, 2009.
46 Vena, Jocelyn. "Lady Gaga Paid Tribute To Beyoncé In 'Video Phone' Clip." MTV News, November 17, 2009.
47 Roberts, Steven. "Beyoncé's 'Why Don't You Love Me' Almost Didn't Happen, Bama Boyz Say." MTV News, July 12, 2010.
48 *Ibid.*
49 Rodriguez, Jayson. "Beyoncé Knew The Perfect Person To Remix 'Ego': Kanye West!" MTV News, May 20, 2009.
50 *Ibid.*
51 Paphides, Pete. "Beyoncé: shy big sister by day, wild girl by night." *The London Times*, November 14, 2008.
52 No author. "Who Originally Had Beyoncé's 'Ego'?" Rap-Up.com, July 22, 2009.
53 Billy Joel interview. "Billy Joel Reveals Major Changes He Made to Some of His Now Hit Songs." *The Howard Stern Show*, February 14, 2024.
54 Reid, Shaheem. "Usher Chalks Up Song Leaks to 'Internal Conspiracy'—Listen to His New 'Club' Banger Here!" MTV News, February 14, 2008.
55 Reid, Shaheem. "Usher Wanted Lil Wayne And Beyoncé's 'Love In This Club' Remix To Be 'Crazier Than The Original.'" MTV News, May 27, 2008.
56 Montgomery, James. "Lady Gaga Recalls Beyoncé's Inspiration In MTV's 'Inside The Outside.'" May 27, 2011.
57 Video interview. "Lady Gaga explains "Telephone" – Fear of Suffocation [HQ] Interview." MTV, 2009. Accessed via: youtube.com/watch?v=Tz4hBXzdWBQ.
58 Concepcion, Mariel. "Kanye West Premieres Beyoncé Track, Album Due Nov. 16." *Billboard*, August 11, 2010.
59 No author. "Keys loves Beyoncé duet." Yahoo! News, January 23, 2010.

4

1 The-Dream video interview. "How The-Dream Writes #1 Hits For Beyoncé & Rihanna | Genius Level." Accessed via YouTube.
2 Rogers, Ray. "Beyoncé Q&A: The *Billboard* Music Awards Millennium Artist Discusses Her Career And New Album." *Billboard*, May 11, 2011.
3 Kaufman, Gil. "Beyoncé's 'I Care' Started Out As Solo Song For Jeff Bhasker." MTV News, February 21, 2013.
4 Alvarez, Gabriel. "Beyoncé: Mighty Fly." *Complex*, July 19, 2011.
5 "I Miss You" countdown text on Beyonce.com, June 18, 2011. Archived on beyoncéonline.org.
6 Original version posted by Patrick "J. Que" Smith at thesuperrandom.com.
7 Gyant, "'Best Thing I Never Had' Songwriter Inspired by Beyoncé." BET, June 3, 2011.
8 *Ibid.*
9 Video interview. "Story behind Beyoncé "Best Thing I Never Had" – told by producer Symbolyc One (Pt 11)." The Sample Lounge, October 11, 2024.
10 Gyant, "'Best Thing I Never Had' Songwriter Inspired by Beyoncé." BET, June 3, 2011.
11 Watson, Paul. "DJ Swivel: Recording Beyoncé's 4." *Sound on Sound*, October 2011.
12 "Party" countdown text on Beyonce.com, June 20, 2011. Archived on beyonceonline.org.
13 Alvarez, Gabriel. "Beyoncé: Mighty Fly." *Complex*, July 19, 2011
14 *Ibid.*
15 "Rather Die Young" countdown text on Beyonce.com, June 21, 2011. Archived on beyonceonline.org.
16 Houser, Brooke. "Song of Herself." *Allure*, February 2010.
17 "Start Over" countdown text on Beyonce.com, June 22, 2011. Archived on beyonceonline.org.
18 Tharpe, Frazier. "The Business of Being Beyoncé Knowles-Carter." *GQ*, September 10, 2024.
19 *Ibid.*
20 Rogers, Ray. "Beyoncé Q&A: The *Billboard* Music Awards Millennium Artist Discusses Her Career And New Album." *Billboard*, May 11, 2011.
21 No author. "Beyoncé '4' Album Preview – EXCLUSIVE." Just Jared, May 11, 2011.
22 Moore, Leslie. Interview with Cainon Lamb. http://instagram.com/upcloseandlovely.
23 *Ibid.*
24 Rogers, Ray. "Beyoncé Q&A: The *Billboard* Music Awards Millennium Artist Discusses Her Career And New Album." *Billboard*, May 11, 2011.
25 No author. "Beyoncé '4' Album Preview – EXCLUSIVE." Just Jared, May 11, 2011.
26 "End of Time" countdown text on Beyonce.com, June 25, 2011. Archived on beyonceonline.org.
27 No author. "Beyoncé Talks 'A Star Is Born' And 'I Was Here.'" Reuters, 2011.
28 "I Was Here" countdown text on Beyonce.com, June 26, 2011. Archived on beyonceonline.org.
29 The-Dream, verified annotation on Genius lyrics for "Run the World (Girls)". Accessed via: genius.com/11937519.
30 McGregor, Nesta. "Diplo: Beyoncé track started off as 'joke song.'" BBC, May 1, 2012.
31 Thorogood, Tom. "We always know how to rock a party." *The Sun*, July 12, 2013.
32 Rogers, Ray. "Beyoncé Q&A: The *Billboard* Music Awards Millennium Artist Discusses Her Career And New Album." *Billboard*, May 11, 2011.
33 "Run the World (Girls)" countdown text on Beyonce.com, June 27, 2011. Archived on beyonceonline.org.
34 Watson, Paul. "DJ Swivel: Recording Beyoncé's 4." *Sound on Sound*, October 2011.
35 *Ibid.*
36 "Dance for You" behind-the-scenes video. Accessed via Dailymotion.
37 *Ibid.*
38 *Ibid.*
39 No authors. "Beyoncé Lends Some Fancy Footwork to 'Move Your Body' Campaign." *Pop Eater*, April 12, 2011.
40 Devin. "New Music: Mary J. Blige f/ Beyoncé – 'Love a Woman.'" Rap-Up.com, November 17, 2011.
41 Markman, Rob, with reporting by Vanessa White Wolf. "Beyoncé/ Mary J. Blige Duet Was Meant For *4.*" MTV News, November 18, 2011.

BEYONCÉ

1 Knopper, Steve. "How a Song Written by Sia Furler Becomes a Hit." *New York Times*, April 21, 2014.
2 Beyoncé Radio, limited-edition iTunes radio station, December 2013.
3 Knopper, Steve. "How a Song Written by Sia Furler Becomes a Hit." *New York Times*, April 21, 2014.
4 Beyoncé Radio, limited-edition iTunes radio station, December 2013.
5 "Pretty Hurts" behind the scenes video. Accessed via: youtube.com/watch?v=mPpRTVYRm5o.
6 Beyoncé Radio, limited-edition iTunes radio station, December 2013.
7 Greene, Jayson. "Beyoncé's Muse." *Pitchfork*, January 21, 2014.
8 *Ibid.*
9 Video interview. "Self-Titled": Part 4, Liberation." Accessed via YouTube: youtube.com/watch?v=UPmX4ASAcaE.
10 Hicklin, Aaron. "Beyoncé Liberated." *Out*, April 8, 2014.
11 *Ibid.*
12 Video interview. "Self-Titled": Part 3, Run 'N Gun." Accessed via YouTube: youtube.com/watch?v=UPmX4ASAcaE.
13 *Ibid.*
14 *Ibid.*
15 Hicklin, Aaron. "Beyoncé Liberated." *Out*, April 8, 2014.
16 *Ibid.*
17 Beyoncé Radio, limited-edition iTunes radio station, December 2013.
18 Marchese, David. "How Chairlift's Caroline Polachek Landed a Track on 'Beyoncé.'" *Rolling Stone*, December 13, 2013.
19 *Ibid.*
20 *Ibid.*
21 SVA Directors Screening + Instagram Q&A, December 21, 2013.
22 *Ibid.*
23 Video interview. "Self-Titled": Part 4, Liberation." Accessed via YouTube: youtube.com/watch?v=UPmX4ASAcaE.
24 Beyoncé Radio, limited-edition iTunes radio station, December 2013.
25 Video interview. "Self-Titled": Part 4, Liberation." Accessed via YouTube: youtube.com/watch?v=UPmX4ASAcaE.
26 Beyoncé Radio, limited-edition iTunes radio station, December 2013.
27 Greene, Jayson. "Beyoncé's Muse." *Pitchfork*, January 21, 2014.
28 Beyoncé Radio, limited-edition iTunes radio station, December 2013.
29 Video interview. "Self-Titled": Part 5, Honesty." Accessed via: youtube.com/watch?v=LFXJGr7sYDk
30 *Ibid.*
31 *Ibid.*
32 Kennedy, John. "Outtakes: Drake Talks Beyoncé, 'Trophies' And Next Album In VIBE Interview." *VIBE*, December 30, 2013.
33 Hicklin, Aaron. "Beyoncé Liberated." *Out*, April 8, 2014.
34 No author. "Beyoncé Slammed for Sampling Shuttle Tragedy on New Album." ABC News, December 30, 2013.
35 Video interview. "Self-Titled": Part 2, Imperfection." Accessed via: youtube.com/watch?v=LFXJGr7sYDk.
36 *Ibid.*
37 *Ibid.*
38 Beyoncé Radio, limited-edition iTunes radio station, December 2013.
39 *Ibid.*
40 *Ibid.*
41 Dobbins, Amanda. "Beyoncé's Creative Director Todd Tourso on Her New Album and Keeping Secrets." *Vulture*, December 18, 2013.
42 BOOTS, verified annotation on Genius lyrics for "Heaven." Accessed via: https://genius.com/2623368.
43 Greene, Jayson. "Beyoncé's Muse." *Pitchfork*, January 21, 2014.
44 Life is But a Dream documentary
45 Video interview. "Bobby Johnson on the underground, OG Bobby Johnson, 7/11 by Beyonce & More! (Part 2/3)." Kult Classic, Interview #37. Accessed via: youtube.com/watch?v=M_OtZ7w92qo.
46 Kult Classic, Interview #37.
47 Video interview. Mr. Vegas on working with Beyoncé on "Standing On The Sun" (Remix)." On the Radar Radio. Accessed via: youtube.com/watch?v=Z9XrUfCwROU.
48 Beyoncé Radio, limited-edition iTunes radio station, December 2013.
49 Baiden, Kamilla Rose. "Introducing Carla Marie Williams, The North London Songwriter Penning Tracks For Queen Bey." *Vibe*, May 16, 2016.
50 *Ibid.*

LEMONADE

1 Platon, Adelle. "Singer Kevin Garrett Talks Writing & Producing Beyoncé's Emotional 'Lemonade' Opener 'Pray You Catch Me.'" *Billboard*, April 28, 2016.
2 Vain, Madison. "Kevin Garrett talks Beyoncé's 'Pray You Catch Me.'" Entertainment Weekly, August 22, 2016.
3 Ezra Koenig, Twitter (now X) post, April 25, 2016. Accessed via: https://x.com/arzE/status/724660587523805184.
4 Video interview. "Father John Misty: 'Pure Comedy' Interview." Apple Music/Beats 1 with Zane Lowe, April 6, 2017.
5 NPR Staff. "Jack White On Detroit, Beyoncé And Where Songs Come From." NPR All Things Considered, September 10, 2016.
6 *Ibid.*
7 Gonzales, Erica. "Diana Gordon's Story Is Bigger Than 'Becky with the Good Hair.'" *Harper's Bazaar*, August 27, 2018.
8 Strauss, Matthew. "Beyoncé's Lemonade Collaborator MeLo-X Gives First Interview on Making of the Album." *Pitchfork*, April 25, 2016.
9 *Ibid.*
10 Leight, Elias. "Producer Ben Billions on Making Hits for The Weeknd, Belly & Beyoncé: 'If The Artist Loves It, I Love It.'" *Billboard*, January 17, 2017.
11 *Ibid.*
12 Platon, Adelle. "Beyonce's Folky 'Lemonade' Track 'Daddy Lessons': Co-writer Kevin Cossom Shares the Story Behind the 'Tough' Song." *Billboard*, April 28, 2016.
13 Goodman, Jessica. "Diana Gordon interview: The 'Becky with the good hair' scribe opens up about new music." *Entertainment Weekly*, August 2, 2016.
14 *Ibid.*
15 Ingrid Burley video interview. "Beyoncé's 'Love Drought' Isn't Actually About Jay Z." Genius, June 15, 2016. Accessed via: www.youtube.com/watch?v=_nbHKdMPnk.
16 *Ibid.*
17 Kennedy, Gerrick D. "How a homeless songwriter's story of heartbreak made it into Beyonce's album." *The Los Angeles Times*, June 15, 2016.
18 *Ibid.*
19 Lozano, Kevin. "James Blake Reveals He Ignored Beyoncé Lyrics and Turned Down Drake." *Pitchfork*, July 13, 2016.
20 *Ibid.*
21 Cliff, Aimee. "What Writing "Freedom" With Beyoncé Was Really Like." *The Fader*, February 10, 2017.
22 *Ibid.*
23 Seabrook, John. "How Mike Will Made It." *The New Yorker*, July 4, 2016.
24 *Ibid.*
25 Gottesman, Tamar. "EXCLUSIVE: Beyoncé Wants to Change the Conversation." *Elle*, April 4, 2016.
26 Roth, Madeline. "Hear the Ballad Ed Sheeran Calls 'the Best Love Song' of His Career." MTV News, March 3, 2017.
27 McCabe, Kathy. "Surprise Ed Sheeran collaboration with Beyoncé." *The New Zealand Herald*, December 1, 2017.
28 Mitchell, Tyler. "Beyoncé in Her Own Words: Her Life, Her Body, Her Heritage." *Vogue*, August 6, 2018.
29 Hadley, Fredara Mareva. "Beyoncé's Coachella Set Was a Landmark Celebration of HBCUs & Southern Black Culture." *Billboard*, April 18, 2018.
30 Puckett, Lily. "Tina Knowles-Lawson thought white people would be "confused" by Beyoncé's Coachella performance." *The Fader*, April 16, 2018.
31 *Ibid.*

THE CARTERS

1 Baquet, Dean. "Interview: Jay-Z." *New York Times*, November 29, 2017.
2 *Ibid.*
3 Feeney, Nolan. "Beyoncé and JAY-Z Collaborators Cool & Dre Detail the Last-Minute Making of 'Everything Is Love.'" *Billboard*, June 18, 2018.
4 *Ibid.*
5 *Ibid.*
6 *Ibid.*
7 Saponara, Michael. "Quavo Talks Crafting 'They Can't Win' For 'Madden 19', How 'Apeshit' Came About & What's in Store For Drake Tour." *Billboard*, July 25, 2018.
8 Chrisafis, Angelique. "Beyoncé and Jay-Z help Louvre Museum break visitor record in 2018." *The Guardian*, January 3, 2019.

THE LION KING

1 Jean-Philippe, McKenzie. "Beyoncé Opens up in a Rare Interview: 'My Family Is My Biggest Priority.'" Oprah Daily, July 16, 2019. Article quoting Beyoncé's interview with ABC's Robin Roberts.
2 Parkwood Entertainment press release, "Beyoncé Produces And Performs On Multi-Artist Album 'The Lion King: The Gift.'" July 9, 2019.
3 *Ibid.*
4 Jean-Philippe, McKenzie. "Beyoncé Opens up in a Rare Interview: 'My Family Is My Biggest Priority.'" Oprah Daily, July 16, 2019. Article quoting Beyoncé's interview with ABC's Robin Roberts.
5 Leight, Elias. "Inside Beyoncé's Bold Bet to Get Americans to Listen to African Music." *Rolling Stone*, July 19, 2019.
6 Video message, *Good Morning America*, July 31, 2020.
7 Interview. "Tina Knowles-Lawson says Beyoncé's 'Black Is King' is meant to share beauty of African culture." *Washington Post*, August 5, 2020.
8 Bradley, Bill. "Here's How Beyoncé's New Song 'Spirit' Wound Up In 'The Lion King.'" *Huffington Post*, July 11, 2019.
9 *Ibid.*
10 Beyoncé Knowles interview. *Beyoncé Presents: Making the Gift*, ABC TV special, September 16, 2019.
11 Social media screenshot of a note by Derek Dixie, as shared on the X account @BeyLegion, June 22, 2020. Accessed via: https://x.com/BeyLegion/status/1275095786347474944.
12 Beyoncé acceptance speech, Grammy Awards, March 14, 2021.
13 Cobo, Leila. "Here's How Beyonce Joined J Balvin & Willy William's 'Mi Gente.'" *Billboard*, September 29, 2017.
14 "Actually Me" video interview. "Megan Thee Stallion Goes Undercover on YouTube, Twitter and Instagram." GQ, November 16, 2020.
15 Adegoke, Yomi. "'When a woman raps, she spitting!' Megan Thee Stallion, the hot girl taking over hip-hop." *The Guardian*, May 8, 2020.
16 Knowles, Beyoncé. "Beyoncé Knowles' NYABJ Award-Winning ESSENCE Article: 'Eat, Play, Love.'" *Essence*, July 2011.
17 *Ibid.*
18 LeDonne, Rob. "Frankie Beverly Responds to Beyonce Covering His Maze Hit 'Before I Let Go.'" *Billboard*, April 24, 2019.
19 Towers, Andrea. "Will Smith explains the 'magic' behind King Richard landing Beyoncé song 'Be Alive.'" *Entertainment Weekly*, October 21, 2021.
20 Draughorne, Kenan. "Dixson just earned an Oscar nod for his song with Beyoncé. He's still saying, 'Not yet.'" *The Los Angeles Times*, February 22, 2022.

RENAISSANCE

1 "Beyoncé's Evolution." *Harper's Bazaar*, September 2021.
2 Lopez, Julyssa. "Kelman Duran Didn't Expect To Be Part of Beyoncé's 'Renaissance.'" *Rolling Stone*, August 10, 2022.
3 Street, Mikelle. "TS Madison Talks Being Sampled On 'Renaissance:' 'You Never Know How Things Line Up.'" *Essence*, August 19, 2022.
4 *Ibid.*
5 Lucky Daye interview, Mina SayWhat, Sirius XM. Accessed via: https://x.com/ourhermitage/status/1780277312459809133?s=46.
6 Antonio Rose, Corey; Girdwood, Barton; Luse, Brittany; Placzek, Jessica; Williams, Veralyn. "Serving house music history with Honey Dijon." *NPR*, December 30, 2022.
7 Caldwell, Brandon. "'I Was Good by Myself. I'm Better With the Guys.' Raphael Saadiq wasn't sure a Tony! Toni! Tone! reunion would happen." *Vulture*, September 22, 2023.
8 *Ibid.*
9 Nile Rodgers' speech, Grammy Awards, February 5, 2023.
10 *Ibid.*
11 Gomez, Patrick. "Beyoncé and Jay-Z receive GLAAD Award for LGBTQ advocacy at starry event." *Entertainment Weekly*, March 29, 2019.
12 Beyoncé Instagram note, June 30, 2022.
13 Gomez, Patrick. "Beyoncé and Jay-Z receive GLAAD Award for LGBTQ advocacy at starry event." *Entertainment Weekly*, March 29, 2019.
14 Garcia, Thana. "Robin S Thanks Beyoncé for 'Giving Me My Flowers' by Sampling 'Show Me Love' on 'Break My Soul.'" *Variety*, June 22, 2022.
15 Beyoncé Instagram note, June 30, 2022.
16 Shipley, Al. "We've Got A File On You: No ID." Stereogum, October 18, 2023.
17 *Ibid.*
18 Wicker, Jewel. "Jozzy's Love Songs: How the Acclaimed Songwriter Kickstarted Her Solo Career With Help From Diddy." *Billboard*, March 22, 2023
19 Garcia, Thania. "Fine-Tuning Beyoncé's 'Virgo's Groove': How Three High-School Friends Ended Up Producing a Song on 'Renaissance.'" *Variety*, August 17, 2022.
20 *Ibid.*
21 Wheeler, André-Naquian. "Grace Jones on Her New Candle and Working With Beyoncé and Issey Miyake." *Vogue*, September 7, 2022.
22 *Ibid.*
23 Blistein, Jon. "Beyoncé to Remove Ableist Slur From Song 'Heated' After Backlash." *Rolling Stone*, August 1, 2022.
24 Jones, Damian. "Hit-Boy says Beyoncé's 'Thique' was originally made in 2014." *NME*, August 17, 2022.
25 *Ibid.*
26 Street, Mikelle. "Kevin JZ Prodigy on Bringing Beyoncé Into Ballroom With 'Pure/Honey.'" The Cut, August 3, 2022.
27 Frank, Jason P. "Kevin Aviance Was 'Overwhelmed' When He Heard Beyoncé Had Sampled His Music." *Vulture*, July 30, 2022.
28 Fallen, Mildred. "Cincinnati Native One of the Producers on Beyoncé's "Renaissance.'" *Cincinnati*, August 18, 2022.
29 Beyoncé Instagram note, June 30, 2022.
30 Price, Joe. "Travis Scott Finally Made His Beyoncé Collab Happen After Manifesting It 8 Years Ago." *Complex*, July 28, 2023.
31 Johnson, Zoe. "Beyoncé And Travis Scott Are Reportedly Working On Music Together." *Vibe*, February 21, 2019.
32 Fekadu, Mesfin. "The-Dream on Oscars Shortlist, Why He'd Give His Kidney to Beyoncé and How Losing His Mother Connected Him to Color Purple". *The Hollywood Reporter*, January 9, 2024.
33 *Ibid.*

COWBOY CARTER

1 Kreps, Daniel. "Paul McCartney Meets Women Who Inspired Beatles' 'Blackbird.'" *Rolling Stone*, May 1, 2016.
2 Newman, Melinda, and Nicholson, Jessica. "Hear From the 4 Black Country Women on Beyoncé's 'Blackbiird': 'We Were Having a Little Destiny's Child Moment.'" *Billboard*.
3 Aswad, Jem and Willman, Chris. "Beyoncé Used Original Beatles Backing Track for 'Blackbird' on New 'Cowboy Carter' Version, With Paul McCartney's Blessing." *Variety*, April 2, 2024.
4 Paul McCartney Instagram post, April 4, 2024.
5 Tharpe, Frazier. "The Business of Being Beyoncé Knowles-Carter." *GQ*, September 10, 2024.
6 Kreps, Daniel. "Paul McCartney Meets Women Who Inspired Beatles' 'Blackbird.'" *Rolling Stone*, May 1, 2016.
7 Browne, David. "Beyoncé Wanted Some 'Country Fire.' She Knew Just Who to Call." *Rolling Stone*, February 13, 2024.
8 Horowitz, Steven J. "Singer-Songwriter Cam Discusses Working on Five Tracks for Beyoncé's 'Cowboy Carter': 'She's Just Such a Creative Genius.'" *Variety*, April 8, 2024.
9 Beyoncé Knowles Instagram post, October 29, 2024.
10 Strauss, Matthew. "Beyoncé Reveals *Cowboy Carter* Artwork, Shares Statement on New Album." *Pitchfork*, March 19, 2024.
11 Rhiannon Giddens Instagram post, February 13, 2024.
12 Hiatt, Brian. "Tony! Toni! Toné! Won't Reunite Again — And Six More Things We Learned From Raphael Saadiq." *Rolling Stone*, September 9, 2024.
13 *Ibid.*
14 Vitale, Tom. "Dolly Parton's 'Jolene' Still Haunts Singers." *NPR*, October 9, 2008.
15 *Ibid.*
16 *Ibid.*
17 Vivinetto, Gina. "How Beyoncé's 'Jolene' changes Dolly Parton's original — and why." TODAY, June 2, 2024, quoting a Parton interview in E! News, May 31, 2024.
18 Hunt, Rebecca. "Joseph Bologne, Chevalier de Saint-Georges." Boston Public Library, February 5, 2024.
19 Tharpe, Frazier. "The Business of Being Beyoncé Knowles-Carter." *GQ*, September 10, 2024.
20 *Ibid.*
21 Arnold, Chuck. "Riding with Bey: How Beyoncé got Willie Jones to saddle up in the 'fourth quarter' for 'Cowboy Carter.'" *New York Post*, April 9, 2024.
22 *Ibid.*
23 Hawgood, Alex. "Miley Cyrus Finally Gets Her 'Flowers.'" *W* Magazine, June 3, 2024.
24 *Ibid.*
25 *Ibid.*
26 *Ibid.*
27 Coscarelli, Joe. "How Post Malone Went Country (Carefully, With a Beer in His Hand)." *The New York Times*, August 8, 2024.
28 *Ibid.*
29 Mamii Instagram post, March 29, 2024.
30 Tharpe, Frazier. "The Business of Being Beyoncé Knowles-Carter." *GQ*, September 10, 2024.
31 O'Connor, Roisin. "Arlo Parks: Beyoncé songwriting credit on Cowboy Carter was 'beautiful surprise.'" *The Independent*, April 5, 2024.
32 Tharpe, Frazier. "The Business of Being Beyoncé Knowles-Carter." *GQ*, September 10, 2024.
33 *Cowboy Carter* official press release, March 29, 2024.
34 *Ibid.*
35 Thompson, Erica. "Chicago's D.A. Got That Dope produced Beyoncé's 'Tyrant,' the violin-heavy banger on 'Cowboy Carter.'" *The Chicago Sun-Times*, March 31, 2024.
36 Fekadu, Mesfin. "How 'Cowboy Carter' Changed My Life: Shaboozey, Brittney Spencer and Tiera Kennedy on Seminal Beyoncé Album." *The Hollywood Reporter*, June 20, 2024.

ACKNOWLEDGEMENTS

THANKS TO EVERYONE AT WELBECK FOR THEIR CARE AND ATTENTION TO ALL OF THEIR BOOKS, BUT ESPECIALLY THIS ONE! I'D ALSO LIKE TO THANK THE INTERNET ARCHIVE, WORLD RADIO HISTORY AND FAN-CURATED WEBSITES (ESPECIALLY BEYONCEONLINE.ORG AND THEBEYONCEWORLD.COM) FOR PRESERVING SO MUCH BEYONCÉ SCHOLARSHIP, AS WELL AS NEWS AND INTERVIEWS. THEIR DEDICATION TO ARCHIVING ENSURES THAT CRUCIAL INFORMATION AND HISTORY ABOUT HER WORK AND CAREER REMAINS ACCESSIBLE TO ALL.

CREDITS

The publishers would like to thank the following sources for their kind permission to reproduce the pictures in this book.

Alamy: Album 30-31, 35, 37, 119; Cinematic 58T, 59, 86; Collection Christophel 89; Everett Collection Inc 9; Featureflash Archive 17B; FlixPix 205, 213; Barry King 226; Maximum Film 87; MediaPunch Inc 32, 48; Moviestore Collection Ltd 90, 95; Pictorial Press Ltd 58B, 107; Brittany Smith 8; Universal Images Group North America LLC 91

Getty Images: Evan Agostini 85; Carlo Allegri 80; Carlos Alvarez 22; Pierre Andrieu/AFP 53B; Christophe Archambault/AFP 152; Robyn Beck/AFP 168; Bryan Bedder 88; Jeremy Bembaron/Sygma 14; David M. Benett/WireImage 189; Michael Buckner/Billboard 214-215; Larry Busacca 77, 97, 145, 162-163, 165, 176, 178-179, 180-181, 183T, 183B, 185T, 185B; Larry Busacca/WireImage 150, 155, 158, 159, 160; Nathaniel S. Butler/NBAE 23; F. Carter Smith/Bloomberg 218, 219; Gareth Cattermole 191B; Michael Caulfield/WireImage 101, 105, 114; Lester Cohen/WireImage 81; Jemal Countess 112; Rick Diamond 216; Kevork Djansezian 146; Tabatha Fireman/Redferns 57; J. Emilio Flores/Corbis 82; Pam Francis 50; Charley Gallay/WireImage 139; John Gichigi 52; Jesse Grant 191T; Scott Gries 69; Frazer Harrison 65; Dave Hogan 44, 125; Dave J Hogan 151; Houston Chronicle/Hearst Newspapers 11, 12, 63, 220; Harry How 173; Samir Hussein 128; Chris Jackson 62-63; Dimitrios Kambouris 157; Dimitrios Kambouris/WireImage 43; Gie Knaeps 38-39, 49; Jeff Kravitz/FilmMagic 34, 40, 41, 61, 98, 99, 100, 108, 111; Stephen Lovekin 227; Mark Mainz 33; Pierre Philippe Marcou/AFP 67; Kevin Mazur 45, 76, 79, 148, 171, 175, 177T, 177B, 184, 186-187, 195, 207; Kevin Mazur/WireImage 21, 47B, 55, 109, 118, 122-123, 126, 130, 131, 133, 134, 135, 142, 144, 147, 153, 154, 156, 167, 198-199, 201, 204, 206, 208, 211, 212; Jamie McCarthy 166; Win McNamee 96; Buda Mendes 143; Mark Metcalfe/WireImage 140-141; Frank Micelotta 18, 42, 47T, 60; Ethan Miller 19, 73; Tim Mosenfelder 25, 26, 115; Paul Natkin 83; Johnny Nunez/WireImage 68; Gail Oskin/WireImage 53T; Maury Phillips Archive 46; Mason Poole 192, 193, 194, 197, 209; Brian Rasic 56, 129; Alberto E. Rodriguez 190; Ezra Shaw 132, 161, 174; John Shearer/WireImage 104, 117; Alex Slitz 224, 228, 232, 233; Francis Specker/CBS 202; Jason Squires/WireImage 74; John Stanton/WireImage 16; Brooke Sutton 221, 234-235; Ray Tamarra 64; Erik Umphery 27; Robert Vos/AFP 102; WPA 188; Nina Westervelt 230-231; Max Whittaker 121; Kevin Winter 92-93, 106, 170, 196, 222, 223

Shutterstock: arvzdix 120; Everett Collection 24, 70, 72, 75, 116; Robert Hoetink 17T; Picturegroup 4; A. Ricardo 137, 138; Sky Cinema 169; Raven Varona/Parkwood/PictureGroup 2-3